Careers in Law, Criminal Justice & Emergency Services

Careers in Law, Criminal Justice & Emergency Services

Editor
Michael Shally-Jensen, Ph.D.

SALEM PRESS
A Division of EBSCO Information Services, Inc.
Ipswich, Massachusetts

GREY HOUSE PUBLISHING

Library of Congress Cataloging-in-Publication Data

Careers in law, criminal justice & emergency services / editor, Michael
  Shally-Jensen, Ph.D. -- [First edition].

    pages : illustrations ; cm. -- (Careers in--)

  Includes bibliographical references and index.
  ISBN: 978-1-61925-475-6

    1. Law--Vocational guidance--United States. 2. Criminal justice, Administration of--Vocational guidance--United States. 3. First responders--Vocational guidance--United States. 4. Public safety--Vocational guidance--United States. I. Shally-Jensen, Michael.
II. Title: Careers in law, criminal justice and emergency services

KF297 .C375 2014
340.023/73

First Printing

PRINTED IN THE UNITED STATES OF AMERICA

CONTENTS

PUBLISHER'S NOTE

Careers in Law, Criminal Justice & Emergency Services contains twenty-four alphabetically arranged chapters describing specific fields of interest in these industries. Merging scholarship with occupational development, this single comprehensive guidebook provides law, criminal justice, and emergency services students and readers alike with the necessary insight into potential careers, and provides instruction on what job seekers can expect in terms of training, advancement, earnings, job prospects, working conditions, relevant associations, and more. *Careers in Law, Criminal Justice & Emergency Services* is specifically designed for a high school and undergraduate audience and is edited to align with secondary or high school curriculum standards.

Scope of Coverage

Understanding the interconnected nature of the different and varied branches of these fields is important for anyone preparing for a career within them. *Careers in Law, Criminal Justice & Emergency* Services comprises twenty-four lengthy chapters on a broad range of branches and divisions within these industry segments, including traditional and long-established fields such as Firefighter, Police Officer, and Judge, as well as in demand and cutting edge fields such as Information Security Analyst and Emergency Dispatcher. This excellent reference also presents possible career paths and occupations within high-growth and emerging fields in these industries.

Careers in Law, Criminal Justice & Emergency Services is enhanced with numerous charts and tables, including projections from the US Bureau of Labor Statistics, and median annual salaries or wages for those occupations profiled. Each chapter also notes those skills that can be applied across broad occupation categories. Interesting enhancements, like **Fun Facts**, **Famous Firsts**, and dozens of photos, add depth to the discussion. A highlight of each chapter is **Conversation With** – a two-page interview with a professional working in a related job. The respondents share their personal career paths, detail potential for career advancement, offer advice for students, and include a "try this" for those interested in embarking on a career in their profession.

Essay Length and Format

Each chapter ranges in length from 3,500 to 4,500 words and begins with a Snapshot of the occupation that includes career clusters, interests, earnings and employment outlook. This is followed by these major categories:

- **Overview** includes detailed discussions on: Sphere of Work; Work Environment; Occupation Interest; A Day in the Life. Also included here is a Profile that outlines working conditions, educational needs, and physical abilities. You will also find the occupation's Holland Interest Score, which matches up character and personality traits with specific jobs.

- **Occupational Specialties** lists specific jobs that are related in some way, like Uniformed Police Officer, State Highway Patrol Officer, Transit Police, Sheriff and Deputy Sheriff, and Detective and Criminal Investigator, all with detailed comparisons. This section also includes a list of Duties and Responsibilities.
- **Work Environment** details the physical, human, and technological environment of the occupation profiled.
- **Education, Training, and Advancement** outlines how to prepare for this occupation while in high school, and what college courses to take, including licenses and certifications needed. A section is devoted to the Adult Job Seeker, and there is a list of skills and abilities needed to succeed in the job profiled.
- **Earnings and Advancements** offers specific salary ranges, and includes a chart of metropolitan areas that have the highest concentration of the profession.
- **Employment and Outlook** discusses employment trends, and projects growth to 2020. This section also lists related occupations.
- **Selected Schools** list those prominent learning institutions that offer specific courses in the profiled occupations.
- **More Information** includes associations that the reader can contact for more information.

Special Features

Several features continue to distinguish this series from other career-oriented reference works. The back matter includes:
- Appendix A: Guide to Holland Code. This discusses John Holland's theory that people and work environments can be classified into six different groups: Realistic; Investigative; Artistic; Social; Enterprising; and Conventional. See if the job you want is right for you!
- Appendix B: General Bibliography. This is a collated collection of annotated suggested readings.
- Subject Index: Includes people, concepts, technologies, terms, principles, and all specific occupations discussed in the occupational profile chapters.

Acknowledgments

Special mention is made of editor Michael Shally-Jensen, who played a principal role in shaping this work with current, comprehensive, and valuable material. Thanks are due to the many academicians and professionals who worked to communicate their expert understanding of law, criminal justice, and emergency services to the general reader. Finally, thanks are also due to the professionals who communicated their work experience through our interview questionnaires. Their frank and honest responses provide immeasurable value to *Careers in Law, Criminal Justice & Emergency Services*. The contributions of all are gratefully acknowledged.

EDITOR'S INTRODUCTION

An Overview

Law, criminal justice, and emergency services–the combined focus of this volume are related but have distinct identities of their own. The legal field, for instance, includes criminal law, with its focus on addressing conduct that is considered harmful to society; but it also includes the broad area of civil law, which concerns the resolution of lawsuits (civil suits) between individuals and organizations. Lawyers and judges generally specialize in one area or the other. The same can be said of legal support staff—paralegals, legal secretaries, and others—along with court professionals—court reporters, court clerks/officers, and others. All of these occupations (and more) make up the field of law.

Criminal justice is similarly broad. It overlaps with the law but encompasses other areas as well. It might be thought of, to use a familiar phrase, as the *law and order* segment of society. On the *law* side, criminal law includes prosecutors, district attorneys, and criminal defense lawyers. On the *order* side are occupations such as police officer, correctional officer, parole officer, and federal law enforcement agent. Criminal justice also encompasses the equally important occupations of forensic scientist, customs officer, and law enforcement (park) ranger. The main job of these professionals is to maintain order within our communities and protect lives and property from harm or hazard. Most of these occupations are considered somewhat dangerous and stressful: there is always a possibility of sustaining injury (or worse) while carrying out one's duties.

Equally as stressful and, often enough, as dangerous are emergency services professions. Among these are firefighter, emergency vehicle operator, and emergency dispatcher. It's important to note that police officers too, together with other law enforcement professionals, frequently are required to deal with emergencies and to ensure public safety. They are "first responders" in emergency situations as much as firefighters and other emergency teams are. Thus, the field of emergency services is separate and distinct, yet closely allied with the other occupational areas.

A fourth area that is often grouped together with occupations discussed so far is security services. By and large, security services refers to occupations in the private sector, whereas most of the occupations named above are associated with federal, state, and local governments. That is, police officers and firefighters are paid (usually) by a municipality or similar government institution. Security services professionals, in contrast, are paid (usually) by businesses or organizations. Within the security field we find such occupations as security guard (in all its variety), information security analyst, and security systems installer. Private detectives, too, can be regarded as belonging to this group.

All of these occupations tend to attract individuals of honest character with a high degree of integrity. Those aspiring to careers in law, criminal justice, emergency services, or security should enjoy working with people and have an appreciation and respect for public service and the law. Good judgment, along with the ability to make decisions quickly, are also important skills. Many jobs in this field (outside the legal and administrative positions) have physical fitness and health requirements, and some of them require a high level of strength and stamina. A candidate must have the ability to deal with hazardous situations and withstand job stress. In addition, most positions have a period of on-the-job training where those who are unsuited to the work are weeded out, and many positions also require drug screenings and medical exams.

Employment Opportunities

Training or experience in this field can open the door to a wide variety of career opportunities in both the public and private sectors. Many of the public service careers have the added benefit of being more recession-proof than jobs in private industry. They are also often unionized. There are over 20,000 federal, state, and local law enforcement agencies in the United States employing over 550,000 people. These include city and suburban police departments, state police departments, county sheriffs' offices and federal law enforcement agencies. The figures for emergency services are somewhat smaller but still considerable. In addition, opportunities exist in more than 5,700 federal, state, and county prison facilities, ranging from "super max" prisons to local community-based correctional institutions.

Most large city police departments have extensive criminal investigation sections and forensics laboratories that employ many different kinds of law enforcement professionals. Moreover, most criminal justice agencies conduct research on the effectiveness of their crime control programs, thereby employing criminologists and other researchers; there are also many federal and state agencies dedicated to criminal justice program evaluation and policy analysis.

Similarly, opportunities exist at the federal, state, and local level within the more than 17,000 adult, juvenile, criminal, and civil courts (both trial and appellate). Likewise, there are extensive public service opportunities in all 50 states at the more than 8,000 federal, state, and local prosecutors' or public defenders' offices. Numerous opportunities exist in the private sector in criminal defense, personal injury, corporate law, or municipal law. Many opportunities also exist in law firms—small and large— in paralegal work, legal research, and office management.

Finally, a significant number of opportunities exist in the area of corporate and industrial security. These jobs range from traditional property, or "asset," protection to advanced computer security and industrial espionage protection. Some people work for large security companies, while others are employed as members of individual businesses or corporations. There are also opportunities in public institutions such as hospitals, airports, port facilities, and rail terminals.

Employment Trends

Protective Services
According to the Bureau of Labor Statistics (BLS), police, emergency services, and security occupations—which the BLS groups together as "protective service" occupations—are expected to add about 265,000 new jobs between now and 2022. This represents a growth rate of about 8 percent, nearly matching the average for all occupations in the economy. The majority of this occupational group consists of law enforcement workers, who predominantly work for governments. Overall, about a third of all new jobs in protective services will be in government. Much of this expansion can be attributed to population growth. (As population increases, the need for crime control rises.) Another 40 percent will be in the private security services and investigation industry, the result of an increasing number of businesses and other organizations emphasizing crime and vandalism reduction.

In terms of specific occupations, the most new jobs created will be for security guards, expected to exceed 195,000. The fastest growing protective service occupation will be information security analyst, projected to expand at a rate of over 35 percent. The highest paying job in protective services will also be information security analyst (averaging over $89,000 annually), followed by supervisors of police and detectives (averaging $78,260 per year).

As for union membership, public-sector workers currently have a union membership rate (35.3 percent) that is more than five times the rate of private-sector workers (6.7 percent). Among all public-sector workers, protective service occupations matched teachers as having the highest unionization rate. Men in this field had a higher union membership rate (11.9 percent) than women (10.5 percent).

Legal Occupations
Legal occupations are projected by the BLS to add about 130,000 new jobs between now and 2022. This represents an 11-percent growth rate, the average for all occupations. Although legal occupations form one of the smallest major occupational groups, they tend to be high-paying jobs, with a median annual wage of about $75,000 .

Lawyers account for more than half of the jobs in this group, with employment of about 725,000. Because their employment is growing at about the same rate as the group as a whole, the 70,000 or more new jobs projected for lawyers will also account for the majority of new jobs in the group.

Jobs for legal support workers are expected to grow by 15 percent or more, in part because legal establishments are expected to continue to expand the role of paralegals and legal assistants and assign them more of the tasks once performed by lawyers. However, they will add only 50,600 new jobs, partly because of lingering effects of the recession of 2007-09. The highest paying occupation in the legal field, on average, will continue to be judges and magistrates, with an average annual salary of close to $120,000.

Future Outlook

The economy is moving slowly toward recovery, and in both law and protective services, as in many industries, jobs are beginning to open up again. Larger firms and departments are opening their doors to new hires, and willing candidates are ready to take them up on the promise of good pay, excellent benefits, and plenty of excitement on the job. In contrast, some smaller, local departments and firms are beginning to struggle to keep well-trained and qualified people on their payrolls.

In general, well-trained, experienced professionals in the fields that are the focus of this book, along with the dramatic growth of college curriculums in fire and police science programs, and the continuing high enrollment of law programs, make competition somewhat tough for applicants but not insurmountable. There continue to be outstanding opportunities across all fields for motivated individuals.
                                                        —Michael Shally-Jensen

Sources

Bureau of Labor Statistics, "Union Members—2013,"
        www.bls.gov/news.release/pdf/union2.pdf
Bureal of Labor Statistics, "Occupational Employment Projections to 2022," December 2013.
        www.bls.gov/opub/mlr/2013/article/occupational-employment-projections-to-2022.htm
Lockard, C. Brett, and Michael Wolf, "Occupational Employment Projections to 2020, Monthly
        Labor Review, January 2012, 84-108. www.bls.gov/opub/mlr/2012/01/art5full.pdf

Correctional Officer

Snapshot

Career Cluster: Law & Criminal Justice; Security Services
Interests: Working in high-risk or dangerous situations, communicating with others
Earnings (Yearly Average): $43,550
Employment & Outlook: Slower Than Average Growth Expected

OVERVIEW

Sphere of Work

Correctional officers monitor incarcerated individuals in federal and state penitentiaries, courthouses, and other detention facilities. They ensure that prisoners are secure in their cells during stated hours, adhere to the prison's rules, and do not engage in acts of violence.

Correctional officers search cells for drugs and contraband, inspect facilities for health, fire, and safety violations, and ensure that prison security systems function properly. They oversee the transportation of prisoners who are awaiting trial and individuals who are serving their respective sentences. Correctional officers must report any incidents, violations, or other pertinent issues to institution administrators and officials.

Work Environment

Correctional officers work primarily in federal and state penitentiaries, courthouses, and other facilities that house criminal suspects and convicts. Conditions vary with the age of the prison facility. These environments tend to be highly crowded with diverse groups of individuals, some of whom do not speak English. All detention centers have strict rules regarding inmate behavior and movement; these rules are designed to maintain order and protect officers as well as inmates. Despite these safety measures, the risk of non-fatal on-the-job injury is substantially higher for correctional officers than for workers in most other occupations. Some correctional officers work in secure control centers within the prison, monitoring prisoners from closed-circuit television and computer systems. Correction officers work regular forty-hour weeks, although their shifts may be late at night, on weekends or on holidays.

Profile

Working Conditions: Work Inside, Work Indoors
Physical Strength: Medium Work
Education Needs: On-The-Job Training, High School Diploma Or G.E.D, Apprenticeship
Licensure/Certification: Required
Physical Abilities Not Required: No Heavy Labor
Opportunities For Experience: Apprenticeship, Military Service
Holland Interest Score*: SER

* See Appendix A

Occupation Interest

Correctional officers work to ensure that the overcrowded prison system is orderly and operates in the safest possible manner. To do so, they must interact on a daily basis with incarcerated individuals from all types of backgrounds. Correctional officers should be physically fit and comfortable working under sometimes dangerous conditions. They must be willing to perform shift work on nights and weekends as necessary. Correctional officers may enjoy camaraderie with one another, experience variety in their daily activities, and receive generous benefits as compensation for the high-risk, stressful work they do.

A Day in the Life—Duties and Responsibilities

Correctional officers are responsible for maintaining order and security in detention facilities and penitentiaries. They conduct periodic head counts, inspect inmates' mail, screen visitors, review security systems, check vehicles, and search prison cells for drugs, weapons, and contraband. They intervene during prisoner fights, disband groups of unruly prisoners, and restrain inmates using handcuffs, weapons, and physical force. Correctional officers also inspect the facility's security system, including windows, cameras, locks, bars, gates, and other areas, to locate and eliminate any risks of escape or internal criminal activity. They must keep careful logs of inspections, head counts, and behavioral infractions, as well as major conflicts and breaches of discipline.

The primary focus of correctional officers' work is maintaining order among prisoners. They have frequent conversations with inmates, answering their questions, assessing their needs, and listening to complaints. Correctional officers are in close proximity to the prisoners at all times, particularly when the inmates are out of their cells. They supervise prison activities and escort them to and from meals, showers, classes, visitor meeting areas, and work assignments. In some cases, correctional officers also manage and administer prisoner prescription medications. They process new arrivals, performing physical inspections for contraband, filing their paperwork, assigning cells, and giving them information about rules and policies. In the event that a prisoner escapes or commits a crime within the walls of the prison, correctional officers coordinate with external law enforcement officers in their investigation of the incident.

Duties and Responsibilities

- Observing the conduct and behavior of inmates to insure that they are orderly and obey rules
- Inspecting locks, window bars, grills, doors, and gates for tampering
- Searching inmates and cells for weapons, drugs, or other prohibited items
- Supervising inmates during work assignments
- Preparing reports of disturbances, violations of rules, and unusual occurrences
- Serving as guards on towers and at gates
- Escorting prisoners between courtrooms and correctional facilities

OCCUPATION SPECIALTIES

Jailers

Jailers guard prisoners in precinct station houses or municipal jails, assuming responsibility for all prisoner needs during detention.

Immigration Guards

Immigration Guards guard aliens held by the immigration service pending further investigation that may lead to the release or deportation of prisoners.

Patrol Conductors

Patrol Conductors guard prisoners being transported in correctional vans between jails, courthouses, prisons, mental institutions, or other institutions.

Bailiffs

Bailiffs, also known as marshals or court officers, are law enforcement officers who maintain safety and order in courtrooms. Their duties include enforcing courtroom rules, assisting judges, guarding juries from outside contact, delivering court documents, and providing general security for courthouses

WORK ENVIRONMENT

Physical Environment

Most correctional officers work in local or state jails, courthouses, and prisons, but many others work in federal penitentiaries. They may also work outside of prisons, particularly as they monitor minimum security work details. In each environment, there is a physical risk related to prisoner conflicts. This risk can add stress to the job.

Relevant Skills and Abilities

Communication Skills
- Speaking effectively

Interpersonal/Social Skills
- Cooperating with others
- Working as a member of a team

Organization & Management Skills
- Following instructions
- Managing conflict
- Meeting goals and deadlines
- Performing routine work

Other Skills
- Remembering names and faces

Human Environment

Besides prisoners and their visitors, correctional officers interact with wardens, police officers, federal agents, judges and attorneys, social workers, mental health professional, drug counselors, on-site medical personnel, and workers delivering supplies.

Technological Environment

Correctional officers work with closed-circuit and computer-based monitoring systems, lighting equipment, alarm technologies, and weapons, which include handguns, shotguns, Tasers, and pepper spray. They may also use computer software, such as spreadsheets and word processing programs, to create comprehensive logs on inmate behavior.

EDUCATION, TRAINING, AND ADVANCEMENT

High School/Secondary

High school students should take courses in government, history, and political science to better understand the law. English and composition classes help build communication skills. Psychology, foreign languages, and social studies may also prove very useful. Physical education and first aid can help correctional officers deal with the physical risks of the job. A high school diploma or graduate equivalency degree (GED) is required for all correctional officers.

Suggested High School Subjects
- English
- First Aid Training
- Government

- Physical Education
- Psychology
- Social Studies
- Sociology

Famous First

The first prison built for and managed by women was the Indiana Reformatory Institution for Women and Girls in Indianapolis, Ind., which opened in 1873. It had a female staff and a female superintendent, and beginning in 1877, an all-female board of trustees. The first federal prison for women was the Federal Prison Camp for Women in Alderson, W. Va, which opened in 1927.

Postsecondary

Federal correctional officers are required to have a bachelor's degree in a related field, such as sociology, criminal justice, or psychology. Some states also require college credits, three years of related job experience, or some combination of the two. Prior military or law enforcement service may satisfy these experience requirements. In the federal system, candidates are generally expected to hold a bachelor's degree.

Related College Majors
- Corrections/Correctional Administration
- Criminal Justice

Adult Job Seekers

Qualified correctional officer candidates may apply directly to the federal, state, or local correctional systems where openings are available. More job opportunities exist at state and local correctional institutions than at federal correctional institutions. Membership in a professional correctional officer association, such as Corrections USA, can provide qualified job seekers with networking and job-finding opportunities.

Professional Certification and Licensure

Most state and federal correctional officers must take and pass a civil service examination. They must also complete extensive job training that includes weapons and self-defense courses.

Additional Requirements

Correctional officers must be at least eighteen to twenty-one years of age, with no felony criminal convictions. They should be physically fit, with good hearing and vision. Correctional officers must submit to mandatory drug testing and must undergo criminal background checks. Officers should be capable of defending themselves and their colleagues; therefore, they must be able to think and respond quickly to stressful situations and show good judgment.

EARNINGS AND ADVANCEMENT

Earnings vary by the level of government, size of the employer and union affiliation. Mean annual earnings of correctional officers were $43,550 in 2012. The lowest ten percent earned less than $27,000, and the highest ten percent earned more than $ $69,000.

Median annual earnings for correctional officers in the public sector in 2012 were: $53,400 in the federal government; $44,180 in state government; and $42,650 in local government.

Correctional officers may receive paid vacations, holidays, and sick days; life and health insurance; and retirement benefits. These are usually paid by the employer. Meals may also be provided while on duty.

Metropolitan Areas with the Highest Employment Level in this Occupation

Metropolitan area	Employment	Employment per thousand jobs	Hourly mean wage
New York-White Plains-Wayne, NY-NJ	11,120	2.16	$33.82
Houston-Sugar Land-Baytown, TX	9,230	3.50	$16.92
Phoenix-Mesa-Glendale, AZ	8,260	4.77	$19.91
Washington-Arlington-Alexandria, DC-VA-MD-WV	5,000	2.13	$24.53
Riverside-San Bernardino-Ontario, CA	4,970	4.28	$32.33
Boston-Cambridge-Quincy, MA	4,560	2.67	$29.20
Bakersfield-Delano, CA	4,360	15.89	n/a
Richmond, VA	4,160	6.95	$17.76

Source: Bureau of Labor Statistics

EMPLOYMENT AND OUTLOOK

Correctional officers held about 435,000 jobs nationally in 2012. Another 45,000 served as supervisors. The majority of jobs were in state correctional institutions such as prisons, prison camps and youth correctional facilities. Employment is expected to grow slower than the average for all occupations through the year 2022, which means employment is projected to increase 3 percent to 9 percent. Budget limitations and a downward trend in crime in recent years will contribute to the slower growth rate. Additional openings will result from high job turnover and the need to replace workers who retire or change jobs.

Employment Trend, Projected 2012–22

Total, All Occupations: 11%

Bailiffs: 5%

Law Enforcement Workers: 5%

Correctional Officers and Jailers: 5%

Note: "All Occupations" includes all occupations in the U.S. Economy. Source: U.S. Bureau of Labor Statistics, Employment Projections Program

Related Occupations
- Federal Law Enforcement Agent
- Parole & Probation Officer
- Police Officer
- Security Guard

Related Military Occupations
- Law Enforcement & Security Specialist

Conversation With . . .
William Crowley
Correctional Officer, 9 years

1. What was your individual career path in terms of education/training, entry-level job, or other significant opportunity?

I studied criminal justice in college then became a police officer. I was on the force in Washington, D.C., then Fairfax County in Virginia. Family matters brought me back to Massachusetts. While trying to get on another police department, I worked for an armored car company. I went out on disability. A neighbor worked in corrections, and I decided to try out that career.

2. What are the most important skills and/or qualities for someone in your profession?

You definitely have to be a very patient individual. It also helps if you're a stickler for rules. You have to know how to say 'no.' You also have to be strong-willed in the sense that you need to almost constantly remind yourself that the people you're dealing with are not your friends. If you give in to peer pressure, are offended easily or have a hard time standing up for yourself, then you're going to run into issues.

Having a good sense of humor also helps.

3. What do you wish you had known going into this profession?

I wish I had known how it would drag on me. They always tell you it's going to wear you down. They tell you you're going to seem to age pretty fast, but they really don't get the point across. A lot of the job is just sitting. You're sitting in the block and you're watching. Physically, it's not a problem. But, you can't go home and talk about the things you've dealt with that day because you don't want to bring that stuff home with you. So it can take a toll, psychologically.

4. Are there many job opportunities in your profession? In what specific areas?

There are many job opportunities and they're in all areas. We are like a miniature city. When you first get there, look around, see what all the different jobs are. We have correctional officers (COs) who strictly work in the kitchen. They do all the food buying, prepare all the meals for 900 people every day. You have the grounds officer who brings in inmates from minimum security and supervise them while they do exterior grounds work, like mowing and shoveling snow. If you like electrical work, wood working, etc., you can put in to be an industrial officer. We have COs who are electricians, guys who manufacture steel, cut doors, install locks, armory guys who maintain all the weapons, tool officers who keep track of tools. We have equipment officers. There are COs who work in transportation, bringing inmates to courts around the state. There are training officers who work at the academy and train new correctional officers. There's also a lot of potential to move up the ranks.

5. How do you see your profession changing in the next five years? What role will technology play in those changes, and what skills will be required?

We use computers for everything. I can pull up an inmate's record by his number and access his folder. I can learn whether he has enemy issues and see a list of who his enemies are. I can see a description of each tattoo he has so I can tell if he's added a tattoo while in prison. I can see what medications he takes, whether he has gang affiliation, etc.

I also think in the next five years, you're going to see more help for staff in dealing with stress. I think we'll see the profession getting a little more respect over the next five years because it really is a noble profession.

6. Do you have any general advice or additional professional insights to share with someone in your profession? What is the most fulfilling part of your job, and what is the most frustrating?

Corrections is a great stepping stone to go to other jobs. The only drawback is, it pays so well that when you're making money this good, it's hard to go to a police department where your base pay will be lower.

I think corrections is a harder and more challenging profession than police work. In corrections, if I have an issue with an inmate and he assaults me, I still have to feed him the next day. We still have to work it out. In Massachusetts, we don't have tasers. I don't carry pepper spray. It's just me and my hands and my mind.

7. Can you suggest a valuable "try this" for students considering a career in your profession?

If you know anyone in corrections, ask him about it. Or call the prison facility and ask about tours. You can always watch some shows about prison on television, like Lockup and Hard Time. But most of the time when you're working, you're bored to tears. It's like babysitting, but with grownups.

SELECTED SCHOOLS

After high school, many first-time correctional officers train with the institutions that have hired them (as trainees). It is beneficial in some cases, however, to obtain college credits or an associate's degree in corrections studies, criminal justice, or a related field. Interested students should check with their school guidance counselor or research area community colleges. For those who seek employment in the federal system, a bachelor's degree is usually necessary.

MORE INFORMATION

American Correctional Association
206 N. Washington Street
Suite 200
Alexandria, VA 22314
800.222.5646
www.aca.org

American Jail Association
1135 Professional Court
Hagerstown, MD 21740-5853
301.790.3930
www.aja.org

Correctional Peace Officers Foundation, Inc.
P.O. Box 348390
Sacramento, CA 95834-8390
800.800.2763
www.cpof.org

Corrections USA
P.O. Box 6912
Pueblo West, CO 81007
719.547.7863
www.cusa.org

Council on Law Enforcement Education & Training
2401 Egypt Road
Ada, OK 74820-0669
405.239.5100
www.ok.gov/cleet

Federal Bureau of Prisons
320 1st Street NW
Washington, DC 20534
202.307.3198
www.bop.gov

National Institute of Corrections Information Center
791 North Chambers Road
Aurora, CO 80011
800.877.1461
www.nicic.org

Michael Auerbach/Editor

Court Administrator

OVERVIEW

Sphere of Work

Court administrators, also called court executives or court coordinators, are responsible for ensuring that courts follow official procedures, and they oversee all the general operations of local, state, and federal courts. Their tasks include jury and trial management, fiscal, budget, and resource allocation, docket management and scheduling, records and reports, education, public relations, and customer service, professional development, facilities and operations,

general clerical and administrative work, and personnel, staff, and human resources. Court administrators are chosen based on their understanding of legal proceedings, court services, and customer service, and for their organizational and leadership abilities.

Work Environment

Court administrators spend their workdays within local, state, and federal court systems, municipalities, and governmental licensing agencies. Court administrators work in administrative offices and courtrooms. Although many court administrators work forty-hour weeks, many others work unpaid overtime hours during busy periods. Court administrators report to a supervising or presiding judge and may direct court clerks.

Profile

Working Conditions: Work Indoors
Physical Strength: Light Work
Education Needs: Technical/
  Community College, Bachelor's Degree
Licensure/Certification: Usually Not
  Required
Physical Abilities Not Required: No
  Physical Labor
Opportunities For Experience:
  Internship, Part-Time Work
Holland Interest Score*: ESR

* See Appendix A

Occupation Interest

Individuals drawn to the court administrator profession tend to be highly intelligent and detail-oriented people. Those most successful at the job of court administrator display tact, leadership, organizational skills, resourcefulness, problem solving, and effective time management. Court administrators should enjoy public administration and working within the legal system.

A Day in the Life—Duties and Responsibilities

The daily occupational duties and responsibilities of court administrators vary by court environment. For instance, local, state, and federal courts each handle different kinds of court cases and follow different operating, safety, and record keeping procedures. A court administrator's daily duties and responsibilities may include tasks related to personnel, budget, calendar management, jury management, trial management, facilities, records, or customer service.

A court administrator assists the judge with all administrative duties and personnel management issues. He or she manages jury summonses and the jury selection process, keeps records of all jury selections, and maintains the master schedule (commonly called the docket) for all upcoming court trials and proceedings. The court administrator also coordinates participants and oversees the court clerk's contact with witnesses, litigants, and lawyers who need to be notified about scheduled dates for court appearances. The court administrator may also plan the court's operating budget, including costs such as payroll, supplies, equipment, maintenance, and repairs.

In addition, all court administrators are responsible for increasing the overall effectiveness of court procedures and improving the court experience for judges, litigants, staff, and the public. A court administrator may solicit post-trial feedback from jurors using questionnaires and surveys, develop new strategies to improve the efficiency of court scheduling and notification procedures, and ensure accurate record keeping of court-related events.

Duties and Responsibilities

- Hiring, disciplining, and evaluating technical and clerical personnel
- Negotiating and administering employee collective bargaining agreements
- Overseeing facilities maintenance and inventory materials and equipment
- Assigning offices, courtrooms, and witness conference rooms
- Systematizing court calendars, case processing, accounting and auditing procedures, and record keeping
- Collecting, compiling and analyzing caseload data to estimate future caseloads and changing staffing and processing procedures
- Overseeing records maintenance and security

WORK ENVIRONMENT

Physical Environment

The immediate physical environment of court administrators includes the courtrooms and administrative offices of municipalities, governmental licensing agencies, and local, state, and federal court systems.

Relevant Skills and Abilities

Communication Skills
- Speaking and writing effectively

Interpersonal/Social Skills
- Cooperating with others
- Working as a member of a team

Organization & Management Skills
- Coordinating tasks
- Making decisions
- Managing people/groups
- Managing time
- Performing duties that change frequently

Other Skills
- Analyzing information
- Gathering information
- Using logical reasoning

Human Environment

Court administrators work with a wide variety of people. They should be comfortable interacting with the public, the media, school groups, court reporters, court clerks, police and public safety personnel, litigants, incarcerated people, lawyers, judges, witnesses, and juries.

Technological Environment

Court administrators use a wide variety of technology to perform their job, including computers, budgeting software, automated scheduling software, Internet communication technology, photocopiers, and printers.

EDUCATION, TRAINING, AND ADVANCEMENT

High School/Secondary

High school students interested in pursuing a career as a court administrator should prepare themselves by developing good study habits. High school courses in typing, bookkeeping, foreign languages, political science, and public safety will provide a strong foundation for college-level work in the field. Owing to the diversity of court administrator responsibilities, high school students interested in this career path may benefit from seeking internships or part-time work opportunities that expose the students to the legal system.

Suggested High School Subjects
- Applied Communication
- Business Data Processing
- Business Law
- College Preparatory
- Composition
- English
- Government
- Keyboarding
- Political Science
- Speech

Famous First

The first juvenile court was the Chicago Juvenile Court, which opened in 1899. It heard cases involving youth accused of committing crimes. Before that time a determination was made, based on the severity of the crime, to try an offender as an adult or let him or her go with a warning or informal fine. In juvenile court youth offenders could be tried and sentenced as youth offenders. The Chicago Juvenile Court heard about 2,300 cases in its first year. Beginning in 1913, a female judge began hearing cases involving girls.

College/Postsecondary

Postsecondary students interested in becoming court administrator should obtain an associate's degree or bachelor's degree in secretarial science, general business, or court administration. Coursework in bookkeeping, pre-law, business, criminology, and foreign languages may also prove useful in their future work. Postsecondary students can gain work experience and potential advantage in their future job searches by securing internships or part-time employment within the legal system.

Related College Majors
- Administrative Assistant/Secretarial Science, General
- Business Administration & Management
- Executive Assistant/Secretary Training
- Legal Administrative Assistant/Secretarial Science
- Office Supervision & Management

Adult Job Seekers

Adults seeking employment as court administrators should have, at a minimum, a high school diploma or an associate's degree. Some court administrator jobs require extensive experience, a bachelor's degree or graduate degree, and second language proficiency. Adult job seekers should educate themselves about the educational and professional license requirements of their home states and the organizations where they seek employment. Adult job seekers may benefit from joining professional associations like the National Center for State Courts and the National Association for Court Management, which generally offer job-finding workshops and maintain lists and forums of available jobs.

Professional Certification and Licensure

Court administrators are not required to have national certification as a condition of employment, but options for court administrator certification do exist at the state level. Specialized training and state certification is mandatory in some states, such as New Jersey, Mississippi, and Missouri. All state-level court administrator certifications require continuing education hours or courses as a condition of ongoing certification. Individuals interested in becoming court administrators should check the certification requirements of the state where they seek employment.

Additional Requirements

Individuals who find satisfaction, success, and job security as court administrators will be knowledgeable about the profession's requirements, responsibilities, and opportunities. Court administrators must demonstrate high levels of integrity and professional ethics as professionals in this role have access to confidential legal information. Membership in professional legal associations is encouraged among all court administrators as a means of building professional community and networking.

EARNINGS AND ADVANCEMENT

Salaries of court administrators depend on education, previous work experience and level of job responsibility, the type and size of the court served, the size of the administrative staff, the budget, and to some extent, the geographic location. Generally, court administrators who work in the federal court system earn the highest salaries. Salaries of state court administrators are predictably higher depending on the population of the state and the greater responsibilities required.

First-year court administrators earned an average annual salary of $52,306 in 2012. With eight or more years of experience, court administrators can earn around $85,706 annually.

Court administrators may receive paid vacations, holidays, and sick days; life and health insurance; and retirement benefits. These are usually paid by the employer.

Metropolitan Areas with the Highest
Employment Level in this Occupation(1)

Metropolitan area	Employment	Employment per thousand jobs	Hourly mean wage
New York-White Plains-Wayne, NY-NJ	50,550	9.80	$32.06
Los Angeles-Long Beach-Glendale, CA	30,470	7.87	$27.10
Chicago-Joliet-Naperville, IL	29,820	8.19	$23.98
Washington-Arlington-Alexandria, DC-VA-MD-WV	22,020	9.40	$27.61
Houston-Sugar Land-Baytown, TX	19,790	7.49	$25.43
Boston-Cambridge-Quincy, MA	16,960	9.91	$27.79
Atlanta-Sandy Springs-Marietta, GA	16,940	7.49	$23.79
Minneapolis-St. Paul-Bloomington, MN-WI	16,090	9.20	$23.58

[1]Includes executive secretaries and executive administrative assistants. Source: Bureau of Labor Statistics

EMPLOYMENT AND OUTLOOK

Nationally, there were about 130,000 court clerks, of which court administrators are a part, employed in courts of general and limited jurisdiction in 2012. However, of this number, approximately 1,000 were court administrators. Each state has at least one state court administrator. Employment of court administrators is expected to grow slower than the average for all occupations through the year 2022, which means employment is projected to increase 3 percent to 9 percent. This is due in part to continuing budget restrictions in most jurisdictions despite growth in the demand for court services.

Employment Trend, Projected 2012–22

Total, All Occupations: 11%

Court Administrators: 7%

Information Clerks: 2%

Note: "All Occupations" includes all occupations in the U.S. Economy. Source: U.S. Bureau of Labor Statistics, Employment Projections Program

Related Occupations
- Administrative Support Manager
- Court Clerk
- Legal Secretary
- Paralegal

Conversation With . . .
Daniel J. Hogan

Clerk Magistrate

26 years Court employee

1. What was your individual career path in terms of education/training, entry-level job, or other significant opportunity?

I started in the courthouse in 1988 at entry-level, which was a Procedures Clerk I. I came here right from college. I had majored in economics. When I graduated, my mother said, "I don't care where you go, but you can't stay here." So I was lucky enough to get that job, and later was promoted to Account Clerk II. I had a lot of opportunity to watch lawyers who did a great job for their clients and to watch lawyers that were not so well prepared. I thought, "I think I can do this." So I applied to law school and was accepted the second time around. I went to Suffolk University Law School nights for four years while working full time. I passed the bar and was preparing to work in the District Attorney's office when it so happened that the assistant clerk-magistrate was leaving. The clerk-magistrate appointed me assistant clerk-magistrate. Later I was appointed to First Assistant Clerk-Magistrate. At that point, the clerk-magistrate became ill and unexpectedly died. I was appointed acting clerk-magistrate for 18 months, then appointed by the Governor in 2000. It's one of the only jobs in the state that is a lifetime appointment. I've held every job on the way up. That was really helpful because I understand how the work is done.

2. What are the most important skills and/or qualities for someone in your profession?

There are 42,000 people who enter the courts across the Commonwealth of Massachusetts every day. Most enter and end their day at the clerk-magistrate's office. Most of them don't want to be there; they're there because they have to be there. You have to be able to listen and to understand and to have some compassion for human frailties. And you have to be able to exercise judgement.

3. What do you wish you had known going into this profession?

I used to think everything was black and white. I've learned that nothing is black and white.

4. Are there many job opportunities in your profession? In what specific areas?

Most of the hiring and firing is done by the clerk-magistrate. The Boston Trial Court has had a hard hiring freeze since 2007. We went from 7,600 employees to 6,300 employees. We're now adding some desperately-needed personnel. For the last several years, jobs were non-existent, but they're coming back.

5. How do you see your profession changing in the next five years? What role will technology play in those changes, and what skills will be required?

Technology is probably one of the most critical elements of our business. E-filing is enormous. A new computerized case management system for the Trial Court is being funded by a $75 million bond allocation. And we're improving how we interact with other entities—the Registry of Motor Vehicles, the Department of Revenue. We can send immediate notices to people rather than them having to come in to check their files. But that also creates a number of significant issues regarding privacy.

6. What do you enjoy most about your job? What do you enjoy least?

People. That includes the people I work with and interacting with the public. The ability to actually impact someone's life on a daily basis is very gratifying. The volume is so great and the pace is so fast that sometimes we have to step back and realize this one case is the most important case in the world to this person. I love my job. I have fun every single day.

The part I enjoy the least is the move toward metrics. We don't build cars here. I just don't think it's appropriate to say we should be able to hear 27 cases in five days, or whatever the number is. A trespass case should be given the same care and effort as a motor vehicle homicide. You can't really measure justice.

7. Can you suggest a valuable "try this" for students considering a career in your profession?

There's nothing more fascinating than watching two competent lawyers argue a case before a jury, nor anything more pitiful than watching two lousy lawyers argue. Spending time in a courtroom is invaluable. Take a seat and watch trials, arraignments, show cause hearings. If you like public service and helping people, I think there's no better branch of government.

SELECTED SCHOOLS

Many colleges, including many community colleges, offer programs in general office management and/or secretarial science. Other schools offer programs in paralegal studies and/or legal secretaryship. Both of these academic areas are relevant to a career in court administration. In addition, more advanced training specifically in court/legal administration is available through some schools. Below are listed selected four-year and post-graduate schools offering programs in this field.

Auburn University
PO Box 244023
Montgomery, AL 36124
334.244.3000
www.aum.edu

John Jay College of Criminal Justice
M.P.A. Program
534 West 59th Street
New York, NY 10019
212.663.7867
www.jjay.cuny.edu

Marymount University
Legal Administration Program
2807 N. Glebe Road
Arlington, VA 22207
703.284.5901
www.marymount.edu

Michigan State University
Judicial Administration Program
1407 S. Harrison Road, Suite 330
East Lansing, MI 48823
517.432.3965
cj.msu.edu/programs/judicial-administration-program/

Mississippi University for Women
1100 College Street
Columbus, MS 39701
662.329.4760
web3.muw.edu

New York University
Opperman Institute of Judicial Administration
40 Washington Square, South
New York, NY 10012
212.998.6100
www.law.nyu.edu/centers/judicial

Sacramento State University
College of Continuing Education
3000 State University Drive East
Sacramento, CA 95189
916.278.4433
www.cce.csus.edu

University of Denver
Sturm College of Law
2255 E. Evans Avenue
Denver, CO 80208
303.871.6000
www.law.du.edu

University of Detroit, Mercy
4001 W. McNichols Road
Detroit, MI 48221
800.635.5020
www.udmercy.edu

University of Nevada, Reno
Justice Management Degree
Program
NJC Building, Room 114C
Reno, NV 89557
775.682.7975
www.unr.edu/justicemanagment

MORE INFORMATION

Conference of State Court Administrators
National Center for State Courts
300 Newport Avenue
Williamsburg, VA 23185
800.877.1233
cosca.ncsc.dni.us

National Association for Court Management
300 Newport Avenue
Williamsburg, VA 23185-4147
800.616.6165
www.nacmnet.org

National Association of Legal Secretaries
8159 East 41st Street
Tulsa, OK 74145
918.582.5188
www.nals.org

National Center for State Courts
300 Newport Avenue
Williamsburg, VA 23185-4147
800.616.6164
www.ncsc.org

National Conference of Appellate Court Clerks
450 E Street NW, Room 103
Washington, DC 20442-0001
www.appellatecourtclerks.org

Simone Isadora Flynn/Editor

Court Clerk

Snapshot

Career Cluster: Government & Public Administration; Law & Criminal Justice

Interests: The legal system, clerical work, written communication

Earnings (Yearly Average): $36,950

Employment & Outlook: Slower Than Average Growth Expected

OVERVIEW

Sphere of Work

Court clerks, also referred to as deputy clerks, judicial clerks, or circuit court clerks, perform a wide variety of administrative, public safety, custodial, and other duties for local, state, and federal courts. Court clerks function as the point of contact for the general public

and, as such, respond to inquiries about court scheduling, fees, forms, and procedures. Court clerks bring their clerical skills, customer service experience, and knowledge of the legal system and government operations to their work. Examples of court clerk tasks and roles include: preparing dockets of upcoming court cases; contacting witnesses, litigants, and lawyers to plan court schedules and

appearances; locating information and data for lawyers, judges, and the court; responding to court-related inquiries; processing licensing applications; and collecting court-related fees.

Work Environment

Court clerks spend their workdays within local, state, and federal court systems, municipalities, and governmental licensing agencies. Court clerks work in administrative offices, courtrooms, and in customer service capacities. Court clerks generally work forty-hour weeks or more.

Profile

Working Conditions: Work Indoors
Physical Strength: Light Work
Education Needs: Technical/Community College, Bachelor's Degree
Licensure/Certification: Usually Not Required
Physical Abilities Not Required: No Heavy Labor
Opportunities For Experience: Internship, Military Service, Part-Time Work
Holland Interest Score*: CSE

* See Appendix A

Occupation Interest

Individuals drawn to the court clerk profession tend to be intelligent and detail-oriented people. Successful court clerks are tactful, well organized, resourceful, problem solvers, efficient, and possess excellent time management skills. Court clerks should find satisfaction in and excel at clerical work, customer service, and working within the legal system.

A Day in the Life—Duties and Responsibilities

The daily activity of the court depends on the efforts of an efficient court clerk. They must have excellent organizational skills to ensure that legal proceedings go smoothly and that the process of working through the docket (the schedule of upcoming court cases) is seamless. Court clerks function as administrative assistants to the judge and in a supervisory role to court reporters. They coordinate planning, scheduling, preparation, and information sharing for the court, and in doing so are responsible for communicating with lawyers, litigants, and witnesses.

A court clerk's daily duties and responsibilities vary from state to state, but generally include preparation of the docket; contacting witnesses, litigants, and lawyers to notify them about court schedule and appearance dates; responding to information requests from lawyers, jurors, litigants, and judges; and locating information and data for lawyers, judges, and the court. Other typical daily responsibilities are responding to court-related inquiries; preparing formal orders of the court including probation documents, release documents, sentencing documents, or summonses; administering oaths to witnesses in court; overseeing the jury selection process; documenting all legal transcripts prepared by court reporters; and maintaining fiscal records of the court's administrative expenses. Court clerks also record trial verdicts and findings, collect and document legal fees, verify rulings with the presiding judge in each case, and forward important information to parole boards and correctional institutions.

In addition to the range of responsibilities described above, all court clerks are responsible for educating the general public on court-related issues such as proper judicial procedure, summonses, warrants, adjournments, fines, affidavits, and witness fees.

Duties and Responsibilities

- Preparing the docket or calendar of cases to be called
- Examining legal documents submitted to the court to insure that they adhere to the law or court procedures
- Preparing case folders
- Posting, filing, or routing documents
- Explaining procedures and forms to parties involved in a case
- Contacting witnesses, attorneys, and others to obtain information and informing them when to appear in court
- Notifying the District Attorney's office of cases to be prosecuted
- Swearing-in and impaneling jurors
- Administering the oath to witnesses
- Recording minutes of the court proc

WORK ENVIRONMENT

Physical Environment

Court clerks work in courtrooms and the administrative offices of local, state, and federal court systems, municipalities, and governmental licensing agencies. As this is a government position, different municipalities or government offices can be in various states of repair. For those systems with limited funding, office conditions may vary and equipment may not be state of the art. Any court employee may be required to pass through security checkpoints or metal detectors to enter the courtroom.

Relevant Skills and Abilities

Communication Skills
- Expressing thoughts and ideas
- Speaking and writing effectively

Interpersonal/Social Skills
- Being sensitive to others
- Cooperating with others
- Working as a member of a team

Organization & Management Skills
- Making decisions
- Paying attention to and handling details
- Performing duties that change frequently
- Performing routine work

Research & Planning Skills
- Scheduling activities
- Using logical reasoning

Human Environment

Court clerks work with a wide variety of people and should be comfortable interacting with the general public, court reporters, court administrators, police and public safety, litigants, incarcerated people, lawyers, judges, witnesses, and juries. As members of the court, they may also face tense, uncomfortable, or hostile encounters within the courtroom or in the course of other interactions. The court clerk must maintain his/her composure in order to effectively communicate with those vested in the process, remembering their key role in the justice system. Court clerks also exchange information with other government officials during the course of their day, such as people who work for parole boards or correctional institutions.

Technological Environment

Court clerks use computers, scheduling software, Internet communication technology, photocopiers, and printers to perform their job duties. Again, technology will be dependent on departmental funding.

EDUCATION, TRAINING, AND ADVANCEMENT

High School/Secondary

High school students interested in pursuing a career as a court clerk should prepare themselves by developing good study habits. High-school level study of typing, bookkeeping, foreign languages, political science, and public safety will provide a strong foundation for work as a court clerk or college-level work in the field. Owing to the diversity of court clerk responsibilities, high school students interested in this career path will benefit from seeking internships or part-time work that expose them to the legal system.

Suggested High School Subjects
- Applied Communication
- Bookkeeping
- Business
- Business & Computer Technology
- Business Data Processing
- Business English
- Business Law
- Keyboarding

Famous First

The first small claims court was a Topeka, Kansas, court for debtors, authorized by the state in 1913. The court dealt with cases involving no more than $20. Judges worked for free and did not have to be lawyers. Plaintiffs and defendants appeared without legal representation. Strict rules of evidence and procedure were waived. The final judgment, however, had the same legal force as any judgment rendered by a regular court.

Postsecondary

Postsecondary students interested in becoming court clerks should work toward an associate's or bachelor's degree in paralegal studies, criminal justice, or court administration. Coursework in bookkeeping, business, and foreign language may also prove useful in future work. Postsecondary students can gain work experience and potential advantage in their future job searches by securing internships or part-time employment within the legal system.

Related College Majors
- Administrative Assistant/Secretarial Science
- Court Reporter
- Legal Administrative Assistant/Secretary

Adult Job Seekers

Adults seeking employment as court clerks should have, at a minimum, a high school diploma or associate's degree. Some court clerk jobs require extensive experience, on-the-job training, a bachelor's degree, or second language proficiency. Adult job seekers should educate themselves about the educational and professional license requirements of their home states and the organizations where they seek employment. They may also benefit from joining professional associations to help with networking and job searching. Professional legal associations, such as the National Center for State Courts, offer job-finding workshops and maintain lists and forums of available jobs.

Professional Certification and Licensure

Court clerks are not generally required to seek certification and licensure as a condition of employment, although options for voluntary court clerk certification do exist at the state level. These state-level court clerk certification programs incorporate education, on the job training, and experience. All court clerk certifications require continuing education hours or courses as a condition of ongoing certification. Consult credible professional associations within your field and follow professional debate as to the relevancy and value of any certification program.

Additional Requirements

Individuals who find satisfaction, success, and job security as court clerks will be knowledgeable about the profession's requirements, responsibilities, and opportunities. Since court clerks have access to confidential legal information, they should hold themselves to high ethical standards and have great respect for our system of justice and the legal right to privacy. Membership in professional legal associations is advisable for all court clerks as a means of building status within the professional community and networking.

EARNINGS AND ADVANCEMENT

Earnings of court clerks depend on the type and size of the court in which they are employed, the individual's experience and the responsibilities of the job. Court clerks who work in the federal court system generally earn the highest salaries. Mean annual earnings of court clerks were $36,950 in 2012. The lowest ten percent earned less than $22,720 and the highest ten percent earned more than $54,470.

Court clerks may receive paid vacations, holidays, and sick days; life and health insurance; and retirement benefits. These are usually paid by the employer.

Metropolitan Areas with the Highest Employment Level in this Occupation

Metropolitan area	Employment	Employment per thousand jobs	Hourly mean wage
New York-White Plains-Wayne, NY-NJ	3,840	0.74	$29.06
Los Angeles-Long Beach-Glendale, CA	2,270	0.59	$21.50
Chicago-Joliet-Naperville, IL	2,100	0.58	$22.39
Denver-Aurora-Broomfield, CO	1,890	1.54	$18.86
Phoenix-Mesa-Glendale, AZ	1,770	1.02	$16.90
Atlanta-Sandy Springs-Marietta, GA	1,750	0.77	$15.72
Minneapolis-St. Paul-Bloomington, MN-WI	1,620	0.92	$19.04
Houston-Sugar Land-Baytown, TX	1,580	0.60	$14.30

Source: Bureau of Labor Statistics

EMPLOYMENT AND OUTLOOK

There were about 123,000 court clerks employed nationally in 2012. Employment is expected to grow slower than the average for all occupations through the year 2022, which means employment is projected to increase0 percent to 6 percent. This is due to tighter budgets in most jurisdictions despite growth in the demand for court services.

Employment Trend, Projected 2012–22

Total, All Occupations: 11%

Legal Occupations: 11%

Information Clerks (including Court Clerks): 2%

Note: "All Occupations" includes all occupations in the U.S. Economy. Source: U.S. Bureau of Labor Statistics, Employment Projections Program

Related Occupations
- Court Administrator
- Legal Secretary
- Paralegal

Conversation With . . . Mickey O'Neil

Court Clerk, 2 years

1. What was your individual career path in terms of education/training, entry-level job, or other significant opportunity?

I got interested the criminal justice field when I was the typical 17-, 18-year old. I was at my uncle's house and he's a lawyer. There was a law book on the table that had different scenarios, things like what threshold of evidence would you need to get a search warrant. My exacts words, and I remember it to this day, were "I could read this stuff all day." My uncle suggested that maybe I should study criminal justice, so I did. I got my bachelor's degree. To be quite honest, I wanted to be a cop all my life, but I was always a day late or a dollar short. The years that I took the exam and got a 99 or 100, there would be no police academy class because there was no money in the city budget. And the years that I either didn't do so well or didn't take the exam, there would be openings.

2. What are the most important skills and/or qualities for someone in your profession?

One of the most important skills that I use in this job is understanding people. You are dealing mostly with people who are angry. Unless it's the day the court handles adoptions, 100 percent of the people you're dealing with don't want to be there. Sometimes you're dealing with people who don't have English as their first language and, on top of that, they don't understand the system. It can be confusing and overwhelming for them. You have to treat them all with respect. You have to always, always be courteous.

3. What do you wish you had known going into this profession?

I wish I had known that I would be the only man working in my office, and that my conversations would be overheard by the 10 or 11 other people in the room. We work in cubicles. Private things that are overheard can be repeated. That doesn't have to do with the profession itself, but a lot of the court offices are like that. It drives me nuts sometimes.

4. Are there many job opportunities in your profession? In what specific areas?

Right now, there are. After I have about six years of experience, I potentially could move up to assistant clerk magistrate. It's a matter of doing your job well and putting in your time.

5. How do you see your profession changing in the next five years? What role will technology play in those changes, and what skills will be required?

Technology is absolutely changing the job. More and more tasks are done on the computer. Even something as simple as time cards. And the courts across the state are sharing more information. But much of the job involves human interaction. My typical day consists of dealing with the public and dealing with lawyers, changing dates, pulling records, and answering questions on the phone.

6. What do you enjoy most about your job? What do you enjoy least?

To be quite honest, what I enjoy most is helping people. As I said before, some people from other countries don't know the language and how the system works. They may be in the wrong court house, or the wrong office. I take pride in figuring out what they need and helping them out. I will take them by the hand over to the right office and explain to the person in that office what they need, instead of making them try to explain everything all over again. They're so grateful. I love it when people tell me, "Thank you very much," or "Thank you for writing that down for me." And even if they don't, it's OK because I know I did a good thing.

What I enjoy least is, again, the cattiness in the office, listening to my coworkers complain, or listening to them talk about Dancing with the Stars for the 900th time.

7. Can you suggest a valuable "try this" for students considering a career in your profession?

Try to get an internship in the probation department. They hire a lot of interns in probation. Sometimes, it's just dummy work, like feeding paper through a shredder. But you can also get the chance to shadow a probation officer. And just being in the courthouse will show you if it's the kind of atmosphere where you'd want to work.

SELECTED SCHOOLS

After high school, some first-time court clerks are hired without postsecondary training and on the basis of prior job experience (secretarial/clerical) only. It is beneficial in most cases, however, to obtain an associate's degree in secretarial/clerical studies, particularly one related to the legal field. Interested students should check with their school guidance counselor or research area community colleges. For those who seek employment in the federal system or in higher state courts, a bachelor's degree may be required. Refer to the listings under "Court Administrator" in the present volume for a selection of these more specialized schools.

MORE INFORMATION

National Association of Legal Secretaries
8159 East 41st Street
Tulsa, Oklahoma 74145
918.582.5188
www.nals.org

National Center for State Courts
300 Newport Avenue
Williamsburg, VA 23185-4147
800.616.6164
www.ncsc.org

National Conference of Appellate Court Clerks
450 E Street NW, Room 103
Washington, DC 20442-0001
www.appellatecourtclerks.org

Simone Isadora Flynn/Editor

Court Reporter

OVERVIEW

Sphere of Work

Court reporters, also referred to as court stenographers or deposition reporters, record court proceedings for local, state, and federal courts. Court reporters create accurate verbatim transcripts of legal proceedings, meetings, judges' speeches, and conversations between lawyers and judges. Court reporters are responsible for creating the written legal record that documents and preserves court proceedings. During court proceedings, they also assist judges, lawyers, juries, and defendants by locating specific information or records in the court record or transcript and by providing closed-captioning and real-time translating services to those in need of speech- and hearing-related services.

Work Environment

Court reporters spend their workdays creating legal transcripts for both civil and criminal court proceedings within local, state, and federal court systems. Court reporters work in administrative offices and courtrooms. Freelance court reports may work from home offices, captioning televised or webcast legal proceedings. Court reporters generally work forty-hour weeks or more. Court reporters may find the pace of the work and expectations of accuracy challenging.

Profile

Working Conditions: Work Indoors
Physical Strength: Light Work
Education Needs: Technical/Community College, Bachelor's Degree
Licensure/Certification: Required
Physical Abilities Not Required: No Heavy Labor
Opportunities For Experience: Internship, Military Service
Holland Interest Score*: CSE

* See Appendix A

Occupation Interest

Individuals drawn to the court reporter profession tend to be intelligent and detail oriented. The most successful court reporters display traits such as focus, excellent hearing, hand-eye coordination, time management, initiative, and concern for individuals and society. Court reporters should enjoy working within the legal system. They should also stay abreast of the news and trends in the greater community.

A Day in the Life—Duties and Responsibilities

The court reporter's area of job specialization and work environment determine his or her daily occupational duties and responsibilities. Court reporting specialties include stenographic recording, real-time captioning, electronic reporting, voice writing, and webcasting.

During legal proceedings, court reporters record testimony from all witnesses, legal objections and motions, instructions and questions asked between the judge and the jury, ruling, sentencing, appeals, and other events and conversations. They may use shorthand, computerized equipment, or a stenotype machine to capture these events. Court reporters ask all legal participants to restate or clarify speech or information that is inaudible, unclear, or spoken too quietly to be understood. They also provide real-time translation or captions for deaf or hearing-impaired people involved in legal proceedings and ensure that all captioning complies with federal regulations.

When a proceeding is over, the court reporter creates transcripts from all recordings. This involves creating the computer dictionary used to translate keystroke codes or voice files into written text, correcting grammar and spelling errors in the resulting text, and generating copies of the new transcript. These copies must be compared regularly with the original to ensure accuracy. The original transcript must be filed in a timely manner, since it will be requested by participants in the proceedings and become public record. Rulings mentioned in the transcript are verified with the presiding judge as a further accuracy check. When people request copies of the legal transcript or want to read the original, the court reporter is responsible for complying with those requests in a timely manner as well.

In addition to these duties, court reporters must maintain all court reporting equipment, including stenotype machine, analog tape recorders, digital equipment, and voice silencing microphones. They also develop personalized methods for storing and accessing stenographic data, audio recording, and voice files.

Duties and Responsibilities

- Recording legal proceedings in the form of written transcripts
- Operating a stenotype machine and creating a transcript using computer-aided transcription
- Reading portions of the transcript during a trial at the judge's request
- Asking speakers to clarify inaudible statements
- Securing all records in one's office
- Preparing court orders and related legal documents
- Filing a legible transcript of the records of a court case with the court clerk's office
- Furnishing a transcript of the records taken to any party on request

WORK ENVIRONMENT

Physical Environment

The immediate physical environment of court reporters varies based on their specialization. Court reporters spend their workdays recording and transcribing legal proceedings in business offices, home offices, local courts, state courts, federal courts, government agencies, and prisons.

Relevant Skills and Abilities

Communication Skills
- Editing written information
- Expressing thoughts and ideas
- Speaking and writing effectively

Interpersonal/Social Skills
- Cooperating with others
- Working as a member of a team

Organization & Management Skills
- Managing time
- Meeting goals and deadlines
- Paying attention to and handling details
- Performing routine work

Human Environment

Court reporters work with a wide variety of people and should be comfortable interacting with court clerks, court administrators, incarcerated people, lawyers, judges, defendants, plaintiffs, witnesses, and juries.

Technological Environment

In their daily activities, court reporters use a wide variety of technology and equipment, including stenotype machines, audio recording devices, voice recognition and translation software, computers, Internet communication technology, photocopiers, and printers.

EDUCATION, TRAINING, AND ADVANCEMENT

High School/Secondary

High school students interested in pursuing a career as a court reporter should prepare themselves by developing good study habits. High school-level study of typing, foreign languages, political science, sociology, shorthand, and psychology will provide a strong foundation for postsecondary-level study in the field. Due to the diversity of court reporter specialties, high school students interested in this career path may benefit from seeking internships or part-time work that expose them to the legal system.

Suggested High School Subjects
- Business & Computer Technology
- Composition
- English
- Government
- Keyboarding
- Shorthand

Famous First

The first shorthand account of a trial was made in St. Johns, Md., in 1681 by John Llywellin, clerk of the Council. The trial involved a charge of mutiny against one Josias Fendall, who was found guilty and sentenced to pay "40,000 pounds of Tobacco for a fine" and to be kept in custody at his own expense until the fine was paid in full. Upon completion of his sentence Fendall was to be "for ever banished out of this Province."

College/Postsecondary

Postsecondary students interested in becoming court reporters should work towards an associate's degree or bachelor's degree in pre-law, criminology, or a related field. Vocational and technical schools also offer formal court reporter training programs. Coursework in education, psychology, and foreign languages may also prove useful in their future work. Postsecondary students can gain work experience and potential advantage in their future job searches by securing internships or part-time employment within the legal system.

Related College Majors

- Administrative Assistant/Secretarial Science
- Court Reporter
- Legal Administrative Assistant/Secretary

Adult Job Seekers

Adults seeking employment as court reporters should have, at a minimum, a high school diploma or associate's degree. Some court reporting organizations and specialties require extensive court reporting experience, on-the-job training, bachelor's degrees, or second language proficiency. Adult job seekers should educate themselves about the educational and professional license requirements of their home states and the organizations where they seek employment. They may benefit from joining professional associations to help with networking and job searching. Professional court reporting associations, such as the National Court Reporters Association and the United States Court Reporters Association, generally offer job-finding workshops and maintain lists and forums of available jobs.

Professional Certification and Licensure

Court reporting certification and licensure requirements vary by job specialization and state. Interested individuals should verify their state's requirements. Professional associations, such as the National Verbatim Reporters Association, National Court Reporters Association, United States Court Reporters Association, and American Association of Electronic Reporters and Transcribers, offer a variety of certifications for court reporters. These certifications generally require completion of dictation and transcription examinations and a written test on spelling, grammar, and legal terminology. All court reporter certifications require continuing education courses as a condition of certification renewal.

Additional Requirements

Individuals who find satisfaction, success, and job security as court reporters will be knowledgeable about the profession's requirements, responsibilities, and opportunities. Court reporters must demonstrate integrity and professional ethics as they have access to confidential legal information. Membership in professional court reporting associations is encouraged among all court reporters as a means of building professional community and networking.

EARNINGS AND ADVANCEMENT

Court reporters' salaries vary widely by type of court, geographic location, skill, experience and level of responsibility. State and local court wages are lower than federal wages. Mean annual earnings of court reporters were $53,000 in 2012. The lowest ten percent earned less than $24,790, and the highest ten percent earned more than $90,530.

Court reporters may receive paid vacations, holidays, and sick days; life and health insurance; and retirement benefits. These are usually paid by the employer. Freelance court reporters working for large firms often receive similar benefits. In some locations, court reporters are provided with recording equipment, and in other locations court reporters must provide their own equipment. Freelance court reporters must usually purchase their own recording equipment.

Metropolitan Areas with the Highest Employment Level in this Occupation

Metropolitan area	Employment[1]	Employment per thousand jobs	Hourly mean wage
Los Angeles-Long Beach-Glendale, CA	920	0.24	$35.59
New York-White Plains-Wayne, NY-NJ	700	0.14	$41.95
Washington-Arlington-Alexandria, DC-VA-MD-WV	470	0.20	$18.94
Atlanta-Sandy Springs-Marietta, GA	400	0.18	$27.22
Pittsburgh, PA	350	0.31	$15.59
Houston-Sugar Land-Baytown, TX	320	0.12	$30.71
Dallas-Plano-Irving, TX	300	0.14	$29.88
Philadelphia, PA	250	0.14	$24.26

[1]Does not include self-employed. Source: Bureau of Labor Statistics

EMPLOYMENT AND OUTLOOK

Court reporters held about 19,000 jobs in 2012. More than half worked for state and local governments. Employment of court reporters is expected to grow about as fast as the average for all occupations through the year 2022, which means employment is projected to increase 8 percent to 13 percent. Demand for court reporters will be spurred by the continuing need for accurate transcription of court proceedings and in pretrial depositions, and by the growing need to create captions of Internet programming, live or pre-recorded television and other technologies, and to provide other real-time translating services for the deaf and hard-of-hearing community.

Federal legislation mandates that all new television programming must be captioned for deaf and hard-of-hearing persons. Additionally, the Americans with Disabilities Act gives deaf and hard-of-hearing students in colleges and universities the right to request access to real-time translation in their classes.

Employment Trend, Projected 2012–22

Total, All Occupations: 11%

Legal Occupations: 11%

Court Reporters: 10%

Note: "All Occupations" includes all occupations in the U.S. Economy. Source: U.S. Bureau of Labor Statistics, Employment Projections Program

Related Occupations
- Court Clerk
- Legal Secretary

Related Military Occupations
- Legal Specialist & Court Reporter

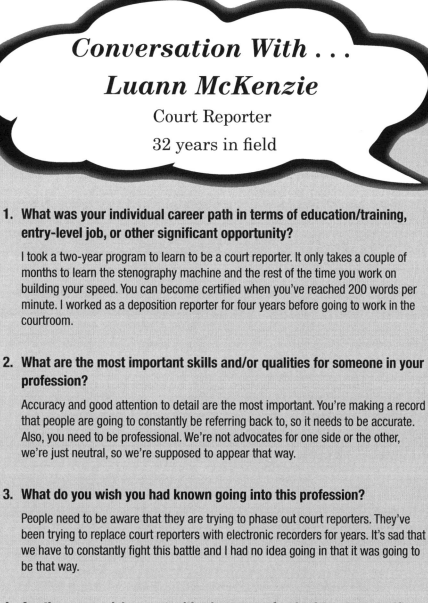

Conversation With . . .
Luann McKenzie
Court Reporter
32 years in field

1. What was your individual career path in terms of education/training, entry-level job, or other significant opportunity?

I took a two-year program to learn to be a court reporter. It only takes a couple of months to learn the stenography machine and the rest of the time you work on building your speed. You can become certified when you've reached 200 words per minute. I worked as a deposition reporter for four years before going to work in the courtroom.

2. What are the most important skills and/or qualities for someone in your profession?

Accuracy and good attention to detail are the most important. You're making a record that people are going to constantly be referring back to, so it needs to be accurate. Also, you need to be professional. We're not advocates for one side or the other, we're just neutral, so we're supposed to appear that way.

3. What do you wish you had known going into this profession?

People need to be aware that they are trying to phase out court reporters. They've been trying to replace court reporters with electronic recorders for years. It's sad that we have to constantly fight this battle and I had no idea going in that it was going to be that way.

4. Are there many job opportunities in your profession? In what specific areas?

In California, we have budget issues. People are being laid off, including court reporters. There are still job opportunities, but there's not a lot of movement in the profession now. People are either staying put or getting laid off.

5. **How do you see your profession changing in the next five years, what role will technology play in those changes, and what skills will be required?**

Some states have already gone to using electronic recorders and gotten rid of court reporters. Some only use court reporters in criminal proceedings. They use electronic recorders for family law and civil matters.

Right now if a judge needs me to looks something up, I can have the answer in literally 10 minutes. The accuracy will go down tremendously if you have someone else transcribing a recording. We transcribe what we heard in court. As record keepers we can say, 'hey slow down, I didn't hear that.' In a recording, if someone slams a door shut, it obliterates everything that's being said.

6. **Do you have any general advice or additional professional insights to share with someone in your profession? What is the most fulfilling part of your job, and what is the most frustrating?**

When I was a new reporter I was kind of timid and I didn't want to speak up if I wasn't hearing something. My advice is, don't be shy. You have to protect the record. Speak up. It's up to you to get the record straight.

The most fulfilling part of the job is turning out a beautiful, accurate, on-time transcript. That's fun for me. You're looking through the changes and it's all perfect. It's a very important part of the process because people are always changing what they say and can't remember what they said and I think, 'Wow, I really serve a purpose here. People need me, I'm putting down here what happened and people need to know that."

The most frustrated part is dealing with fast talkers, mumblers and people with heavy accents. That's really frustrating.

7. **Can you suggest a valuable "try this" for students considering a career in your profession?**

People who are interested should go to a courtroom and sit in on a proceeding to see what it's all about. Go to a deposition and watch the reporter in action. Just listen with a critical ear and in your mind, try to write everything down. Most of the students have to do intern hours and have to set up their machine during a proceeding. It's invaluable because then you get a real good feel for what it's like. I love it when students come in with me because you can share what you learned with them.

SELECTED SCHOOLS

Those interested in a career as a court reporter may obtain the necessary training at a technical/community college or at a commercial vocational school. Interested students should check with their school guidance counselor or research area postsecondary schools. In some cases it is beneficial to obtain a bachelor's degree in legal administration. The website of the National Court Reporters Association (see below) provides a list of certified schools and programs.

MORE INFORMATION

American Association of Electronic Reporters and Transcribers
P.O. Box 9826
Wilmington, DE 19809
302.475.2173
www.aaert.org

National Center for State Courts
300 Newport Avenue
Williamsburg, VA 23185-4147
800.616.6164
www.ncsc.org

National Court Reporters Association
8224 Old Courthouse Road
Vienna, VA 22182-3808
800.272.6272
www.ncra.org

United States Court Reporter Association
8430 Gross Point Road
Suite 115
Skokie, IL 60077-2036
847.470.9500
Info.uscra@gmail.com
www.uscra.org

Simone Isadora Flynn/Editor

Criminologist

Snapshot

Career Cluster: Social Science; Law & Criminal Justice
Interests: Research, analyzing data, communicating with others
Earnings (Yearly Average): $58,500
Employment & Outlook: Average Growth Expected

OVERVIEW

Sphere of Work

Criminologists are sociologists who specialize in the study of crime, deviant behavior, and the criminal justice system. They usually specialize in certain types of crime, such as juvenile or white-collar crime, a certain type of offense, such as serial murder or hate crimes, or a certain aspect of the criminal justice system, such as rehabilitation or police brutality. Some criminologists also study crime scenes, but they should not be confused with forensic scientists (criminalists) or crime scene investigators (CSIs), whose jobs are more narrowly focused on the physical evidence, or forensics, of crime scenes.

Work Environment

Criminologists work in federal, state, and local law enforcement agencies, including the Federal Bureau of Investigation (FBI), U.S. Department of Homeland Security (DHS), and state and local police departments. They also work for correctional institutions, universities, private security companies or banks, and public policy research organizations (or think tanks). Their jobs usually involve both office work and fieldwork. Their hours vary widely depending on the employer, tenure, and type of research, and may require much flexibility, although some criminologists do work a regular forty-hour week.

Profile

Working Conditions: Work Indoors
Physical Strength: Light Work
Education Needs: Master's Degree, Doctoral Degree
Licensure/Certification: Usually Not Required
Physical Abilities Not Required: No Heavy Labor
Opportunities For Experience: Internship
Holland Interest Score*: EIS

* See Appendix A

Occupation Interest

People who are interested in criminology are frequently inquisitive by nature. They may wonder what causes a person to commit a murder, or whether capital punishment deters crime, or they may search for ways in which a community can work together to end gang violence. They enjoy conducting research that will shed light on motives for human behavior, particularly behavior considered to be deviant, and they work to better society. Logical thinkers with a flair for thinking creatively, criminologists tend to find satisfaction in working with both statistics and people. They usually have excellent written and oral communication skills.

A Day in the Life—Duties and Responsibilities

As social scientists, criminologists spend much of their time researching hypotheses, gathering information, analyzing data, and presenting their studies to their colleagues, various agencies and organizations, and/or the general public. Criminologists conduct some of their research on a computer, accessing many different databases and websites for statistics, newspaper articles, police reports, historical information, recent research studies, and other documents.

They also study crime scenes, interview criminals, victims, and their families, or investigate entire communities. Sometimes their research may lead them to foreign countries or involve many different cities.

As criminologists analyze statistics and other information, they look for patterns that might help in preventing crime or in making public policy more effective. For example, their research may help law enforcement in profiling criminals or, to the contrary, show that profiling doesn't work. Criminologists may demonstrate the need for more funding for prisons or police officers, or, instead, funding for education, social service organizations, and/or rehabilitation centers. Their research findings can lead to changes in sentencing guidelines or the establishment of programs intended to help victims.

Criminologists publish their data in journals, reports, and/or books. They also give speeches and sometimes prepare videos, films, or podcasts. Criminologists are also sometimes asked to testify as expert witnesses in court cases. Other responsibilities might include teaching, and/or handling the duties of forensic scientists, which include working with cadavers, DNA samples, and other crime scene data and evidence.

Duties and Responsibilities

- Researching crime and patterns of crime
- Analyzing crime data using statistical methods and other means
- Conducting field visits to prisons, police departments, rehabilitation centers, and social service organizations to collect research data
- Interviewing criminals, victims, families, law enforcement personnel, and others to shed light on crime, criminal behavior, and responses to crime
- Developing hypotheses and putting them to the test using quantitative and/or qualitative data and information
- Writing reports and making policy recommendations
- Lecturing and writing academic papers and books
- Testifying in court or formal hearings

WORK ENVIRONMENT

Physical Environment

Some criminologists rarely work outside the office, while others may deal regularly with venues such as prisons, rehab facilities, police departments, courts, urban neighborhoods, and so on. They may also spend time in libraries collecting material for their research.

Relevant Skills and Abilities

Analytical Skills
- Analyzing information

Communication Skills
- Speaking and writing effectively

Interpersonal/Social Skills
- Being objective
- Being patient
- Cooperating with others
- Working independently and/or as a member of a team

Organization & Management Skills
- Managing time and resources
- Meeting goals and deadlines
- Paying attention to and handling details

Research & Planning Skills
- Collecting data
- Developing a plan
- Solving problems

Human Environment

A criminologist employed in an academic environment reports to a department head or director, and may supervise graduate students and assistants. Other criminologists work under a director or supervisor, and may oversee staff and interns. Most criminologists interact with a variety of people, including law enforcement personnel, lawyers and judges, medical professionals, forensic scientists, criminals, victims, and the general public.

Technological Environment

Criminologists rely heavily on computers, cell phones, scanners/copiers, and other office equipment. Those who work extensively with statistics will need to be familiar with statistical software programs, whereas those who rely more heavily on qualitative data (interviews, ethnographic description) will primarily use word processing software. Criminologists may also use still and video cameras.

EDUCATION, TRAINING, AND ADVANCEMENT

High School/Secondary

The best preparation for a career as a criminologist is a well-rounded college-preparatory program that includes calculus and statistics, computer science, a foreign language, and courses in the social sciences (political science, sociology, anthropology, and/or psychology). Part-time jobs or volunteer work in the community helps to develop an understanding of people and social institutions.

Suggested High School Subjects
- Algebra
- Applied Math
- Calculus
- College Preparatory
- Composition
- Computer Science
- English
- Geometry
- Psychology
- Social Studies
- Sociology
- Statistics
- Trigonometry

Famous First

The first national conference on crime was held on October 11-12, 1935, in Trenton, N.J., with a roster of delegates from 41 states and from the federal government. It was an era of rampant mob violence and crimes committed by outlaws such as Bonnie and Clyde, Ma Barker, and John Dillinger. (The era has been duly dubbed the Public Enemy era.) The purpose of the conference was to curb crime throughout the country by developing reciprocal legislation and interstate cooperation agreements.

College/Postsecondary

Most criminology positions require a master's degree or doctorate in criminology or a related subject. Since the study of criminology encompasses several different disciplines, there are many suitable undergraduate majors, including political science, criminal justice, computer criminology, forensics, sociology, and psychology. Students should plan to take courses in as many of these disciplines as possible, and consider a double major or plan to minor in one or more subjects. Advanced degree programs in criminology and criminal justice, and their related disciplines, are aimed especially at those students interested in doing original research, consulting, and/or teaching at the college level. Internships and part- or full-time jobs working in related agencies will provide hands-on experience.

Related College Majors
- Anthropology
- Criminology
- Political Science & Government
- Sociology
- Urban Studies/Affairs

Adult Job Seekers

Criminologists come from many different backgrounds. Adults who have worked in the legal profession or in law enforcement, public administration, or counseling may find criminology to be the next logical step in their careers.

Advancement for criminologists is dependent upon the size and type of organization, as well as one's education. Entry-level positions for those with a bachelor's degree in criminology and criminal justice tend to be more limited in scope; candidates with doctorate degrees have far greater opportunities for conducting original research or moving into management or consulting positions.

Professional Certification and Licensure

There is no national certification or statewide licensing program for criminologists. However, many colleges and universities offer certificates in criminology and related programs, and some states, counties, and local law enforcement organizations do require licensure for employment.

Additional Requirements

Criminologists may be subject to background and security checks. Fieldwork will require a driver's license and good physical health.

EARNINGS AND ADVANCEMENT

Earnings of criminologists increase with experience and position. Advanced study is highly recommended because of strong competition in this field. Criminologists working in research and development centers (including colleges and universities) earned between $45,000 and $92,000 annually in 2012. Those working for state and local governments earned less, between $30,000 and $67,000 annually in 2012.

Criminologists may receive paid vacations, holidays, and sick days; life and health insurance; and retirement benefits. These are usually paid by the employer.

Metropolitan Areas with the Highest Employment Level in this Occupation

Metropolitan area	Employment	Employment per thousand jobs	Hourly mean wage
Los Angeles-Long Beach-Glendale, CA	210	0.06	$39.98
Ann Arbor, MI	190	0.97	$37.59
Boston-Cambridge-Quincy, MA	170	0.10	$44.36
Philadelphia, PA	160	0.09	$34.20
San Francisco-San Mateo-Redwood City, CA	150	0.15	$40.97
Washington-Arlington-Alexandria, DC-VA-MD-WV	140	0.06	$49.70
Seattle-Bellevue-Everett, WA	120	0.08	$30.27
New York-White Plains-Wayne, NY-NJ	100	0.02	$50.01

Source: Bureau of Labor Statistics

EMPLOYMENT AND OUTLOOK

Sociologists, of which criminologists are a part, held about 4,000 jobs nationally in 2012. Employment is expected to grow about as fast as the average for all occupations through the year 2022, which means employment is projected to increase 9 percent to 15 percent. Employment opportunities for criminologists are good, but government budgets will limit federal and state employment. Those persons with only a bachelor's or a master's degree may have difficulty finding a job. Persons with a Ph.D. and skills in quantitative research have the best chances for employment.

Employment Trend, Projected 2012–22

Sociologists (incl. Criminologists): 15%

Social Scientists and Related Workers: 11%

Total, All Occupations: 11%

Note: "All Occupations" includes all occupations in the U.S. Economy. Source: U.S. Bureau of Labor Statistics, Employment Projections Program

Related Occupations
- Forensic Scientist
- Sociologist

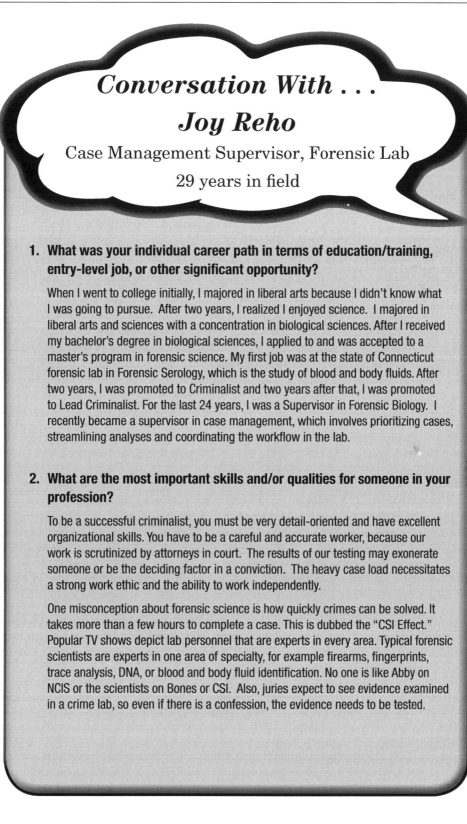

Conversation With . . .
Joy Reho
Case Management Supervisor, Forensic Lab
29 years in field

1. What was your individual career path in terms of education/training, entry-level job, or other significant opportunity?

When I went to college initially, I majored in liberal arts because I didn't know what I was going to pursue. After two years, I realized I enjoyed science. I majored in liberal arts and sciences with a concentration in biological sciences. After I received my bachelor's degree in biological sciences, I applied to and was accepted to a master's program in forensic science. My first job was at the state of Connecticut forensic lab in Forensic Serology, which is the study of blood and body fluids. After two years, I was promoted to Criminalist and two years after that, I was promoted to Lead Criminalist. For the last 24 years, I was a Supervisor in Forensic Biology. I recently became a supervisor in case management, which involves prioritizing cases, streamlining analyses and coordinating the workflow in the lab.

2. What are the most important skills and/or qualities for someone in your profession?

To be a successful criminalist, you must be very detail-oriented and have excellent organizational skills. You have to be a careful and accurate worker, because our work is scrutinized by attorneys in court. The results of our testing may exonerate someone or be the deciding factor in a conviction. The heavy case load necessitates a strong work ethic and the ability to work independently.

One misconception about forensic science is how quickly crimes can be solved. It takes more than a few hours to complete a case. This is dubbed the "CSI Effect." Popular TV shows depict lab personnel that are experts in every area. Typical forensic scientists are experts in one area of specialty, for example firearms, fingerprints, trace analysis, DNA, or blood and body fluid identification. No one is like Abby on NCIS or the scientists on Bones or CSI. Also, juries expect to see evidence examined in a crime lab, so even if there is a confession, the evidence needs to be tested.

3. What do you wish you had known going into this profession?

I wish I had known when I was still in school how much I would have to rely on strong math skills in my day-to-day job. You have to have a solid footing in statistics and molecular genetics. Additionally, I wish I had stronger computer skills when I started out.

4. Are there many job opportunities in your profession? In what specific areas?

Yes, there are. One of the fields within forensic science that is seeing the most growth involves computer crimes. The field of molecular biology—and DNA in particular—is also burgeoning.

5. How do you see your profession changing in the next five years? What role will technology play in those changes, and what skills will be required?

Technology will definitely play a role in the changes that are coming. There will be more emphasis on robotics for DNA extraction because it allows a faster throughput of sampling and extraction. Additionally, newer techniques are more sensitive, allowing for a smaller sample size. Finally, computer forensics will only continue to become more commonplace and important in the next five or more years.

6. What do you enjoy most about your job? What do you enjoy least?

What I enjoy most about my job is the fulfillment I get from assisting police departments in solving crimes. It's a feeling of accomplishment when I use science to bring closure to victims. What I enjoy least is the volume of casework. It can really be overwhelming at times. There's a constant struggle for funding to obtain supplies and equipment that we need to do our job. This can be frustrating and time-consuming.

7. Can you suggest a valuable "try this" for students considering a career in your profession?

Students considering working as a criminalist could undertake a research project on an area of interest in forensic science. Are you interested in fingerprinting techniques? What about animal hair identification? Researching topics like this will help you discover how engaging you find the subject, and that, in turn, may help you figure out if this is really something you'd want to do for a career. You could prepare a display for a science fair and volunteer to show it at a Girl Scout or Boy Scout meeting. Are you able to clearly explain the topic?

Our lab has internships for college students. However, due to the nature of what we do, job shadowing is not an option. A major concern is contamination of the evidence by anyone near the evidence. Anyone entering the lab needs to provide a DNA sample that will be entered into the staff index of DNA profiles.

SELECTED SCHOOLS

Many colleges, including many community colleges, offer programs in sociology and criminal justice. Some of them offer programs specifically in criminology. Below are listed selected graduate schools offering programs in this field.

Florida State University
College of Criminology and Criminal Justice Eppes Hall
145 Convocation Way
Tallahassee, FL 32306
850.644.4050
crim.fsu.edu

John Jay College of Criminal Justice
City University of New York
524 W. 59th Street
New York, NY 10019
212.237.8000
www.jjay.cuny.edu

Michigan State University
School of Criminal Justice
Baker Hall
644 Auditorium Road, Rm. 560
East Lansing, MI 48824
517.355.2197
cj.msu.edu

Pennsylvania State University, University Park
Department of Sociology and Criminology
211 Oswald Tower
University Park, PA 16802
814.865.2527
www.sociology.la.psu.edu

Rutgers, the State University of New Jersey, Newark
School of Criminal Justice
123 Washington Street
Newark, NJ 07102
973.353.3311
rcsj.newark.rutgers.edu

University at Albany State University of New York
School of Criminal Justice
1400 Washington Avenue
Albany, NY 12222
518.442.3300
www.albany.edu/scj

University of California, Irvine
Department of Criminology, Law and Society
2340 Social Ecology II
Irvine, CA 92697
949.824.5575
cls.soceco.uci.edu

University of Cincinnati
School of Criminal Justice
PO Box 210002
Cincinnati, OH 45221
513.556.4307
cech.uc.edu/crimnaljustice.html

University of Maryland, College Park
Department of Criminology and
Criminal Justice
2220 Samuel J. LeFrank Hall
College Park, MD 20742
301. 405.4699
www.ccjs.umd.edu

University of Missouri, St. Louis
Department of Criminology and
Criminal Justice
One University Boulevard
324 Lucas Hall
St. Louis, MO 63121
314.516.4499
www.umsl.edu/ccj

MORE INFORMATION

American Society of Criminology
1314 Kinnear Road, Suite 212
Columbus, Ohio 43212-1156
614.292.9207
www.asc41.com

American Sociological Association
1430 K Street NW, Suite 600
Washington, DC 20005
202.383.9005
www.asanet.org

National Criminal Justice Association
720 7th Street NW
Washington, DC 20001
202.628.8550
www.ncja.org

Sally Driscoll/Editor

Customs Inspector

Snapshot

Career Cluster: Government & Public Administration Law and Criminal Justice; Security Services
Interests: Law enforcement, safety and security, dealing with crises
Earnings (Yearly Average): $73,923
Employment & Outlook: Slower Than Average Growth Expected

OVERVIEW

Sphere of Work

Customs inspectors are federal law enforcement agents who uphold the laws and regulations governing imports and exports. Working under the umbrella of the U.S. Department of Homeland Security, customs inspectors perform thorough checks of commercial trucks, ships, trains, and cargo planes to ensure that all incoming and outgoing shipments are accounted for and present no danger, and to determine the duties or taxes that must be paid on incoming cargo. They also inspect international travelers' passports and visas, search for drugs and other contraband in baggage and clothing, and detain potentially dangerous individuals. Customs inspectors collaborate

with other law enforcement officials as well as private shipping and logistics companies to facilitate compliance with federal laws.

Work Environment

Customs inspectors work in shipyards, commercial and private airfields and airports, rail yards, border stations, and other locations where international travel and shipping occur. These venues are busy, with many people and packages passing through every day. Some customs inspectors must work outside for most of the day, in all types of weather. Most work standard forty-hour weeks; however, customs inspectors may work late-night, weekend, and holiday shifts, as the work they perform is required twenty-four hours a day year-round. Coping with uncooperative travelers or shippers can add stress to the job.

Profile

Working Conditions: Work both Indoors and Outdoors
Physical Strength: Light to Medium Work
Education Needs: On-The-Job Training High School Diploma or G.E.D. Technical/Community College
Licensure/Certification: Required
Physical Abilities Not Required: No Heavy Labor
Opportunities For Experience: Part-Time Work
Holland Interest Score*: CEI

* See Appendix A

Occupation Interest

Customs inspectors safeguard the country's borders and ports of entry from international terrorism, drug trafficking, and other kinds of smuggling, and they collect revenue for the government in the form of duties and taxes from commercial shippers. Therefore, prospective customs inspectors must have keen judgment, strong observational and decision-making skills, and personal integrity. They should also be extroverted, communicate effectively, and thrive under pressure. Demand for qualified customs inspectors remains moderately high, which means jobs are available, on a competitive basis, in a wide range of locations.

A Day in the Life—Duties and Responsibilities

The daily responsibilities of customs inspectors vary based on their work setting. For example, inspectors who work in airports meet individual travelers, check their identification and other documentation, inspect luggage and cargo, and interview travelers as they enter the airport. On occasion, they may also perform pat-downs to check for drugs, weapons, or other contraband. Airport customs inspectors also supervise the loading and unloading of cargo, checking manifests, and weighing and measuring boxes and materials. They must keep thorough records of all passenger interactions and inspected cargo and luggage.

Customs inspectors working in other areas, such as at border stations and at ports of entry, perform additional tasks. At ports of entry, customs inspectors board incoming ships to inspect cargo and ensure that all documentation is accurate. They also seize any illegal materials or undeclared goods, including shipments from countries whose exports are forbidden in the United States under federal boycotts. Port customs officials may even impound ships or have them stay offshore pending a thorough investigation. Border station–based customs inspectors, meanwhile, halt vehicles along the U.S. borders with Canada and Mexico. These officials check passports and visas of travelers, board and search trailers, interview suspicious individuals, and verify vehicle documentation. In many cases, customs inspectors become specialists in one particular area, such as narcotics, antiques, agriculture, exotic animals, or machinery.

Some customs inspectors have the authority to carry firearms, issue warrants, and make arrests in relation to customs law violations. They may testify in court proceedings related to seized goods.

Duties and Responsibilities

- Examining, counting, weighing, gauging, measuring, and sampling commercial and noncommercial cargo
- Insuring cargo is properly described
- Inspecting baggage and articles worn by passengers and crew members
- Insuring all property complies with entrance and clearance requirements
- Insuring all merchandise is declared and proper duties are paid
- Intercepting all contraband

WORK ENVIRONMENT

Physical Environment

Customs inspectors work in well-lit and well-ventilated airports, shipping ports, border stations, and other ports of entry. These locations also experience heavy traffic, with many travelers and/or shipments passing through each day. Many venues are outdoors and require inspectors to work in all weather conditions, day or night. Due to the nature of their work, customs inspectors risk exposure to dangerous substances, such as explosives, drugs, and toxic chemicals.

Relevant Skills and Abilities

Communication Skills
- Speaking effectively

Interpersonal/Social Skills
- Being patient
- Working as part of a team

Organization & Management Skills
- Following instructions
- Managing time
- Paying attention to and handling details

Other Skills
- Adhering to rules and procedures

Human Environment

Customs inspectors work with a wide range of individuals, which may include international travelers, commercial ship crews, forklift operators, dockworkers, airline and airport staff, truck drivers, and members of federal, state, and local law enforcement. During the course of their work, customs inspectors must deal calmly and firmly with travelers and shippers.

Technological Environment

Customs inspectors must have training in the use of lethal and nonlethal weapons, including handguns and pepper spray. In the inspection process, they use radiation and weapons detection equipment, such as explosives detectors, radioisotope detection devices, and x-ray and gamma-ray imaging machinery. They must use computer systems that link them with international and national law enforcement resources, such as the National Crime Information Center (NCIC) database. Customs inspectors should also be familiar with basic word processing and spreadsheet software, as they must record daily interactions and transactions.

EDUCATION, TRAINING, AND ADVANCEMENT

High School/Secondary

High school students interested in becoming customs inspectors are encouraged to take courses in social studies, government, and history. Psychology and sociology courses are also useful, as is English, which promotes communication skills. Additionally, foreign language training is highly beneficial for aspiring customs inspectors.

Suggested High School Subjects
- English
- Foreign Languages
- Government
- Humanities
- Psychology
- Social Studies
- Sociology

Famous First

The first customhouse in colonial America was established in Yorktown, Va, pictured. It was built in 1706 by Richard Ambler, who occupied it as "Collector of Ports for Yorktown" in 1720. At this period Yorktown was the port of entry for New York, Philadelphia, and other northern cities. An old tombstone in Hampton, Va., reads "Peter Heyman, Collector of His Majesty's custom, died April 29, 1700." Heyman is presumed to have been one of the earliest collectors of customs at Yorktown.

Library of Congress

College/Postsecondary

Customs inspectors are encouraged to pursue undergraduate courses in law enforcement, criminal justice, or a related field, although three or more years of direct experience in customs inspection may serve as an alternative to a postsecondary degree. Candidates must enter and complete a fifteen-week training course at the Customs Border Protection Academy in Artesia, New Mexico. Requirements may vary between work settings and specialties. Interested individuals should research the requirements of the agency and/or specialty in which they wish to work.

Related College Majors
- Law Enforcement/Police Science
- Security & Loss Prevention Services

Adult Job Seekers

Qualified customs inspectors may find positions on the federal government's employment website or by applying directly to positions offered by the Department of Homeland Security, U.S. Customs and Border Protection, or U.S. Immigration and Customs Enforcement. They may also obtain job placement upon completion of the Customs Border Protection Academy. Bilingual applicants with college degrees may find employment as customs inspectors more easily.

Professional Certification and Licensure

Customs inspectors must be trained and licensed to carry a firearm. They must also pass a civil service examination and have a valid U.S. driver's license.

Additional Requirements

Customs inspectors must be citizens of the United States who are over the age of twenty-one. They should be physically fit, able to work on their feet for long periods in all weather conditions. Customs inspectors are required to undergo a comprehensive background check, as well as frequent medical checkups and drug tests. Prior military or law enforcement experience is also useful for many positions. Fluency in a foreign language is highly useful for all customs inspectors and is required for U.S. Border Patrol positions.

EARNINGS AND ADVANCEMENT

Customs inspectors had mean annual earnings of $73,923 in 2012.

Customs inspectors employed by federal, state, and local governments and large firms may receive paid vacations, holidays, and sick days; life and health insurance; and retirement benefits. These are usually paid by the employer.

Metropolitan Areas with the Highest Employment Level in this Occupation

Metropolitan area	Employment	Employment per thousand jobs	Hourly mean wage
New York-White Plains-Wayne, NY-NJ	8,600	1.67	$52.09
Los Angeles-Long Beach-Glendale, CA	3,730	1.03	$48.08
Chicago-Joliet-Naperville, IL	2,500	1.07	$54.37
Washington-Arlington-Alexandria, DC-VA-MD-WV	2,290	1.34	$39.77
Miami-Miami Beach-Kendall, FL	2,030	0.90	$30.64
Newark-Union, NJ-PA	2,010	1.59	n/a
Phoenix-Mesa-Glendale, AZ	1,740	1.00	$43.82
Houston-Sugar Land-Baytown, TX	1,450	0.83	$40.70

Source: Bureau of Labor Statistics

EMPLOYMENT AND OUTLOOK

Customs inspectors held about 100,000 jobs nationally in 2012. Employment is expected to grow somewhat slower than the average for all occupations through the year 2022, which means employment is projected to increase 3 percent to 9 percent. A more security-conscious society and concern about drug-related crimes will continue to create jobs. Job openings will also arise from the need to replace those workers who transfer to other occupations, retire, or leave the labor force for other reasons.

Employment Trend, Projected 2012–22

Total, All Occupations: 11%

Customs Inspectors: 8%

Police and Detectives: 5%

Note: "All Occupations" includes all occupations in the U.S. Economy. Source: U.S. Bureau of Labor Statistics, Employment Projections Program

Related Occupations
- Federal Law Enforcement Agent
- Fish & Game Warden
- Inspector & Compliance Officer
- Security & Fire Alarm System Installer

Conversation With . . .
Jack Ramsey

Recruiting Program Manager, U.S. Customs
and Border Protection, 12 years in field

1. What was your individual career path in terms of education/training, entry-level job, or other significant opportunity?

I was in the military, a Navy diver. When I retired, I was looking for something different to do. I already had my graduate degree and I wanted to go into law enforcement. I worked as a college campus police officer for a year. But U.S. Customs looked like the place to go at the time, and I was hired as a customs inspector.

2. What are the most important skills and/or qualities for someone in your profession?

You've got to be willing to become part of a dynamic team that works in a very fast paced environment. Every day represents new challenges. You have to be technologically astute. Everything we do has some type of technology behind it. You've got to be flexible. You have to be able to think on your feet, be able to determine if someone is telling you the truth or not. You have to be open to all ideas, accepting of all cultures.

3. What do you wish you had known going into this profession?

For the new person coming in, I think they need to know they have to be in better shape than they thought. There are physical fitness standards going into this job. The application process is a year long. Because it's a national security position, it requires a thorough background investigation and a polygraph test. There are medical exams, a physical fitness test, structured interviews, both video and face-to-face. If you're hired, you're accepted into the training academy, which is 17-19 weeks long.

4. Are there many job opportunities in your profession? In what specific areas?

Right now, we're getting ready to hire an additional 2,000 customs patrol and border officers, nationwide. The biggest need is on the borders. Most of those jobs will go to our busiest ports.

5. How do you see your profession changing in the next five years? What role will technology play in those changes, and what skills will be required?

The technology is getting better every year. Customs and Border Patrol is constantly upgrading its technology to keep up with what's really happening out there. Everything from biometrics to non-intrusive inspection systems using gamma x-ray systems so we can do vehicle and cargo inspections faster and more efficiently.

You've got to be a technology user. Learning new systems is part of the job. There's always training on new systems, new tools being introduced, and maintaining your training. And everyone has to do it, front the entry level officer all the way up to senior officer.

6. Do you have any general advice or additional professional insights to share with someone in your profession? What is the most fulfilling part of your job, and what is the most frustrating?

The most fulfilling part of the job is the job itself. What we do makes a difference. Customs and Border Patrol Officers not only enforce the customs and immigration laws, but we also enforce the laws for 40 other federal agencies. It's always changing, there's always something new to learn, there's always something different that can happen.

It's a job that makes a difference and it's one that attracts a certain individual. If you can stand on your feet and pass the background check, we'll make you a good officer.

7. Can you suggest a valuable "try this" for students considering a career in your profession?

We have a lot of student intern opportunities around the country. Speak to a recruiter. Speak to an officer who actually works at a port of entry. They'll tell you how it is. It takes a long time to get this job, but it extremely worth it.

SELECTED SCHOOLS

After high school, prospective customs inspectors should obtain college credits or an associate's degree in law enforcement, criminal justice, or a related field. Interested students should check with their school guidance counselor or research area community colleges. For those who wish eventually to perform in a supervisory role, a bachelor's degree is sometimes beneficial.

MORE INFORMATION

U.S. Customs and Border Protection
1300 Pennsylvania Avenue NW
Washington, DC 20229
877.227.5511
www.cbp.gov

U.S. Immigration and Customs Enforcement
500 12th Street SW
Washington, DC 20536
202.732.4242
www.ice.gov

U.S. Department of Homeland Security
245 Murray Lane SW
Washington, DC 20528
202.282.8000
www.dhs.gov

Michael Auerbach/Editor

Fun Facts

On a typical day in 2013, customs and border patrol agents seized:
11,945 pounds of drugs
$291,039 in undeclared or illicit currency
4,379 materials for quarantine – plant, meat, animal byproduct and soil
48 fraudulent documents
$4.7 million worth of products with Intellectual Property Rights violations

Emergency Dispatcher

Snapshot

Career Cluster: Law & Criminal Justice; Public Safety & Security
Interests: Solving problems, helping others, handling emergencies, communicating with others
Earnings (Yearly Average): $38,010
Employment & Outlook: Average Growth Expected

OVERVIEW

Sphere of Work

Emergency dispatchers are communications professionals who receive and transmit information, traditionally via telephone or radio transceiver. Emergency dispatchers are utilized by municipalities and other organizations to coordinate communications between the public and police, fire, and emergency medical personnel. Dispatchers are in charge of receiving, monitoring, and transmitting emergency communications. Dispatchers are also used by airports, port facilities, ground transportation centers, and the military to coordinate the movements of vehicles and address any emergency situations. Public-utility companies also use dispatchers to coordinate emergency crews in the field.

Work Environment

Dispatchers traditionally work out of organizational headquarters and communications hubs. Emergency dispatchers customarily work out of police, fire, and ambulance stations or in offices designated for emergency communication, such as 911 call centers and public-safety answering points. Transportation and public-utility dispatchers coordinate communications from major transportation and logistical hubs, including airports, power stations, and garages.

Profile

Working Conditions: Work Indoors
Physical Strength: Light Work
Education Needs: On-The-Job Training
High School Diploma Or G.E.D.
Licensure/Certification: Required
Physical Abilities Not Required: No
Heavy Labor
Opportunities For Experience: Part-Time Work
Holland Interest Score*: CES, CSR, ECS

* See Appendix A

Occupation Interest

Professional emergency dispatchers come from a variety of educational and experiential backgrounds. Dispatchers are multitasking problem solvers who are organized and enthusiastic about interacting with people. They should also be able to display patience and pragmatism in stressful situations and chaotic environments. Emergency dispatchers are detail-oriented people who know that clear communication is essential to their profession.

A Day in the Life—Duties and Responsibilities

Emergency dispatchers are often assigned lengthy shifts that can range anywhere from eight to twelve hours in duration. Responsibilities of a dispatcher vary somewhat depending on their particular area of employment.

The most specialized field of dispatching is police, fire, and ambulance dispatch. Emergency dispatchers determine the exact location of callers, confirm the nature and severity of emergencies, and are responsible for relaying that information to the appropriate officials in a quick and efficient manner. Emergency dispatchers must also provide 911 callers with medical and safety advice while emergency personnel are en route to their location, as well as strategies to get to a safer environment or mitigate further damage.

Similarly, transportation dispatchers communicate with drivers, engineers, and pilots to ensure that trucks, trains, and planes complete their journeys in a safe and timely manner. These dispatchers monitor and review a variety of information, such as weather reports, government notices, and emergency radio frequencies. This information helps them assess if there are any issues that they need to communicate to the vehicle operator. They may at times become involved in assisting during an emergency situation. All dispatchers must be well versed in effective transportation routes and the overall geographic layout of the district in which they work.

Emergency dispatchers frequently record the information they receive in written or electronic form. They are responsible for the accuracy of this information. They may also analyze recorded data to help determine the best possible solution as problems develop over time.

Work as a dispatcher can be stressful. They often work long hours, take many calls, and deal with troubling situations. Some calls require assisting people who are in life-threatening situations, and the pressure to respond quickly and calmly can be demanding.

Duties and Responsibilities

- Receiving emergency calls and recording all pertinent information
- Informing the caller about what steps are being taken
- Instructing the caller how to proceed in the situation
- Directing the information to the proper police, fire, or ambulance unit
- Monitoring and coordinating ongoing communications between caller and the responding unit
- Providing over-the-phone first aid or medical advice as necessary
- Keeping records of transmissions
- Maintaining communication systems by performing routine tests

OCCUPATION SPECIALTIES

Emergency Dispatchers

Emergency Dispatchers receive calls from individuals and relay information to police, fire, and ambulance crews. They must remain calm while collecting vital information from callers to determine the severity of a situation and the location of those who need help. They then give the appropriate first-responder agencies information about the call.

Transportation and Other Dispatchers (Nonemergency)

Transportation Dispatchers schedule and dispatch workers, work crews, equipment, or service vehicles for conveyance of materials, freight, or passengers, or for normal installation, service, or emergency repairs rendered outside the place of business. Duties may include using radio, telephone, or computer to transmit assignments and compiling statistics and reports on work progress.

WORK ENVIRONMENT

Immediate Physical Environment

Call centers vary in size depending on the population served. Dispatchers in major urban areas tend to work in large call centers, while those in remote and rural locations may work out of traditional offices. Call centers house various communication technologies and can sometimes be cramped.

Human Environment

Dispatching requires deft interpersonal communication skills and the ability to make decisions quickly under pressure. Individuals with an even temperament and a strong desire to help those in need make particularly good candidates for the role. Emergency dispatchers need to possess strong collaboration skills, as they are in frequent communication with callers, supervisors, emergency personnel, and coworkers.

Relevant Skills and Abilities

Communication Skills
- Speaking effectively

Interpersonal/Social Skills
- Cooperating with others
- Working as a member of a team

Organization & Management Skills
- Coordinating tasks
- Managing people/groups
- Managing time
- Organizing information or materials
- Performing duties that change frequently

Technical Skills
- Working with data and information
- Using communications equipment

Technological Environment

Dispatchers use a variety of communication technologies, ranging from telephone systems to radio equipment. They use computers to log important facts, such as the nature of the incident and the name and location of the caller. Some dispatchers also use crime databases, maps, and weather reports when helping emergency response teams. Other dispatchers monitor alarm systems, alerting law enforcement or fire personnel when a crime or fire occurs.

EDUCATION, TRAINING, AND ADVANCEMENT

High School/Secondary

Emergency Dispatchers are normally required to have only a high school diploma or a general educational development (GED) certificate. High school students interested in a career as a dispatcher should take courses in English composition, keyboarding, and basic computer science to prepare for the technical aspects of the role. Speech classes and immersion in foreign-language study is also advisable. Participation in an audiovisual club is a good way to learn the basics of communication technologies.

Suggested High School Subjects
- Business & Computer Technology
- Business English
- Business Math
- First Aid
- Foreign Language
- Sociology
- Speech

Famous First

The first emergency 911 phone system was installed in Haleyville, Ala., A demonstration call, the first on a 911 system, was placed in February 1968. The caller was Rankin Fite, speaker of the House in the Alabama legislature, who called from the city hall in Haleyville. The recipient was Tom Bevill, an Alabama congressman, who took the call at the police station. The demonstration was arranged by Robert Gallagher, head of the Alabama Telephone Company.

Postsecondary

Certificate and associate degree-level educational programs in dispatching are offered nationwide. Certificate-oriented course work in dispatching familiarizes students with basic terminology and standard operating procedures. Those applying for dispatching jobs in large emergency management organizations may benefit from having completed colleges courses in communications or information technology.

Related College Majors
- Administrative Assistant/Secretarial Science
- Communications
- Emergency Services
- Information Systems
- Radio & Television

Adult Job Seekers

Applicants with extensive professional experience, particularly in communications or customer service, can transition to the field with relative ease. Those who complete private certificate- or associate-level instruction in dispatching are normally given preference for vacancies.

Being an emergency dispatcher can sometimes require late shifts and irregular hours, including work on holidays and weekends. The lengthy work shifts and frequent stress inherent to the position may cause difficulty for professionals with families or young children. In addition, communication technologies and standards are always changing, so dispatchers should be willing to continue learning throughout their career.

Professional Certification and Licensure

The certification requirements of dispatch professionals vary from state to state. The Association of Public-Safety Communications Officials (APCO) has information on which states require training and certification. One commonly required certification is the Emergency Medical Dispatcher (EMD) certification, which enables dispatchers to give medical assistance over the phone.

Additional Requirements

Emergency dispatchers must have a strong ability to listen and understand the communications they are receiving. They must possess excellent organizational skills and be able to maintain their patience and calm under pressure. Regardless of the size of the population they serve, dispatchers are often required to solve complex problems, answer questions, and make important decisions on a moment's notice.

EARNINGS AND ADVANCEMENT

Earnings of emergency dispatchers depend on the individual's education, experience, and the geographic location of the employer. Higher earnings were paid to those in large metropolitan areas. Dispatchers can become senior dispatchers or supervisors before advancing to administrative positions.

Mean annual earnings of emergency dispatchers were $38,010 in 2012. The lowest ten percent earned less than $23,190, and the highest ten percent earned more than $56,580.

Dispatchers may receive paid vacations, holidays, and sick days; life and health insurance; and retirement benefits. These are usually paid by the employer.

Metropolitan Areas with the Highest Employment Level in this Occupation

Metropolitan area	Employment	Employment per thousand jobs	Hourly mean wage
New York-White Plains-Wayne, NY-NJ	2,490	0.48	$20.65
Chicago-Joliet-Naperville, IL	1,980	0.54	$24.22
Dallas-Plano-Irving, TX	1,300	0.62	$18.22
Nassau-Suffolk, NY	1,230	1.01	$21.46
Atlanta-Sandy Springs-Marietta, GA	1,230	0.54	$15.81
Phoenix-Mesa-Glendale, AZ	1,200	0.69	$21.15
St. Louis, MO-IL	1,170	0.92	$16.78
Philadelphia, PA	1,120	0.62	$18.67

Source: Bureau of Labor Statistics

EMPLOYMENT AND OUTLOOK

Emergency dispatchers held about 100,000 jobs in 2012. Employment is expected to grow about as fast as the average for all occupations through the year 2022, which means employment is projected to increase 7 percent to 12 percent. Population growth, a growing elderly population, and the increased use of cell phones are expected to spur employment growth for emergency dispatchers. However, most emergency dispatchers are employed by local and state governments. Therefore, any future budget constraints will likely limit the number of dispatchers hired in the coming decade.

Employment Trend, Projected 2012–22

Total, All Occupations: 11%

Emergency Dispatchers: 8%

Administrative Support Occupations: 7%

Note: "All Occupations" includes all occupations in the U.S. Economy. Source: U.S. Bureau of Labor Statistics, Employment Projections Program

Related Occupations
- Air Traffic Controller
- Production Coordinator
- Reservation & Ticket Agent

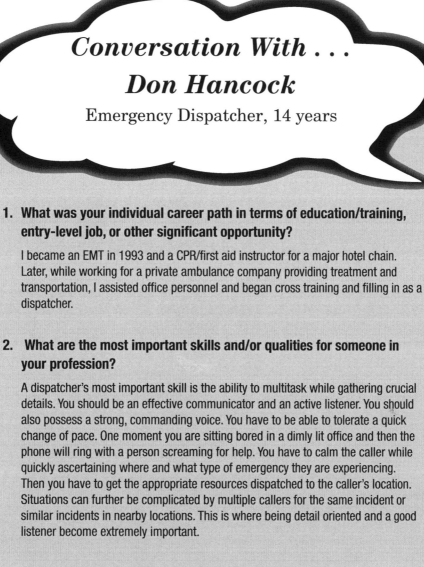

Conversation With . . .
Don Hancock
Emergency Dispatcher, 14 years

1. What was your individual career path in terms of education/training, entry-level job, or other significant opportunity?

I became an EMT in 1993 and a CPR/first aid instructor for a major hotel chain. Later, while working for a private ambulance company providing treatment and transportation, I assisted office personnel and began cross training and filling in as a dispatcher.

2. What are the most important skills and/or qualities for someone in your profession?

A dispatcher's most important skill is the ability to multitask while gathering crucial details. You should be an effective communicator and an active listener. You should also possess a strong, commanding voice. You have to be able to tolerate a quick change of pace. One moment you are sitting bored in a dimly lit office and then the phone will ring with a person screaming for help. You have to calm the caller while quickly ascertaining where and what type of emergency they are experiencing. Then you have to get the appropriate resources dispatched to the caller's location. Situations can further be complicated by multiple callers for the same incident or similar incidents in nearby locations. This is where being detail oriented and a good listener become extremely important.

3. What do you wish you had known going into this profession?

I wish I knew about the impact it would have on my cardiovascular health. The combination of stress and a sedentary career is not good for the heart. It's also important to be prepared for calls from people you know or may even be related to. Further, remember the requirement of confidentiality and do not violate it.

4. **Are there many job opportunities in your profession? In what specific areas?**

Yes, there are many opportunities in the dispatch career path. Many departments are continuing to phase sworn personnel (police officers or firefighters) out of the communication centers. Also there seems to be a recent interest in regional dispatch centers.

5. **How do you see your profession changing in the next five years? What role will technology play in those changes, and what skills will be required?**

\With all the technology in this field, it is no longer possible to have an officer or firefighter cross-trained to "fill in" on the desk. The job is no longer a matter of simply sitting in the room and picking up the phone. The average telecommunicator sits in front of and controls four to six computer screens. Those are connected to two or three computers and running between 10 to 20 different applications.

Further, the next generation 911 systems (commonly referred to as NexGen) will receive text and video to 911 in the near future. Along with the words, sounds and screams we are currently exposed to as professionals, there will be visual images viewed, interpreted and stored for possible further court action. This certainly will be instrumental in situations with language barriers.

6. **Do you have any general advice or additional professional insights to share with someone in your profession? What is the most fulfilling part of your job, and what is the most frustrating?**

Listen carefully, and then listen more. Try not to rush callers and speak slowly and clearly. Rushing a caller may mean missing an important detail.

The most fulfilling part of my job is helping people. I know it sounds corny but when you have a scared caller at 3 a.m. who has heard an unusual noise, it's fulfilling to talk to and calm them while waiting for help to arrive.

The most frustrating part of my job is dealing with tempers and rage. Although, in some disturbances, I have been able to talk with the aggressor and at a minimum, distract him while units respond. Not to mention that keeping the aggressor on the phone also allows the victim to flee the situation. Also in a few situations, the aggressor has made statements implicating him or herself.

7. **Can you suggest a valuable "try this" for students considering a career in your profession?**

Similar to a police ride along, get to know a dispatcher and come in and sit with him or her. Watch how they occupy their downtime and pay attention to how they stay prepared for that next call. Listening to a scanner can be helpful, but it shows only a small portion of the tasks we are responsible for.

SELECTED SCHOOLS

College-level training is not expected of beginning emergency dispatchers. Most important are the professional certifications in the field. Training for certification is available at many vocational schools and technical community colleges. Information on certification is also available from the associations listed below.

MORE INFORMATION

Association of Public-Safety Communications Officials
351 N. Williamson Boulevard
Daytona Beach, FL 32114-1112
888.272.6911
www.apcointl.org

International Academies of Emergency Dispatch
110 South Regent Street
Suite 800
Salt Lake City, UT 84111
800.960.6236
www.emergencydispatch.com

National Emergency Number Association
1700 Diagonal Road, Suite 500
Alexandria, VA 22314
202.466.4911
www.nena.org

Michael Shally-Jensen

Emergency Vehicle Operator

Snapshot

Career Cluster: Emergency Services

Interests: Driving a vehicle, operating equipment, assisting in emergencies

Earnings (Yearly Average): $24,900

Employment & Outlook: Average Growth Expected

OVERVIEW

Sphere of Work

Emergency vehicle operators drivespecially designed and outfitted vehicles such as ambulances, rescue vehicles, fire trucks, police vehicles, hazardous materials (hazmat) vehicles, and others. They may also operate apparatuses such as cranes, wenches, safety nets, and more. In most cases emergency vehicle operators are not simplydrivers but active participants or assistants in the incident at hand. Operators who drive ambulances, for example,may transport sick, injured, convalescent, or otherwise disabled patients to hospitals, nursing homes, and other care facilities, but they also work with

or serve as emergency medical technicians (EMTs) and paramedics to stabilizepatients. Similarly, in a fire service unit there often are crewmemberswho specialize in operating fire trucks and other firefighting apparatuses, even while they may also be qualifiedto perform general firefighting duties. Most emergency vehicle operators are expected, at a minimum, to be able to administer first aid to those in need. Additionally, operators are responsible for ensuring the proper functioning of equipment carried in or attached to their vehicles, and for replacing all supplies used at an incident. In general, they must guarantee the readiness and safety of their vehicles.

Profile

Working Conditions: Work both Indoors and Outdoors

Physical Strength: Medium to Heavy Work

Education Needs: High School Diploma or G.E.D.

Licensure/Certification: Required

Physical Abilities Not Required: N/A

Opportunities For Experience: Volunteer Work

Holland Interest Score*: RSI, SEC

* See Appendix A

Work Environment

When on calls, emergency vehicle operators work in the cabs of trucks, or "rigs,"that are customizedto accommodate the equipment used by particular kinds of emergency crews. Operators work in all types of weather conditions and environments, often at accident scenes and building fires, and do a great deal of physical activity, including heavy lifting. They often work a standard forty-hour week, although they may work longer and more erratic shift hours as emergency situations dictate. They are frequently required to work nights, weekends, and holidays, as emergency vehicles are needed around the clock. Work may be very stressful, and there is a risk of physical injury from equipment as well as from disoriented victims or others at the scene. Additionally, there is a risk—especially in the case of ambulances and blood banks—of exposure to blood and other bodily fluids.

Occupation Interest

The job of emergency vehicle driver is rarely routine or predictable. Drivers or rig operators are frequently called into dangerous or chaotic situations, and are expected to attend to victims under any and all conditions and circumstances. While the hours may be irregular and the work stressful, emergency vehicle operators are part of a team that helps save people's lives and, as much as is possible, return conditions to normal.

A Day in the Life—Duties and Responsibilities

Emergency vehicle operators respond to emergency calls or alarms. The operator is someone who takes his or her job seriously right from the start. He or she follows the vehicle and traffic laws in his or her state that apply to the safe operation of emergency vehicles. From the time of the alarm the operator/driver is constantly evaluating the type of incident, traffic conditions, weather conditions and any other situation that may affect his or her ability to maneuver the vehicle. Drivers cautiously observe their crew to make sure they are safely seated and belted, and apply the same standard to themselves. They proceed to the site of the incident knowing that if they do not arrive safely, they and their crew cannot provide service to their community. Operators know the limitations oftheir vehiclesand how best to handle them given their weight, length, size, steering, braking, and other characteristics.

When they arrive on the scene, drivers work with other emergency personnel in addressing the problem at hand, be it a flood or a fire, a car accident or a train derailment. For example, rescue personnel may spread out to search for a victim, or team up to retrieve a victim from a situation of danger or harm. Fire crews may be involved in the suppression not only of building fires but of wildfires burning in forests or underbrush. Emergency medical personnelmust administer first aid and other lifesaving measures to victims, and transport victims to nearby hospitals.

Emergency services coordination requires personnel from many different organizations to work closely together and to have open lines of communication. Most service agencies have methods and procedures—protocols—in place to make sure this happens. Even so, there can sometimes be tension between different emergency services organizations. The best emergency vehicle operators find common cause with their colleagues in advancing general public safety.

A standard measure of efficiency in emergency services is response time, the amount of time it takes for emergency personnel ("first responders") to arrive at the scene of an incident after the alarm has sounded. Drivers/operatorsplay a key role in producing fast response times by ensuring the readiness of their vehicles and their preparedness as drivers to move quickly and safely through traffic. Afteran incident has passed and the vehicle is returned to thegarage,operators may perform minor repairs as necessary.

Duties and Responsibilities

- **Responding to emergency calls or alarms**
- **Identifying the location of an incident**
- **Driving the vehicle to the required location**
- **Operating equipment or apparatuses associated with the vehicle**
- **Coordinating efforts with other emergency personnel**
- **Reporting facts concerning an incident to supervisors**
- **Keeping basic records pertaining to calls and responses**
- **Providing first aid when needed**
- **Maintaining the vehicle in a safe and ready condition**

WORK ENVIRONMENT

Physical Environment

Emergency vehicle operators work primarily in vans, trucks, or other rigs, though they may also operate vehicles such as snowmobiles and apparatuses such as cranes and wenches. They work at accident, fire, search-and-rescue, and disaster scenes, often in chaotic and dangerous conditions. When not on calls, emergency vehicle operators work at firehouses, ambulance facilities, or garages ensuring the preparedness of their equipment.

Human Environment

In addition to victims, emergency vehicle operators work with or serve as EMTs and paramedics, firefighters, police, and others. Communicating with one's crew and coordinating between service organizations are both of paramount importance to emergency vehicle operators and other first responders.

Relevant Skills and Abilities

Communication Skills
- Speaking effectively

Interpersonal/Social Skills
- Being sensitive to others
- Cooperating with others
- Remaining calm under pressure
- Working as a member of a team

Organization & Management Skills
- Making decisions
- Managing time
- Meeting goals and deadlines
- Performing duties that change frequently
- Working quickly when necessary

Work Environment Skills
- Driving a vehicle
- Being able to withstand incidents involving trauma

Technological Environment

Emergency vehicle operators use various types of heavy equipment, including booms and cable-wenches, in addition to the vehicles themselves. They may also use devices such as radios, global positioning systems (GPS), and emergency sirens and lights.

EDUCATION, TRAINING, AND ADVANCEMENT

High School/Secondary

High school students should take a driver's education course in order to receive their driver's license. They should also take first aid courses and study sciences such as anatomy and physiology. As emergency vehicle operators are expected to communicate with victims and other emergency personnel, communications courses are also beneficial.

Suggested High School Subjects
- Driver Training
- English
- First Aid Training

- Health Science Technology
- Physiology

Famous First

The first ambulance equipped for mobile coronary care appeared in 1968, operated by St. Vincent's Hospital and Medical Center in New York City. Along with ambulance personnel it included equipment (defibrillator, respirator, and electrocardiograph) for treating patients suffering from a heart attack. A doctor and nurse could ride within the vehicle if required.

Postsecondary

Emergency vehicle operators must be twenty-one years of age with a valid driver's license. Required courses vary by state, but drivers may have to take the Emergency Vehicle Operators course, which in some cases is offered online as well as in person. Drivers should also receive certification in CPR and first aid, and are encouraged to take internships at fire stations and ambulance companies.

Related College Majors

- Emergency Medical Technology
- Public Safety & Security

Adult Job Seekers

Candidates can apply directly to local fire departments and private ambulance companies for positions. They may start as interns, where they can receive on-the-job training and become aware of job opportunities as openings occur. Candidates should be prepared to take drug tests and undergo criminal background checks as well.

Professional Certification and Licensure

Emergency vehicle operators should be certified in first aid and CPR. They must also possess a valid driver's license with a clean driving record. Some states require licenses to operate certain kinds of emergency equipment or vehicles.

Additional Requirements

Emergency vehicle operators must be physically fit and able to lift heavy objects, including, if necessary, victims onto stretchers and gurneys. They should be able to work under pressure, both at emergency scenes and while navigating heavy traffic. Operators must have good interpersonal skills and be able to project a calm, reassuring demeanor toward victims. Finally, operators must be quick thinkers and solid communicators.

EARNINGS AND ADVANCEMENT

Earnings of emergency vehicle operators depend on the type of employer, experience, and geographic location of employment. Some operators may be paid on a run or an on-call basis. Drivers of ambulances had mean annual earnings of $24,900 in 2012, a figure that can be taken as more or less representative of the field as a whole.

Emergency vehicle operators may receive paid vacations, holidays, and sick days; life and health insurance, and retirement benefits. These are usually paid by the employer. Some employers may provide uniforms or a uniform allowance.

Metropolitan Areas with the Highest Employment Level in this Occupation

Metropolitan area	Employment	Employment per thousand jobs	Hourly mean wage
New York-White Plains-Wayne, NY-NJ	1,420	0.27	$13.92
Philadelphia, PA	760	0.41	$11.42
Edison-New Brunswick, NJ	420	0.43	$11.91
Boston-Cambridge-Quincy, MA	420	0.24	$15.50
Nassau-Suffolk, NY	340	0.27	$15.19
Los Angeles-Long Beach-Glendale, CA	230	0.06	$14.14
Las Vegas-Paradise, NV	220	0.27	$11.17
Augusta-Richmond County, GA-SC	200	0.99	$11.91

Source: Bureau of Labor Statistics

Fun Facts

The National Registry of Emergency Medical Technicians certifies EMTs through its testing program. A single test item takes about a year to develop and pilot test, and costs about $1,000 to produce.

Source: nremt.org

EMPLOYMENT AND OUTLOOK

There were about 19,000 drivers of ambulances employed in 2012—not counting independent contractors or self-employed operators. Considerably more than that number served as drivers/operators of fire apparatus, many of them qualified firefighters. Employment of emergency vehicle operators is expected to grow close to the average for all occupations through the year 2022, which means employment is projected to increase 7 percent to 10 percent.

Employment Trend, Projected 2012–22

Total, All Occupations: 11%

Emergency Vehicle Operators: 9%

Protective Service Occupations: 8%

Note: "All Occupations" includes all occupations in the U.S. Economy. Source: U.S. Bureau of Labor Statistics, Employment Projections Program

Related Occupations
- Emergency Medical Technician
- Firefighter

Conversation With . . .
Brian Luttrell
Emergency Medical Technician/Paramedic
38 years in field

1. What was your individual career path in terms of education/training, entry-level job, or other significant opportunity?

My career path started with a basic emergency medical technician (EMT) course. That got me into an entry level position with a private ambulance company.

2. What are the most important skills and/or qualities for someone in your profession?

Being clear-headed, being able to make an educated decision on a moment's notice and being able to detach yourself from the work are very important. Don't be excitable. Someone told me a long time ago, "Keep one thing in mind: this is the patient's emergency, not yours."

As a driver, you need to have good concentration and the ability to multitask. You'll be operating the vehicle, the radio and a siren while communicating from the driver's seat to your partner at the back of the ambulance -- all at the same time.

3. What do you wish you had known going into this profession?

It's important to realize you'll be working long hours. It's a 24-hour, seven day a week, 365 day a year job and you will work all of them. You will work nights, weekends, you will work Christmas, Hanukkah, Thanksgiving. You will work on someone's birthday. You will not be able to go to your kid's ballgame because you will be working.

4. Are there many job opportunities in your profession? In what specific areas?

There are tons of job opportunities. You can work in the private sector for an ambulance company. You can work for a fire department.

5. How do you see your profession changing in the next five years? What role will technology play in those changes, and what skills will be required?

There is more computer-aided dispatching going on now. More of the vehicles are equipped with technology that reports back information. They'll know back at headquarters if you're driving too fast, braking too hard, cornering too hard. They know when you're backing the vehicle up and whether your partner is guiding you. There are blind spots in an ambulance, so your partner has to be outside the vehicle, directing you when you back up. Your partner has to hold a button in the back of the truck while you're backing up. If your partner isn't there holding the button in, a text memo goes to your supervisor.

The computers in the trucks now are giving you directions, but also giving you information pertinent to your call. If I'm transferring a patient from one hospital to another, I'll be getting information on the computer about his heart rate, the med pumps, the medications the patient is on, etc.

6. Do you have any general advice or additional professional insights to share with someone in your profession? What is the most fulfilling part of your job, and what is the most frustrating?

The most frustrating part is seeing people being taken care of poorly, whether it's at home or at a skilled nursing facility. It's very frustrating to answer a call where someone is being abused.

What's fulfilling is helping to deliver a baby or save someone's life. Being part of a team is fulfilling. Helping to save someone's life by getting that patient to the right hospital, that feels good.

7. Can you suggest a valuable "try this" for students considering a career in your profession?

Before diving headfirst into this, take a CPR or first aid course. If you're in college, see if there's an emergency medical services department where you can volunteer.

SELECTED SCHOOLS

Most emergency vehicle operators train with the organizations that hire them (as trainees). It is also possible in some cases to train for a truck or emergency vehicle operating license through a private agency. Interested students should check with local hospitals and fire companies or research area business listings for driving schools offering specialized training.

MORE INFORMATION

American Ambulance Association
8400 Westpark Drive, 2nd Floor
McLean, VA 22102
703.610.9018
www.the-aaa.org

Federal Emergency Management Agency
500 C Street SW
Washington, DC 20472
202.646.2500
www.fema.gov

Fire and Emergency Manufacturers and Services Association
PO Box 147
Lynnfield, MA 01940
781.334.2771
www.femsa.org

National Association for Search and Rescue
PO Box 232020
Centreville, VA 20120
703.222.6277
www.nasar.org

Office of Emergency Medical Services (EMS)
National Highway Traffic Safety Administration
1200 New Jersey Avenue SE
Washington, DC 20590
202.366.5440
www.ems.gov

U.S. First Responders Association
420 North Kimbrel Avenue
Panama City, FL 32404
www.usfra.org

Michael Shally-Jensen

Federal Law Enforcement Agent

Snapshot

Career Cluster: Law & Criminal Justice; Government & Public Administration; Security Services

Interests: Criminal and terrorism issues, being in dangerous situations, handling conflict

Earnings (Yearly Average): $82,563

Employment & Outlook: Slower Than Average Growth Expected

OVERVIEW

Sphere of Work

Federal law enforcement agents are professional security personnel responsible for protecting the country from external threats, investigating criminal activity within the country and monitoring and preventing the unauthorized movement of people and goods across the country's borders. These public safety officials work for a number of government agencies, including the Federal Bureau of Investigation, the U.S. Border Patrol, the U.S. Drug Enforcement Agency, the Bureau of Alcohol, Tobacco and Firearms, and the U.S. Secret Service.

Federal law enforcement agents often work in concert with one another, particularly with regard to ending terrorism and halting drug smuggling.

Work Environment

Federal law enforcement agents work in a wide range of environments. Some work in office settings, organizing and analyzing evidence and interviewing witnesses. They also work in the field, where they conduct investigations, patrol borders and streets, and question and arrest suspects. Some law enforcement agents work in uniform; others operate undercover. The work of a federal law enforcement agent is often extremely dangerous. Therefore, federal law enforcement agents must be well trained in self-defense and skilled with a wide range of weapons. They tend to work long, erratic hours and travel extensively, and unexpectedly, as part of their jobs.

Profile

Working Conditions: Work both Indoors and Outdoors
Physical Strength: Light to Medium Work
Education Needs: Bachelor's Degree
Licensure/Certification: Required
Physical Abilities Not Required: No Strenuous Labor
Opportunities For Experience: Military Service
Holland Interest Score*: ERI, SRE

* See Appendix A

Occupation Interest

Federal law enforcement agents take pride in the fact that they are on the front lines in the battle against interstate crime, terrorism, and illegal drug smuggling. These men and women protect world leaders, identify and infiltrate criminal organizations, and work to safeguard the public against Internet crime and identity theft. Federal agents also routinely place themselves in harm's way to prevent terrorist attacks. The life of a federal law enforcement agent is exciting but challenging.

A Day in the Life—Duties and Responsibilities

The United States has over seventy federal law enforcement agencies. A federal law enforcement agent's responsibilities vary based on the agency for which he or she works. The U.S. Capitol Police agents enforce security and patrol the grounds of federal buildings and property. While on duty, these agents protect members of Congress and their families. Other agencies, like the U.S. Border Patrol and

U.S. Customs and Border Protection, monitor the nation's northern and southern borders, domestic and international airports, and seaports for illicit activity such as drug smuggling, attempts to transport dangerous weapons, and illegal immigration. The U.S. Fish and Wildlife officers spend most of their time in national parks and wildlife refuges, where they track and apprehend poachers and provide basic law enforcement services to park visitors. Agents in the Bureau of Alcohol, Tobacco, Firearms, and Explosives detect and prevent domestic acts of terror. Drug Enforcement Agency officials attempt to disrupt the lucrative and often highly dangerous traffic of illegal narcotics, both within U.S. borders and in other countries. In addition to providing security services for the president, U.S. Secret Service agents frequently investigate terrorist organizations as well as counterfeiting and credit card fraud activity. Under the U.S. Department of Homeland Security, FBI agents coordinate with Secret Service, Customs, and other federal agents to gather information and disrupt terrorist organizations, drug rings, and other dangers to national security.

Duties and Responsibilities

- Enforcing federal laws
- Preventing and investigating crimes
- Locating and arresting criminals
- Collecting evidence of criminal activity
- Conducting surveillance operations
- Protecting the lives of others
- Preparing reports and maintaining records

OCCUPATION SPECIALTIES

Border Patrol Agents

Border Patrol Agents protect more than 8,000 miles of international land and water boundaries. They detect and prevent the smuggling and unlawful entry of undocumented foreign nationals into the United States, apprehend those persons found in violation of immigration laws, and intercept contraband, such as narcotics.

Bureau of Alcohol, Tobacco and Firearms (ATF) Agents

Bureau of Alcohol, Tobacco and Firearms (ATF) Agents regulate and investigate violations of Federal firearms and explosives laws, as well as Federal alcohol and tobacco tax regulations.

Central Intelligence Agency (CIA) Agents

Central Intelligence Agency (CIA) Agents collect, evaluate, and report on foreign intelligence to assist the President and other top U.S. government officials in making decisions related to the country's national security.

Customs Agents

Customs Agents investigate violations of narcotics smuggling, money laundering, and customs fraud.

Diplomatic Security Agents

Diplomatic Security Agents are engaged in the battle against terrorism. They advise U.S. Ambassadors on all security matters, manage security programs, investigate passport and visa fraud, conduct personnel security investigations, issue security clearances, and protect the Secretary of State and foreign dignitaries.

Drug Enforcement Administration (DEA) Agents

Drug Enforcement Administration (DEA) Agents enforce laws and regulations relating to illegal drugs.

Federal Bureau of Investigation (FBI) Agents

Federal Bureau of Investigation (FBI) Agents investigate organized crime, public corruption, financial crime, fraud against the government, bribery, copyright infringement, civil rights violations, bank robbery, extortion, kidnapping, air piracy, terrorism, espionage, interstate criminal activity, drug trafficking, and other violations of federal laws.

Immigration and Naturalization Service (INS)

juries doctorate facilitate the entry of legal visitors and immigrants to the United States and detain and deport those arriving illegally.

Secret Service Agents

Secret Service Agents are employed by the Department of the Treasury. They protect the President, Vice President, and their immediate families along with presidential candidates, former Presidents, and foreign dignitaries visiting the United States. They also investigate counterfeiting, forgery of government checks or bonds, and fraudulent use of credit cards.

Uniformed Secret Service Officers

Uniformed Secret Service Officers protect the White House grounds, the residences of top government officials, and the embassies of foreign nations located in Washington, DC. They are the police force for the Secret Service.

U.S. Marshals

U.S. Marshals protect the Federal courts and ensure the effective operation of the judicial system. They provide protection for federal judges, transport federal prisoners, protect federal witnesses, pursue and arrest federal fugitives, and manage assets seized from criminal investigations.

WORK ENVIRONMENT

Physical Environment

Federal law enforcement agents work in a wide variety of environments. Border agents, for example, spend a great deal of time outdoors, patrolling rugged and remote areas in all weather conditions. Customs agents, on the other hand, work in high-traffic areas such as airports and shipyards. Many FBI, Secret Service, and Diplomatic Security Service agents travel overseas into dangerous cities and areas to locate and apprehend terrorists and other criminals.

Relevant Skills and Abilities

Communication Skills
- Speaking effectively
- Writing concisely

Interpersonal/Social Skills
- Being able to remain calm
- Being able to work independently and as a member of a team
- Cooperating with others
- Having good judgment

Organization & Management Skills
- Coordinating tasks
- Demonstrating leadership
- Handling challenging situations
- Making decisions
- Managing people/groups
- Organizing information or materials

Research & Planning Skills
- Identifying problems
- Solving problems
- Using logical reasoning

Human Environment

Federal agents interact with many different people. In addition to fellow agents and the criminals they seek to apprehend, they must interact with witnesses, victims, and the public both in the United States and in overseas locations. Sometimes they must work closely with politicians and their families or meet with lawyers to prepare for testifying in a trial.

Technological Environment

Federal law enforcement agents must work with a wide range of equipment. Most agents must have training in weapons such as handguns, automatic rifles, and similar devices. Many learn about the components of explosive devices. Computer systems, thermal sights, metal and explosive material detectors, and radar and sonar systems may also be used in performing duties.

EDUCATION, TRAINING, AND ADVANCEMENT

High School/Secondary

High school students who seek to become federal agents should take a variety of courses that will help them understand criminal behavior, learn about different technologies, and adapt to dangerous and unusual situations. These classes include foreign languages, communications, geography, political science, and physical fitness.

Suggested High School Subjects
- Applied Communication
- College Preparatory
- Driver Training
- English
- First Aid Training
- Foreign Languages
- Geography
- Government
- History
- Physical Education
- Psychology
- Social Studies
- Sociology
- Speech

Famous First

The first federal law officer to be killed in the line of duty was a U.S. Marshal from Georgia named Robert Forsyth. On January 11, 1794, he and two deputies went to a house in Augusta, Ga., to serve court papers on the brothers William and Beverly Allen. Forsyth asked them to step outside; instead, they barricaded themselves in an upstairs bedroom. Beverly Allen put a pistol shot through the door and hit Forsyth in the head, killing him instantly. The Allen brothers were arrested but succeeded in escaping.

College/Postsecondary

Most federal agents have an undergraduate degree in a field relevant to the agency for which they seek to work. Such degrees may be in criminal justice, public safety, political science, or public administration. In addition to training at the agency's academy and professional experience, federal agents may obtain advanced degrees in computer science, foreign languages, engineering, or law.

Related College Majors
- Criminal Justice/Law Enforce Administration
- Law (L.L.B., J.D.)
- Law Enforcement/Police Science
- Political Science & Government
- Pre-Law Studies

Adult Job Seekers

Many aspiring agents access current federal agency job listings through government websites or through federal agency human resources websites. Local job placement companies may also have access to postings. Furthermore, federal agencies often work with colleges and graduate schools to recruit candidates.

Professional Certification and Licensure

Law enforcement agents must complete training and certification at the federal agency's training academy, such as the FBI's training academy in Quantico, Virginia. These facilities train recruits on law enforcement techniques, weapons, and physical fitness.

Additional Requirements

Federal law enforcement agents must be physically fit, in terms of both stamina and strength. It is important for these individuals to work well with others as a team, particularly in confrontational situations with suspects. Since they must work cooperatively with members of other law enforcement agencies and with the public, agents should have strong communications skills. Prospective federal law enforcement agents should be able to handle extremely stressful situations while remaining calm and collected.

EARNINGS AND ADVANCEMENT

All federal law enforcement agents are paid according to the General Schedule, which is a special pay scale for employees of the federal government. The General Schedule has fifteen grades (GS-1 through GS-15) with ten steps per grade. Earnings increase as the employee moves up a grade or a step within a grade. Additionally, federal law enforcement agents receive law enforcement availability pay (LEAP), which is equal to 25 percent of the agent's grade and step, because of the large amount of overtime that these agents are expected to work. The agency in which an agent is employed determines the beginning pay level. For example, in 2012, FBI agents entered Federal service as GS-10 employees on the pay scale at a base annual salary of $48,823, yet they earned about $61,029 annually with availability pay. They could advance to the GS-13 grade level in field nonsupervisory assignments at a base annual salary of $76,452, which was $95,565 with availability pay. FBI supervisory, management, and executive positions in grades GS-14 and GS-15 earned a base annual salary of about $90,343 and $106,270, respectively, which amounted to $112,929 and $132,838 annually including availability pay. Median annual earnings of federal law enforcement agents were $82,563 in 2012. Advancement to higher levels and steps primarily depends on the agent having additional education and experience.

Federal law enforcement agents are entitled to a federal benefits package, including paid overtime, annual vacation, sick leave, life and health insurance and a retirement plan.

EMPLOYMENT AND OUTLOOK

There were approximately 225,000 federal law enforcement agents employed nationally in 2012. Employment is expected to grow slower than the average for all occupations through the year 2022, which means employment is projected to increase 3 percent to 9 percent. A more security-conscious society and concern about drug-related crimes will continue to spur moderate job demand. The turnover rate in federal law enforcement is very low due to the training required and the salaries and benefits; thus, there are more persons applying for these positions than there are positions available. Competition is fierce and only those who are fully qualified will be considered.

Related Occupations
- Correctional Officer
- Customs Inspector
- Inspector & Compliance Officer
- Parole & Probation Officer
- Police Officer
- Private Detective
- Security & Fire Alarm System Installer

Related Military Occupations
- Intelligence Officer
- Intelligence Specialist
- Law Enforcement & Security Officer
- Law Enforcement & Security Specialist
- Military Police

Conversation With . . .
Alison C. Pritchard
Lead Transportation Security Officer, 7 years with
Transportation Security Administration

1. What was your individual career path in terms of education/training, entry-level job, or other significant opportunity?

I was a school bus driver and started working at the airport for a car rental company. I needed stability and health insurance. I wanted to do more at the airport itself. I applied online at usajobs.gov. They do a background investigation looking at your job history going back 10 years. You have to pass a computer-generated X-ray test where they show you images and ask you to find, say, a pen inside the bag. You also have to pass a color blindness test, because different colors represent certain explosives. Then they do a drug and alcohol test. Back then the testing was two weeks; now it's four weeks. There's classroom training and 65 hours of on the job training. You have to do at least 20 hours of X-ray time. After one year, I was promoted to Lead Security Officer.

2. What are the most important skills and/or qualities for someone in your profession?

Attention to detail is big, and the ability to multi-task. Patience, not only with the people you work with, but with the public, is huge. Flexibility is important. Security procedures can change quickly and you have to implement them right away. When we started taking liquids away, overnight we just had to start taking them away from everyone, even flight attendants and pilots.

3. What do you wish you had known going into this profession?

I wish I had known how to control my temper when I started. I was young. If I had better control over my temper and my attitude, I would have gone even further than I have.

4. Are there many job opportunities in your profession? In what specific areas?

Most people start as a Transportation Security Officer (TSO) and work their way up. You can put in for temporary assignments. There's a big call center in Washington

D.C. where you can work for three or six months a time. If someone comes through with no ID, we have to call this office and they ask the passenger things about their childhood or about the neighborhood they live in. If there's a security breach, we have to call them. It could be something as simple as someone who's meeting a passenger walks through an exit and that causes a checkpoint shutdown. There's a job called Behavior Detection Officer. They're trained to identify passengers who are behaving in a way that indicates stress or deception.

5. **How do you see your profession changing in the next five years? What role will technology play in those changes, and what skills will be required?**

We're moving toward Risk-Based Screening, or RBS. People who are over age 75 get screened differently than someone who's 30. It's no longer black-and-white; we're looking at individual circumstances.

Technology is definitely helping. We have machines that can detect tiny particles of drugs or explosives. X-ray machines are so much more advanced than they were when I started. Body scans are better. Soon we may be able to test liquids and allow them through.

6. **What do you enjoy most about your job? What do you enjoy least?**

What I enjoy most is interaction with the public and a lot of the staff. You get those passengers who are rude or angry, but then you get that one passenger who thanks you. The daughter of an American Airlines flight attendant who was killed in 9/11 came through a few weeks ago. It was her first time flying since 9/11. I escorted her the whole way. For her to say thank you to me, the hair on my arms stood up.

Anyone who lost somebody in 9/11, and Wounded Warriors, can be escorted through by the airlines. Another program allows kids with autism and their families to come through weeks or months before a flight to walk through the process.

The hours are really rough. I have a 9-month-old and I'm into work at 3:30 in the morning.

7. **Can you suggest a valuable "try this" for students considering a career in your profession?**

It's not just a job, it's about lives. If you fly, pay attention to what we do and not just rush through as quickly as possible. Also, we periodically do drills, where we act out what would happen if there were an emergency like a shooting. College kids come in and act as passengers for these drills; the port authority can tell you how to participate.

SELECTED SCHOOLS

Many colleges, including many community colleges, offer programs in criminal justice and/or law enforcement. Below are listed some of the more prominent institutions in this field.

American University
4400 Massachusetts Avenue NW
Washington, DC 20016
202.885.1000
www.american.edu

California State University, Long Beach
1250 Bellflower Boulevard
Long Beach, CA 90840
562.985.4111
www.csulb.edu

George Mason University
4400 University Drive
Fairfax, VA 22030
703.993.1000
www.gmu.edu

George Washington University
2121 I Street NW
Washington, DC 20052
202.994.1000
www.gwu.edu

Indiana University
107 S. Indiana Avenue
Bloomington, IN 47405
812.855.4848
www.indiana.edu

John Jay College of Criminal Justice
City University of New York
524 W. 59th Street
New York, NY 10019
212.237.8000
www.jjay.cuny.edu

Northeastern University
360 Huntington Avenue
Boston, MA 02115
617.373.2000
www.northeastern.edu

Sam Houston State University
1806 Avenue J
Huntsville, TX 77340
866.232.7528
www.shsu.edu

University of California, Irvine
260 Aldrich Hall
Irvine, CA 92697
949.824.6703
uci.edu

University of Cincinnati
2600 Clifton Avenue
Cincinnati, OH 45220
513.556.6000
www.uc.edu

MORE INFORMATION

Central Intelligence Agency
Office of Public Affairs
Washington, DC 20505
703.482.0623
www.cia.gov

Federal Law Enforcement Officers Association
1100 Connecticut Avenue NW
Suite 900
Washington, DC 20036
202.293.1550
www.fleoa.org

U.S. Bureau of Alcohol, Tobacco, Firearms & Explosives
Office of Public & Governmental Affairs
99 New York Avenue, NE
Room 5S 144
Washington, DC 20226
800.800.3855
www.atf.gov

U.S. Department of Homeland Security
Washington, DC 20528
202.282.8000
www.dhs.gov

U.S. Drug Enforcement Administration
Office of Personnel
8701 Morrissette Drive
Springfield, VA 22152
202.307.1000
www.dea.gov

U.S. Federal Bureau of Investigation
J. Edgar Hoover Building
935 Pennsylvania Avenue, NW
Washington, DC 20535-0001
202.324.3000
www.fbi.gov

U.S. Immigration and Custom Enforcement
500 12th Street SW
Washington, DC 20536
202.732.4242
www.ice.gov

U.S. Marshal Service
Employment & Compensation Division
Field Staffing Branch
600 Army Navy Drive
Arlington, VA 22202
www.usmarshals.gov

U.S. Secret Service
Personnel Division
950 H Street NW, Suite 8400
Washington, DC 20223
202.406.5708
www.secretservice.gov

Michael Auerbach/Editor

Firefighter

Snapshot

Career Cluster: Emergency Services; Public Safety & Security
Interests: Working in dangerous situations, helping others
Earnings (Yearly Average): $47,850
Employment & Outlook: Slower Than Average Growth Expected

OVERVIEW

Sphere of Work

Firefighters are public safety workers who extinguish structure, forest, and other fires. They also administer first aid to accident victims and conduct search-and-rescue operations. Firefighters are also responsible for creating and implementing public fire prevention campaigns and promoting safe practices for the home and workplace. Additionally, firefighters often conduct building inspections, enforce building and fire codes, and investigate alleged violations of those rules.

Work Environment

Firefighters are based in fire stations, where they store equipment and trucks, located in all types of municipalities. These stations are well organized and maintained so that when a call comes in, all of the necessary equipment is close at hand and fully operational. When the station receives a call, firefighters enter highly dangerous work environments, including burning and destabilized buildings and accident scenes. At such sites, they must wear heavy suits, boots, and helmets and carry heavy equipment. Frequently, firefighters visit schools and other public locations to promote fire safety.

Profile

Working Conditions: Work both Indoors and Outdoors
Physical Strength: Heavy Work
Education Needs: On-The-Job Training, Technical/Community College, Apprenticeship
Licensure/Certification: Required
Physical Abilities Not Required: N/A
Opportunities For Experience: Apprenticeship, Military Service, Volunteer Work, Part-Time Work
Holland Interest Score*: RES

* See Appendix A

Occupation Interest

Firefighters perform a wide range of duties, all of which center around saving lives. Firefighters enter burning buildings and accident scenes, risking their own lives and safety for others. As first responders, they are trained to treat victims on the scene; their quick work can make the difference between life and death. The job of a firefighter is exciting and challenging, with dangerous situations occurring regularly. Firefighters typically have excellent job benefits, including full insurance and a strong retirement plan.

A Day in the Life—Duties and Responsibilities

Firefighters work in stations, where they organize and maintain trucks, hoses, rescue equipment, first aid kits, and outerwear so that crews can immediately depart when an alarm sounds. They also meet members of the public at the station, performing outreach activities such as installing child car seats and giving fire safety presentations. Fire stations are normally staffed around the clock by full-time firefighters whose shifts may last twenty-four hours or more. During their shifts, firefighters eat and sleep at the station when not performing training or maintenance duties.

When a call comes in, the dispatcher informs the firefighters of the address and nature of the emergency. The firefighters then suit up, gather the appropriate equipment, and take the necessary vehicles to the site. At the scene of a fire, firefighters work closely with their company mates. As a team, they coordinate various assignments, such as using hoses, breaking down walls, opening fire hydrants, operating rescue equipment, and administering first aid to victims. Upon returning to the station, firefighters complete reports on each incident and how the company responded. They restock supplies and make repairs to equipment as needed.

Some firefighters are also fire inspectors, who investigate suspicious fires and enforce fire safety codes. These individuals enter buildings and assess whether sprinklers, fire escapes, and smoke alarms are installed and operating properly and according to code. Many others teach fire safety and prevention at schools and other venues. Some firefighters have specialized training in emergencies that require different approaches, such as toxic chemical spills, forest fires, and boat fires.

Duties and Responsibilities

- Responding to fire alarms and other emergency calls
- Selecting appropriate equipment to direct water or chemicals onto fire
- Positioning and climbing ladders to gain access to upper levels of burning buildings
- Using axes to create openings in buildings for ventilation or entrance
- Rescuing victims
- Completing fire incident reports
- Providing public education on fire safety

OCCUPATION SPECIALTIES

Fire Inspectors and Investigators

Fire Inspectors examine buildings to detect fire hazards and ensure that federal, state, and local fire codes are met. Fire Investigators determine the origin and cause of fires and explosions.

Forest Firefighters

Forest Firefighters use heavy equipment and water hoses to control forest fires. They also frequently create fire lines—a swathe of cut-down trees and dug-up grass in the path of a fire—to deprive a fire of fuel. Some forest firefighters, known as smoke jumpers, parachute from airplanes to reach otherwise inaccessible areas.

Hazmat Specialists

Hazmat Specialists work in hazardous materials (hazmat) units and are specially trained to control, prevent, and clean up hazardous materials, such as oil spills and chemical accidents.

WORK ENVIRONMENT

Physical Environment

Firefighters work mostly in fire stations when they are not on a call. When a call comes in, they risk injury or death when putting out fires, rescuing and treating fire and traffic accident victims, and responding to other emergencies. Exposure to fire, smoke, hazardous materials, and structural collapse are a few of the dangers firefighters face.

Relevant Skills and Abilities

Communication Skills
- Speaking effectively

Interpersonal/Social Skills
- Being able to remain calm
- Providing support to others
- Working as a member of a team

Organization & Management Skills
- Coordinating tasks
- Following instructions
- Handling challenging situations
- Making decisions
- Meeting goals and deadlines
- Performing duties that change frequently

Technical Skills
- Operating machines and equipment
- Working with your hands

Human Environment

The team dynamic is vitally important for firefighters; company members must work together extremely well. In addition to their fellows, firefighters must work with other emergency and public safety personnel, such as police, emergency medical technicians, and hospital staff. They must also work with the public, both victims and people seeking information.

Technological Environment

Firefighters use a variety of rescue and fire equipment in addition to fire trucks and hoses, including fire extinguishers, oxygen tanks, and various hydraulic rescue tools for extricating victims from buildings and vehicles. Forest firefighters, meanwhile, use helicopters and all-terrain vehicles during the course of their work. Firefighters often use global positioning system (GPS) navigational aids and must be capable of using radio and computer systems as well.

EDUCATION, TRAINING, AND ADVANCEMENT

High School/Secondary

Aspiring firefighters are encouraged to take science and math courses in high school, which will help them to understand fires and emergency equipment. They should also study English and other subjects that build communication skills. Finally, physical education courses are essential to building the strength and endurance firefighters need.

Suggested High School Subjects
- Driver Training
- English
- First Aid Training
- Mathematics
- Physical Education
- Science

Famous First

The first all-female fire department was the Ashville, N.Y., Fire Department (located in the far western part of the state). In 1943 thirteen women replaced the department's male firefighters, most of whom were serving in the armed forces during World War II. The women worked without pay, operating a large fire pump and becoming proficient in rescue work and all of the other firefighting duties and responsibilities.

Postsecondary

Although it is not required, most firefighters take some courses at the postsecondary level. Many have associate's degrees in fire science or related disciplines from community and technical colleges or even four-year universities. Such degrees can help a firefighter become a fire specialist or gain a promotion.

Related College Majors
- Fire Science/Firefighting

Adult Job Seekers

Qualified firefighters should apply for jobs directly with municipal fire departments. The job market for firefighters is competitive, so applicants should send their resumes to many departments rather than simply their preferred location. While pursuing full-time jobs as firefighters, many individuals take positions as seasonal, part-time, or volunteer firefighters.

Professional Certification and Licensure

Prospective firefighters must take a physical and written civil service fire exam, which includes a drug test. Those individuals who score highest on this exam are invited to attend a fire academy, where they spend several weeks of intensive classroom and physical training before they enter the job market.

Additional Requirements

Firefighters must be physically fit, with great strength and stamina. They must also be at least eighteen years old. Upon completion of their training at the fire academy, firefighters must spend several years in apprenticeships. They must have extensive first aid training, be able to think quickly, and work in intense situations as part of a team.

EARNINGS AND ADVANCEMENT

Earnings for firefighters are established by local communities and vary greatly. Wages are generally highest in large cities. In 2012, firefighters earned mean annual salaries of $47,850. The lowest ten percent earned less than $22,030, and the highest ten percent earned more than $79,150.

Firefighters who work more than a certain number of hours per week are required to be paid overtime. Firefighters often earn overtime for working extra shifts to maintain minimum staffing levels or for special emergencies.

Firefighters usually receive paid vacations, holidays, and sick days; life and health insurance; retirement benefits; and death duty payments. In addition, most fire departments provide allowances for uniforms and protective clothing.

Metropolitan Areas with the Highest
Employment Level in this Occupation

Metropolitan area	Employment	Employment per thousand jobs	Hourly mean wage
Chicago-Joliet-Naperville, IL	10,270	2.82	$25.61
New York-White Plains-Wayne, NY-NJ	9,540	1.85	$38.20
Los Angeles-Long Beach-Glendale, CA	7,150	1.85	$40.04
Dallas-Plano-Irving, TX	5,570	2.65	$25.36
Atlanta-Sandy Springs-Marietta, GA	5,320	2.35	$18.41
Houston-Sugar Land-Baytown, TX	5,000	1.89	$23.90
Boston-Cambridge-Quincy, MA	4,780	2.79	$27.84
Cleveland-Elyria-Mentor, OH	4,530	4.55	$22.76

Source: Bureau of Labor Statistics

Fun Facts

With smoke detectors, automatic sprinklers, better building codes and fire-resistant materials in office buildings, there are fewer major fires. In 1975 in Boston, for example, there were 417 major fires, but in 2012, only 40. Nationwide, just 1.4 million of the 30 million calls that fire departments responded to that year were fire related.

EMPLOYMENT AND OUTLOOK

Firefighters held about 310,000 jobs nationally in 2012. About 90 percent of firefighters were employed by local fire departments. Some large cities have thousands of career firefighters, while many small towns have only a few and utilize mostly volunteer firefighters. Employment of firefighters is expected to grow slower than the average for all occupations through the year 2022, which means employment is projected to increase 3 percent to 9 percent. Most job growth will occur as volunteer firefighting positions are converted to paid positions in growing suburban areas. In addition to job growth, openings are expected to result from the need to replace firefighters who retire, stop working for other reasons or transfer to other occupations.

Employment Trend, Projected 2012–22

Total, All Occupations: 11%

Protective Service Occupations: 8%

Firefighters: 7%

Note: "All Occupations" includes all occupations in the U.S. Economy. Source: U.S. Bureau of Labor Statistics, Employment Projections Program

Related Occupations
- Emergency Vehicle Operator

Related Military Occupations
- Emergency Management Specialist
- Firefighter
- Seaman

Conversation With . . .
John Rhatigan
Retired Captain
Firefighter, 19 years

1. What was your individual career path in terms of education/training, entry-level job, or other significant opportunity?

I went to college at St. John's University and graduated with an accounting degree. While I was in school, I did some auditing work for Pathmark and Supermarkets General Corporation and I thought, "Geez, this isn't for me, life in a cubicle." So I took the firefighters exam while I was in college as a "just in case." When I graduated, I went into sales for the Shulton Company, selling Old Spice and Breck. I did very well with it. Right out of college, they gave me a company car, an expense account, all that good stuff. That lasted about five years. It got to a point where I just wanted to work with other people. I quit and worked with my dad in construction for about six months before I got on with the fire department.

2. What are the most important skills and/or qualities for someone in your profession?

You have to be physically fit, obviously. It requires strength and speed and agility. It can be mentally challenging. It requires a lot of people skills. As you move up the ladder, you'll need to deal with the firefighters working under you. Even a regular firefighter has to deal with the public, when you're out doing building inspections and fire inspections. Especially in Manhattan, where I worked, you have to dress well and present yourself well.

You have to be able to remain calm. It's really controlled chaos when you're in a fire. We run into buildings while other people are running out. It takes a certain type of person to do that. Most of the people who do this, they're like caregivers. They do a lot for other people. They're always shoveling snow for their neighbors or cutting their lawns.

3. What do you wish you had known going into this profession?

I wish I had known that once you retire, you can't get back on! I retired because I had to have back surgery as a result of a 9/11 injury. I was at a meeting of retirees today and we all miss it tremendously. It's a lot of camaraderie and laughing and joking and breaking people's chops every day.

4. Are there many job opportunities in your profession? In what specific areas?

The (NY) fire department is hiring. There are preferences for veterans, minorities and women. A lot of firefighters take a different path after they retire, working in fire science or getting certified as fire engineers, working in high rises and working on fire alarm systems. It can be very lucrative.

5. How do you see your profession changing in the next five years? What role will technology play in those changes, and what skills will be required?

Technology is changing the fire department just the way society is advancing. All information from building inspections is computerized now and you get a printout on your way to a fire. It's called the CIDS–Critical Information Dispatch System. It will tell you the type of construction, number of apartments per floor, if there are any handicapped people living there, all kinds of things.

There's thermal imaging cameras and better equipment, chin straps and better helmets. The firefighter's gear is much more protective, which can be good and bad because sometimes you're so protected that you might expose yourself to a dangerous situation like a backdraft, because you can't feel it.

6. What do you enjoy most about your job? What do you enjoy least?

It's easy to say now that what I enjoy most was just being with a common group of people. You come in together, work your shift, and go home safe. You could rely on each other. It was like one big family.

The worst is anytime a kid passes away in a fire. It's just horrible. That's the hardest part, whether it's a kid dying in a fire or a car accident. For me, that was the worst. And then there was the whole 9/11 thing, which is a whole other story. I had the day off and was painting my house when a guy called me. The towers had collapsed just before I got there. I told my son he should take the (qualifying) exam, but he said, "Why would anyone want to do that job, after everything that has happened?"

7. Can you suggest a valuable "try this" for students considering a career in your profession?

In smaller towns, you can be a volunteer firefighter. But I caution anyone thinking about that to be aware that the municipalities might not have very good life insurance policies on them. I tell everyone, even my own son, just take the test. You never know what can happen. I took it as a goof. But it's a great job. You can work 24-hour shifts, then have time for maybe bartending on the side. You can raise a family and be there to watch them grow.

SELECTED SCHOOLS

Training beyond high school is not necessarily expected of beginning firefighters. However, completing a fire science program at a community college or vocational school can prove beneficial. A tool for locating such schools and programs is available on the website of the U.S. Fire Administration (see below).

MORE INFORMATION

American Helicopter Services and Aerial Firefighting Association
3223 N. Tacoma Street
Arlington, VA 22213-1343
703.409.4355
www.ahsafa.org

Emergency Services Training Institute
Texas Engineering Extension Service
The Texas A&M University System
301 Tarrow Street
College Station, TX 77840-7896
877.833.9638
www.teex.com/esti

International Association of Fire Fighters
1750 New York Avenue, NW
Washington, DC 20006
202.737.8484
www.iaff.org

International Association of Women in Fire and Emergency Services
4025 Fair Ridge Drive
Fairfax, VA 22033
703.896.4858
www.i-women.org

International Fire Service Training Association
Fire Protection Publications
Oklahoma State University
930 N. Willis
Stillwater, OK 74078
800.654.4055
www.ifsta.org

National Fire Protection Association
Public Fire Protection Division
1 Batterymarch Park
Quincy, MA 02169-7471
617.770.3000
hr@nfpa.org
www.nfpa.org

National Volunteer Fire Council
7852 Walker Drive, Suite 450
Greenbelt, MD 20770
202.887.5700
www.nvfc.org

U.S. Fire Administration
16825 South Seton Avenue
Emmitsburg, MD 21727
301.447.1000
www.usfa.fema.gov

Michael Auerbach/Editor

Fish and Game Warden

Snapshot

Career Cluster: Agriculture & Natural Resources; Environment; Law & Criminal Justice

Interests: Law enforcement, the environment, being outdoors

Earnings (Yearly Average): $49,400

Employment & Outlook: Slower Than Average Growth Expected

OVERVIEW

Sphere of Work

Fish and game wardens are responsible for the protection of wildlife and their habitats in parks, animal refuges, wildlife sanctuaries, and other protected public lands. They typically patrol these areas, enforcing state and federal laws regarding hunting, fishing, and other activities. This includes the enforcement of hunting and fishing quotas, boating laws and regulations, and otherwise working to ensure that protected wildlife and ecosystems remain safe. In many cases, fish and game wardens work with scientists and naturalists to monitor protected species. They also work with law

enforcement officials regarding situations such as hunting accident investigations.

Because of their expertise, fish and game wardens are often called upon to share their knowledge with the media, schools, and other interested organizations. Public officials and scientists may also request their input on the creation of new hunting and fishing rules and other regulations.

Profile

Working Conditions: Work both Indoors and Outdoors
Physical Strength: Medium Work
Education Needs: Bachelor's Degree, Master's Degree
Licensure/Certification: Required
Physical Abilities Not Required: No Heavy Labor
Opportunities For Experience: Volunteer Work, Part-Time Work
Holland Interest Score*: RES

* See Appendix A

Work Environment

A fish and game warden's workplace is the great outdoors. Most of their time is spent patrolling public roads, waterways, and coastlines using an assortment of vehicles and aircraft, ranging from helicopters, all-terrain vehicles (ATVs), and boats to bicycles and horses. Fish and game wardens face all types of weather conditions during the course of their daily responsibilities. They may face other issues as well, including forest fires, accidents and emergencies, and pollution. Upon their return to an office or station, wardens file reports, store confiscated weapons and items, and meet with scientists, law enforcement, and other relevant professionals.

Occupation Interest

Individuals interested in becoming fish and game wardens tend to have a strong appreciation for the environment and the outdoors. Many have studied biology and the natural sciences in addition to having received some level of law enforcement training. Additionally, fish and game wardens are unconcerned with extreme weather or the dangers of the wilderness. Lastly, those interested in becoming a fish and game warden should have an interest in law enforcement, one of the most important aspects of a fish and game warden's job.

A Day in the Life—Duties and Responsibilities

Generally speaking, fish and game wardens are uniformed, armed law enforcement officials, assigned to enforce state and federal regulations and laws regarding hunting, fishing, and trapping on public lands or areas. This task includes patrolling a particular territory or jurisdiction, inspecting commercial fishing and hunting operations, serving warrants, making arrests, and seizing illegal equipment. Fish and game wardens are also involved in accident recovery, search-and-rescue operations, and investigations.

In addition to defending a natural environment from illegal activity and protecting the site's visitors, fish and game wardens are also invaluable to the efforts of scientists in monitoring the condition of wildlife and ecosystems. Wardens monitor food supplies, habitats, and the number of certain animals within the territory. They then report this information to scientists and other interested parties. Similarly, they track the number of hunters, fishermen, and others who enter the area in order to understand how effective existing regulations and laws are with regard to the habitats they oversee.

Furthermore, a fish and game warden is often invited to share his or her knowledge of how the current laws affect the many animals and natural resources of an ecosystem. Fish and game wardens frequently speak to schools, civic organizations, and other interested groups about the environment as well as the current rules and regulations of hunting and fishing.

Duties and Responsibilities

- Overseeing fish and game habitats and enforcing the laws that apply to them
- Collecting, compiling, and interpreting data
- Helping to establish methods of conservation
- Recommending rules and regulations to protect fish and wildlife
- Reporting the results of established programs
- Serving warrants and making arrests
- Preparing and presenting evidence in court
- Investigating hunting accidents
- Addressing schools and civic groups to educate and promote public relations
- Enlisting the aid of hunting and fishing groups
- Running lake and stream rehabilitation and game habitat improvement programs

WORK ENVIRONMENT

Physical Environment

The immediate environment in which fish and game wardens operate is the outdoors; some wardens work in the woods where hunting takes place, while others patrol the waters in a boat to investigate fishing activity. Natural elements can pose a risk to the individual's safety, including weather, terrain, and wildlife. Also presenting a danger are uncooperative visitors, criminals, accident scenes, and exposure to pollution.

Wardens also return to a central office or station to file paperwork, book criminals, and perform administrative duties. They are often called into meetings at other sites as well.

Relevant Skills and Abilities

Communication Skills
- Speaking and writing effectively

Interpersonal/Social Skills
- Cooperating with others
- Working both independently and as a member of a team

Organization & Management Skills
- Coordinating tasks
- Managing people/groups
- Paying attention to and handling details
- Performing duties that change frequently

Research & Planning Skills
- Analyzing information
- Developing evaluation strategies

Work Environment Skills
- Working outdoors

Human Environment

Fish and game wardens often work alone when out in the field. However, many work in teams, particularly during peak hunting and fishing seasons, when additional temporary or seasonal workers may be hired. Additionally, they coordinate with other professionals, such as police, fire officials, scientists, environmental engineers, and political leaders. Finally, they interact with visitors to the territory they patrol, ensuring their safety and compliance with state and federal regulations and laws.

Technological Environment

Fish and game wardens must be able to operate all-terrain vehicles, boats, and other modes of transportation. They should be knowledgeable on hunting weapons, fishing equipment, and other devices used by fishermen, trappers, and hunters. They also need to use global positioning systems, radios, computers, and other monitoring and communications tools.

EDUCATION, TRAINING, AND ADVANCEMENT

High School/Secondary

High school students who wish to become fish and game wardens are encouraged to study such subjects as agriculture, biology, chemistry, forestry, and other natural sciences. They may also seek summer employment with fish and game departments and government agencies.

Suggested High School Subjects

- Agricultural Science
- Algebra
- Applied Biology/Chemistry
- Applied Math
- Biology
- Chemistry
- College Preparatory
- English
- Forestry
- Geometry
- Physics

Famous First

The first full-time, paid game warden was William Alden Smith of Grand Rapids, Mich., who starting in 1887 earned $1,200 per year, plus expenses, to enforce laws regarding "the preservation of moose, wapiti [elk], deer, birds, and fish." Later that same year Wisconsin passed a similar law and hired four state game wardens.

College/Postsecondary

Most fish and game wardens receive a bachelor's degree, and many possess a master's degree as well. In college and graduate school, they may study geography, environmental science, law and government, biology, agriculture, and public safety.

Related College Majors

- Fisheries Management
- Natural Resources Law Enforcement & Protection
- Natural Resources Management & Policy
- Wildlife & Wildlands Management

Adult Job Seekers

Fish and game warden positions are typically federal or state jobs. Qualified adults who seek to become wardens can directly apply to government agencies or take civil service examinations. They may also consult college and professional placement services. They usually need to acquire additional training at a training academy, which familiarizes cadets with the job responsibilities as well as builds physical strength and endurance.

Professional Certification and Licensure

Most states require that aspiring fish and game wardens become familiar with fish and game policies. They must also receive formal training, which can last three to twelve months, and field training. Most prospective wardens are required to pass physical exams. Fish and game wardens are expected to be U.S. citizens with no criminal records.

Additional Requirements

Fish and game wardens must be physically fit. Because they interact directly with the public, they should have skills in interpersonal communication, conflict resolution, and customer service. They may join a national fish and game warden-related professional organization, such as the American Fisheries Society, or state game warden associations and networks.

EARNINGS AND ADVANCEMENT

Earnings depend on the employer as well as employee's education, experience, type of work performed and level of responsibility. Mean annual earnings of fish and game wardens were $49,400 in 2012. The lowest ten percent earned less than $31,870, and the highest ten percent earned more than $70,750. Fish and game wardens may be required to purchase some or all of their supplies, such as uniforms, waders, boots, cameras, and binoculars.

Fish and game wardens may receive paid vacations, holidays, and sick days; life and health insurance; and retirement benefits. These are usually paid by the employer.

Metropolitan Areas with the Highest Employment Level in this Occupation

Metropolitan area	Employment	Employment per thousand jobs	Hourly mean wage
Tallahassee, FL	150	0.97	$25.35
Nashville-Davidson--Murfreesboro--Franklin, TN	70	0.09	$28.66
Phoenix-Mesa-Glendale, AZ	60	0.04	$23.28
Baltimore-Towson, MD	60	0.04	$35.61
Providence-Fall River-Warwick, RI-MA	40	0.07	$32.27
Bridgeport-Stamford-Norwalk, CT	30	0.08	$18.35
Jacksonville, FL	30	0.06	$17.18
Tampa-St. Petersburg-Clearwater, FL	30	0.03	$17.82

Source: Bureau of Labor Statistics

EMPLOYMENT AND OUTLOOK

Fish and game wardens held about 7,000 jobs nationally in 2012. Employment is expected to grow slower than the average for all occupations through the year 2022, which means employment is projected to increase 3 percent to 9 percent. Because most employees work in government, they are fairly well-protected from negative changes in the job market.

Employment Trend, Projected 2012–22

Total, All Occupations: 11%

Protective Service Occupations: 8%

Fish and Game Wardens: 5%

Note: "All Occupations" includes all occupations in the U.S. Economy. Source: U.S. Bureau of Labor Statistics, Employment Projections Program

Related Occupations
- Customs Inspector
- Park Ranger

Conversation With . . .
Tim Kraemer

Natural Resources Police, 10 years

Park Service Ranger, 3 years

1. What was your individual career path in terms of education/training, entry-level job, or other significant opportunity?

I worked summers at Sandy Point State Park starting at age 14 in the food concession. When I was old enough to get a driver's license, I worked at the park's marina renting out motor boats. I did that for seven summers before becoming a seasonal technician doing maintenance projects. Later I became a welder, a plumber, and, for six years, a commercial waterman. In winters, I worked as a seasonal technician for another state park. Finally the park service offered me a full-time job as a ranger recruit. I went on to the police academy for six months, then went to Point Lookout State Park as a full-time ranger. We did law enforcement, conservation enforcement, plus programming, interpretation, and maintenance, which was a large part of the park ranger job.

At the time I became a Natural Resources Police Officer, the job was similar to a park ranger here in Maryland. That has since changed, and many of the assignments we had as rangers are now done by Natural Resources Police Officers, such as law and conservation enforcement. Also, we police officers are on waterways doing commercial seafood inspections and waterways enforcement. I'm on the Potomac River, the Patuxent River and the Chesapeake Bay. Natural Resources Police handle private lands and waterways.

All of those years in the private sector gave me a lot of good experience for the career I have now. For instance, when I check the watermen and the fisheries, I have a better grasp of how those guys work, and I know their gear.

2. What are the most important skills and/or qualities for someone in your profession?

A good work ethic, honesty, integrity, knowledge of fishing laws and hunting laws. You definitely need to be a self-starter. You have to want to be outside, on vessels, and know the mechanical workings of a vessel and fishing gear.

3. What do you wish you had known going into this profession?

I wish I was better with the academic part of it. I'm more of a hands-on learner.

4. Are there many job opportunities in your profession? In what specific areas?

In the last year or two, the state started hiring more Natural Resources Police Officers and they are constantly taking applications in every part of the state.

5. How do you see your profession changing in the next five years? What role will technology play in those changes, and what skills will be required?

We're already starting to see technology play a big role with the Natural Resources Police, with new programs and new report management systems. Officers are issued laptops now that are linked with the new Maritime Law Enforcement Information Network (MLEIN) that we just got trained on. It's a series of cameras and radar stations up and down the Chesapeake Bay that the Natural Resources Police use to track vessels or illegal activities.

In 2007 we had the introduction of new vessels with better outboard/inboard motors and more advanced high tech. The outboards are better, faster, more efficient, more reliable, and more comfortable for officers in harsh environments. They're rigged out for law enforcement use.

I don't ever see us getting away from low-tech completely; there's nothing more reliable than a pad of paper and a pen. Sometimes we're on foot in the middle of a field and you have to travel light and you have to travel fast. A pad of paper doesn't need to be recharged.

6. What do you enjoy most about your job? What do you enjoy least?

It's probably one of the best jobs around. The best part is being in on the water. I like running the boats, as well as the feeling you're making a difference and making sure there's something there tomorrow, such as when you enforce crabbing regulations. Or oysters, which are a big thing. We make sure the kids will have seafood out there to harvest one day. I love being in the state parks, talking to people, doing campground enforcement, and just being there for public information.

Natural resource law changes constantly, and keeping yourself updated on laws and regulations is very challenging. That is probably the hardest part of this job.

7. **Can you suggest a valuable "try this" for students considering a career in your profession?**

You've really got to want to be outside and talk to people. For people who like to hunt and fish and like fishing and game law, this is a great job. Be a volunteer or, if you're old enough, be a reserve officer.

Fun Facts

According to the National Park Service, more than half of forest rangers, aka park rangers, work east of the Mississippi River, and predominately work outside.

Source: www.ehow.com

SELECTED SCHOOLS

Programs in fisheries and wildlife management are available at many four-year colleges and universities. The student can also gain initial training at a community college. The website of the National Association of University Fisheries and Wildlife Programs (see below) provides a state-by-state listing of member institutions. Other programs besides those listed exist and should be considered as well. Interested students are advised to consult with a school guidance counselor.

MORE INFORMATION

American Fisheries Society
5410 Grosvenor Lane
Bethesda, MD 20814
301.897.8616
www.fisheries.org

Association of Fish & Wildlife Agencies
444 North Capitol Street NW
Suite 725
Washington, DC 20001
202.624.7890
fishwildlife.org

National Association of University Fisheries and Wildlife Programs
Virginia Tech
100 Cheatham Hall
Blacksburg, VA 24061
540.231.5573
naufwp.org

North American Wildlife Enforcement Officers Association
P.O. Box 22
Holidaysburg, PA 16648
naweoa.org

U.S. Fish and Wildlife Service Department of the Interior
1849 C Street NW
Washington, DC 20240
800.344.9453
www.fws.gov

Wildlife Society
5410 Grosvenor Lane
Suite 200
Bethesda, MD 20814
301.897.9770
www.wildlife.org

Michael Auerbach/Editor

Forensic Scientist

Snapshot

Career Cluster: Law & Criminal Justice; Science & Technology

Interests: Criminal science, investigative work, laboratory work, analyzing data

Earnings (Yearly Average): $55,730

Employment & Outlook: Slower Than Average Growth Expected

OVERVIEW

Sphere of Work

Forensic scientists, also referred to as crime laboratory analysts, crime scene investigators, or evidence technicians, most often investigate crime scenes and collect and analyze physical evidence for the legal system. Most forensic scientists specialize in either crime scene investigation or laboratory analysis, though these roles can and do overlap in many jurisdictions. All forensic scientists follow the same general workflow, which involves collecting and storing evidence, performing tests on collected evidence, analyzing test results, and documenting all evidence collected, tests

performed, and results obtained. Sometimes, there is the additional task of providing expert testimony in criminal trials.

Work Environment

Forensic scientists spend their workdays both gathering physical evidence from crime scenes and documenting, testing, and analyzing physical crime-scene evidence in laboratories. Forensic laboratories are usually located in police departments, educational institutions, or government agencies. Laboratories are usually sterile and well ventilated. Human interaction in forensic laboratories tends to be limited to laboratory staff and criminal investigators. Forensic scientists generally work forty-hours or more per week. In addition to day shifts, forensic scientists must be on call during evenings, weekends, and holidays to meet the needs of the legal system for accurate and timely crime scene investigations and evidence testing.

Profile

Working Conditions: Work Indoors and Outdoors
Physical Strength: Light Work
Education Needs: Bachelor's Degree, Master's Degree
Licensure/Certification: Recommended
Physical Abilities Not Required: No Heavy Labor
Opportunities For Experience: Internship
Holland Interest Score*: IRE

* See Appendix A

Occupation Interest

Individuals drawn to the profession of forensic scientist tend to be intelligent, analytical, and detail oriented. Successful forensic scientists display traits such as logical thinking, focus, dependability, and responsibility. A high tolerance for stress, excellent analytical and communication skills, and the ability to handle evidence of violence and injury calmly and objectively are also desirable qualities in a forensic scientist. Forensic scientists should enjoy spending time in laboratory settings and have a strong background in basic science in addition to criminal science and investigation.

A Day in the Life—Duties and Responsibilities

The specific daily occupational duties and responsibilities of a forensic scientist are determined by the individual's area of job specialization and work environment. In most cases, at the beginning of a project, forensic scientists collect crime scene evidence, preserve it following standard and legally approved protocols, photograph crime scenes to document the location and position of evidence, and perform blood spatter analysis and weapons tests as necessary. Depending on the nature of the crime scene evidence, they may also analyze fiber, glass, hair, tissue, and body fluids found on the crime scene. Forensic scientists use such tools as facial reconstruction, DNA fingerprinting, ballistics, DNA profiling, footwear analysis, and bloodstain pattern analysis to inform crime scene investigations and criminal prosecutions.

Once they have returned to the office, forensic scientists may perform fingerprint testing, comparing evidence found at crime scenes with criminal fingerprint databases. Sometimes, they are asked to reconstruct crime scenes to aid in criminal investigations where police have insufficient leads or need additional evidence before arresting a suspect.

Carefully documenting all physical evidence collected and methods used to test evidence is extremely important: if the evidence collected and conclusions drawn are used at trial, the methods used to obtain the evidence will come under greater scrutiny. Forensic scientists typically prepare reports for investigators and criminal lawyers and/or provide expert testimony in criminal trials. They frequently respond to requests from criminal investigators for information about crime scenes or evidence testing.

In addition to the range of responsibilities described above, all forensic scientists are responsible for setting up, calibrating, and sterilizing all forensic laboratory equipment and materials on an ongoing basis.

Duties and Responsibilities

- Collecting and analyzing physical evidence from crime scenes and individual suspects
- Following rigorous protocols regarding the logging in and preservation of evidence
- Applying specialized lab techniques to evidence
- Determining how and when a crime occurred based on the evidence
- Preparing reports explaining the results of forensic tests
- Testifying in criminal court cases to describe findings

OCCUPATION SPECIALTIES

There are many different subareas of forensic science. Forensic scientists can specialize in ballistics (firearms analysis), criminalistics (crime scene analysis), digital or computer forensics (hardware and software analysis), forensic archeology and anthropology (historical remains analysis), forensic DNA analysis, forensic entomology (insect-based analysis), forensic odontology (dental analysis), forensic pathology (examination of the corpse), forensic serology (body fluids analysis), forensic toxicology (drug/poison analysis), or latent (fingerprint) or trace (hair, fibers, etc.) analysis, among other areas.

WORK ENVIRONMENT

Physical Environment

The immediate physical environment of forensic scientists varies based on their employer and specialization. Forensic scientists spend their workdays at crime scenes, laboratories, or other locations. Forensic laboratories may be located in police departments, state or federal agencies, educational institutions, or independent businesses. At all times forensic scientists must ensure that their own presence at a crime scene or handling of evidence does not affect the integrity of the evidence. In many cases investigators/scientists are exposed to potentially harmful substances or conditions, such as body fluids from corpses or rooms containing spent needles or broken glass.

Human Environment

Forensic scientists should be comfortable interacting with laboratory staff, supervisors, police, and criminal investigators. They may also work with prosecutors and other members of the legal system during the course of a court trial. Experienced forensic scientists sometimes must help train new laboratory technicians in laboratory techniques and protocols.

Relevant Skills and Abilities

Communication Skills
- Speaking and writing effectively

Interpersonal/Social Skills
- Being able to work independently and as part of a team
- Being patient
- Cooperating with others

Organization & Management Skills
- Organizing information or materials
- Performing routine work
- Paying attention to and handling details

Research & Planning Skills
- Generating ideas
- Identifying problems
- Solving problems
- Using logical reasoning

Technical Skills
- Performing scientific, mathematical, and technical work
- Applying technology to a task

Technological Environment

Forensic scientists use analytical tools, such as facial reconstruction, DNA fingerprinting, ballistics, DNA profiling, footwear analysis, and bloodstain pattern analysis, to assist with crime scene investigations and criminal prosecutions. Forensic scientists should be confident using blood collection kits, DNA collection kits, evidence or specimen jars, measuring tapes, ultraviolet lights, electronic databases, and scientific and photo-imaging software programs.

EDUCATION, TRAINING, AND ADVANCEMENT

High School/Secondary

High school students interested in pursuing a career as forensic scientist should prepare themselves by developing good study habits and by taking anthropology, biology, chemistry, anatomy, psychology, and mathematics courses. Owing to the diversity of forensic scientist responsibilities, high school students interested in this career path may benefit from seeking internships or part-time jobs that expose them to the legal system or laboratory settings and procedures.

Suggested High School Subjects
- Algebra
- Applied Biology/Chemistry
- Applied Communication
- Applied Math
- Applied Physics
- Biology
- Calculus
- Chemistry
- College Preparatory
- Composition
- Computer Science
- English
- Geometry
- Government
- Mathematics
- Physics
- Psychology
- Science
- Social Studies
- Sociology
- Statistics
- Trigonometry

Famous First

The first police department to set up a criminal identification bureau was the Chicago Police Department, which in 1884 opened a small photographic archive holding photos of known or suspected criminals. Three years later the department incorporated the Bertillon system of anthropometric identification, which identified individuals based on various bodily and facial measurements. In 1904 the unit adopted an early fingerprinting system (the Henry system), which by then other departments had begun using as well.

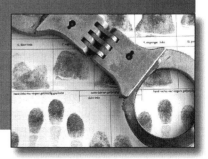

College/Postsecondary

Postsecondary students interested in becoming forensic scientists should earn a bachelor's degree in forensic science chemistry, biology, or a related field, such as biochemistry, archeology, or premedical studies. Coursework in anatomy, psychology, statistics, laboratory procedures, criminology, and mathematics may also prove useful in their future work. Postsecondary students can gain work experience and potential advantage in their future job searches by securing internships or part-time employment in laboratory or criminal law settings.

Related College Majors
* Criminology
* Forensic Technology

Adult Job Seekers

Adults seeking employment as forensic scientists should have, at a minimum, a bachelor's degree. Employers may require that forensic scientists have a master's of science in forensic science (MSFS) degree. Background checks and periodic drug tests are mandatory for employment in this field. Adult job seekers should educate themselves about the specific educational and professional certification requirements of their home states and the organizations where they seek employment.

Joining professional associations may help with networking and job searching. Professional forensic associations, such as the American Academy of Forensic Sciences and the American Board of Criminalistics, generally offer job-finding workshops and maintain lists and forums of available jobs.

Professional Certification and Licensure

Certification for forensic scientists is voluntary but often required as a condition of employment in a crime laboratory. Job candidates who choose to obtain certification in one or more areas of specialization tend to have better prospects than those who do not. The following organizations offer general and specialized certification designations in forensic science: the American Board of Criminalistics, the American Board of Forensic Entomology, the American Board of

Forensic Document Examiners, the American Board of Forensic Toxicology, and the National Registry in Clinical Chemistry. Specialized forensic science certification is offered in areas such as drug analysis, crime scene reconstruction, firearms, molecular biology, fire debris, photography, trace evidence, and laboratory safety. Certification is earned by satisfying educational requirements, passing an examination, and undergoing peer review. Continuing education coursework is required as a condition of recertification.

Additional Requirements

 Because forensic scientists collect and test important criminal evidence, they must be honest, objective, and adhere to strict professional ethical standards. They should be able to remain focused and composed when viewing graphic evidence or working at disturbing crime scenes. Analytical skills, attention to detail, and membership in professional forensic associations are important and useful tools for all forensic scientists.

EARNINGS AND ADVANCEMENT

Mean annual earnings of forensic scientists were $55,730 in 2012. The lowest ten percent earned less than $32,200, and the highest ten percent earned more than $85,210. Directors of crime laboratories who supervised forensic scientists frequently earned over $100,000 annually, as did medical examiners and forensic pathologists with medical degrees.

Forensic scientists may receive paid vacations, holidays, and sick days; life and health insurance; and retirement benefits. These are usually paid by the employer.

Metropolitan Areas with the Highest
Employment Level in this Occupation

Metropolitan area	Employment	Employment per thousand jobs	Hourly mean wage
Phoenix-Mesa-Glendale, AZ	590	0.34	$27.11
Los Angeles-Long Beach-Glendale, CA	520	0.13	$38.09
Washington-Arlington-Alexandria, DC-VA-MD-WV	420	0.18	$35.82
New York-White Plains-Wayne, NY-NJ	370	0.07	$29.67
Baltimore-Towson, MD	320	0.26	$28.24
Bethesda-Rockville-Frederick, MD	270	0.48	$34.98
Riverside-San Bernardino-Ontario, CA	260	0.22	$29.11
Atlanta-Sandy Springs-Marietta, GA	240	0.11	$19.38

Source: Bureau of Labor Statistics

EMPLOYMENT AND OUTLOOK

Forensic scientists held about 13,000 jobs nationally in 2012. Employment of forensic scientists is expected to grow slightly slower than the average for all occupations through the year 2022, which means employment is projected to increase 5 percent to 10 percent. With advances in technology making the analysis of crime scene evidence more exact, courts of law are relying on forensic scientists to analyze and present their findings in civil and criminal cases. Competition in this field is strong, however, and opportunities will be best for those who have an advanced degree or are certified in a specialty of forensic science.

Employment Trend, Projected 2012–22

Total, All Occupations: 11%

Life, Physical, and Social Science Technicians: 10%

Forensic Scientists: 6%

Note: "All Occupations" includes all occupations in the U.S. Economy. Source: U.S. Bureau of Labor Statistics, Employment Projections Program

Related Occupations
- Criminologist
- Private Detective

Conversation With . . .
Lawrence Kobilinsky, PH.D.
Forensic Scientist, 34 years

1. **What was your individual career path in terms of education/training, entry-level job, or other significant opportunity?**

   I have my master's degree and my Ph.D. in biology. I did post-doctoral training at Sloan Kettering Institute. When I obtained a part-time job as an adjunct professor teaching biology at John Jay College, I got very interested and motivated and excited about forensic science.

   Forensics was the only major in science at the college. It was clear to me I needed to get further involved in that because that's what I was teaching. More importantly, because I read the literature in forensic science, I recognized that there was research that I could do and excel in. And that would help my career. My choice was crystal clear about focusing 100 percent of my attention on forensic science.

2. **What are the most important skills and/or qualities for someone in your profession?**

   First of all, ethics is really crucial. We're dealing with people's lives and freedom, so one has to understand the ethical responsibilities of the work. Secondly, we're scientists and, as such, we have to understand the science behind our analysis of physical evidence. Thirdly, we have to remember that although we are in the criminal justice system, we are not advocates. We are neutral, unbiased people that can generate factual information for judges and juries to make their decisions.

   As for skills, it depends what you're doing but instrumental analysis is more and more important. Using equipment to help you analyze the evidence is a major skill that one needs to learn.

3. **What do you wish you had known going into this profession?**

   I was smart in that I looked into the profession before jumping into it. I did my homework. I knew it wasn't just bench science and that I would have to go into the court and testify. That is not simple. You are cross examined by experts and sometimes that's hard, but it's a very important skill that one has to learn. I was well prepared for what I was getting into.

I guess what I didn't know is that to be successful, you really need to be an all-around scientist. Biology was not enough. The field has a lot of chemistry. It even has some physics and mathematics. One has to have a good foundation of science and math.

4. Are there many job opportunities in your profession? In what specific areas?

There are a lot of opportunities. People who want to work in forensic science can work either in county, state or federal laboratories, or in private, commercial labs.

We strongly recommend getting an advanced degree. When one leaves college with a bachelor's of science degree and is looking for work in forensics, he or she will end up being a technician. They'll prepare solutions, sterilize glassware, weigh things out. They're not really doing science. They don't have a lot of responsibility. It's what I would consider a foundation job. I find that students want more than that. They want to play a role in the system. They want to analyze evidence, write reports, testify. You need an advanced degree to do that.

5. How do you see your profession changing in the next five years? What role will technology play in those changes, and what skills will be required?

We are in a transition right now. (U.S. Attorney General) Eric Holder has just appointed a commission, the Forensic Science Commission. They are setting standards for all practitioners as well as making recommendations about education in forensic science. There's a lot of change that I expect over the next two to three years. Lots of quality control, a change in focus for practitioners, making sure the work is done at the highest level possible. All crime labs will have to be accredited.

6. Do you have any general advice or additional professional insights to share with someone in your profession? What is the most fulfilling part of your job, and what is the most frustrating?

What is fulfilling is that you are communicating the science to juries and judges. But it's frustrating when you're on the stand and you're not always given the opportunity to say everything you'd like to say. The lawyers want to hear something from you, but not necessarily all you want to say.

7. **Can you suggest a valuable "try this" for students considering a career in your profession?**

I would suggest that students, first of all, come to academic institutions that teach forensic science. Get information that way. I think they should also contact the lab director of the local crime lab and see if that person has the time to conduct a visit. You can also attend a regional professional meeting. In this part of the country, we have a group called the Northeastern Association of Forensic Scientists. They hold a meeting every year.

Understand what you're getting into. Don't make decisions based on television shows or newspaper articles. It's hard science. Not everybody does well with that.

Fun Facts

The FBI's Regional Computer Forensic Laboratory program provides services to more than 4,000 agencies in 17 states.

Source: fbi.gov

SELECTED SCHOOLS

Programs in forensic science are available at a variety of four-year colleges and universities. The student may also gain initial training at a technical community college. For those seeking to specialize in a particular area, or to eventually advance to a management-level position, a master's degree is often expected. Below are listed some of the more prominent institutions in this field.

Boston University
Biomedical Forensic Sciences
School of Medicine
72 E. Concord Street, R806
Boston, MA 02118
617.638.1950
www.bumc.bu.edu/gms/
biomedforensic/

Drexel University
Office of Professional Studies in the
Health Sciences
College of Medicine
New College Building, Rm. 4104
245 N. 15th Street, Mail Stop 344
Philadelphia, PA 19102
215.762.4692
www.drexelmed.edu

George Washington University
Department of Forensic Sciences
2100 Foxhall Road, NW
Somers Hall—Lower Level
Washington, DC 20007
202.242.5758
departments.columbian.gwu.edu/
forensicsciences/

Michigan State University
Forensic Science
School of Criminal Justice
655 Auditorium Road, 560 Baker
Hall
East Lansing, MI 48824
517.353.7133
www.forensic.msu.edu/

**Penn State University,
University Park**
Forensic Science
Eberly College of Science
107 Whitmore Lab
University Park, PA 16802
814.867.2465
forensics.psu.edu

Syracuse University
Graduate Forensics
1-008 Center for Science and
Technology
Syracuse, NY 13244
315.443.0360
gradforensics.syr.edu

University at Albany
State University of New York
Forensics
1400 Washington Avenue
Albany, NY 12222
518.442.3300
www.albany.edu/academics/

University of California, Davis
Forensic Science
1909 Galileo Court, Suite B
Davis, CA 95618
530.747.3922
forensicscience.ucdavis.edu

University of Cincinnati
Clermont College
4200 Clermont College Drive
Batavia, OH 45103
513.732.5200
www.ucclermont.edu/.html

Virginia Commonwealth University
Department of Forensic Science
1020 W. Main Street
Harris Hall S., Rm. 2015
PO Box 843079
Richmond, VA 23284
804.828.8420
www.has.vcu.edu/forensics/

MORE INFORMATION

Academy of Criminal Justice Sciences
P.O. Box 960
Greenbelt, MD 20768-0960
800.757.2257
www.acjs.org

American Academy of Forensic Sciences
P.O. Box 669
Colorado Springs, CO 80901-0669
719.636.1100
www.aafs.org

American Board of Criminalistics
P.O. Box 1123
Wausau, WI 55402-1123
715.845.3684
abcreq@dwave.net
www.criminalistics.com/abc/A.php

American Board of Medicolegal Death Investigators
900 W. Baltimore Street
Baltimore, MD 21223
410.807.3007
www.abmdi.org

American College of Forensic Examiners
2750 East Sunshine
Springfield, MO 65804
800.423.9737
www.acfei.com

International Association for Identification
2131 Hollywood Boulevard, Suite 403
Hollywood, FL 33020
954.589.0628
www.theiai.org

National Center for Forensic Science

12354 ResearchParkway, Suite 225
Orlando, FL 32826
407.823.6469
ncfs.ucf.edu

National Forensic Science Technology Center

7881 114th Avenue North
Largo, FL 33773
727.549.6067
www.nfstc.org

Simone Isadora Flynn/Editor

Information Security Analyst

Snapshot

Career Cluster: Information Technology; Public Safety & Security

Interests: Electronics, computers, analyzing data

Earnings (Yearly Average): $89,290

Employment & Outlook: Faster Than Average Growth Expected

OVERVIEW

Sphere of Work

Information security analysts design and monitor technological systems that shield computer networks from outside threats. They encrypt system data, erect firewalls, and utilize a wide variety of hardware and software tools to ensure that homes, businesses, and government agencies remain protected from criminals, viruses, hackers, and other security threats.

Work Environment

Information security analysts work primarily in administrative and office settings. Analysts work at a variety of locations in and around offices and organizational complexes, most often at their own private workstations. They may also spend time working at the workstations of other employees, servicing their computers or installing equipment. Information security analysts also work in temperature-controlled server housing rooms and may be required to work remotely.

Profile

Working Conditions: Work Indoors
Physical Strength: Light Work
Education Needs: Bachelor's Degree
Licensure/Certification:
Recommended
Physical Abilities Not Required: No
Heavy Labor
Opportunities For Experience:
Internship, Military Service, Volunteer
Work, Part-Time Work
Holland Interest Score*: IRC

* See Appendix A

Occupation Interest

The field of information security attracts critical thinkers with a passion for electronics and computing who enjoy tackling complex problems. Information security analysts often get a tremendous amount of satisfaction from staying ahead of and repeatedly outsmarting security threats. Analysts also possess the patience to scrutinize extremely complicated data.

A Day in the Life—Duties and Responsibilities

Information security analysts handle a wide variety of duties and responsibilities on an everyday basis. Their main responsibility is to see computer systems through cyberattacks from the outside and to prevent such attacks from recurring. They are also tasked with identifying new potential security threats and encrypting archival data.

Data encryption is one of the central tasks of information security analysts. They are also responsible for constructing firewalls to protect organizational information. Some information security analysts are responsible for building, monitoring, and maintaining custom firewall and encryption systems for specific organizations and businesses, while others operate standard network-based firewall applications for a collection of clients.

Information security analysts are constantly on the lookout for security breaches, evidenced by the presence of outside influences on a computer network or traces of past network violations. In the event of a security breach, analysts will alert senior staff members and recommend enhancements to prevent future violations. This constant need for adaptation requires analysts to stay abreast of new developments in computer security technology through ancillary academic coursework, industry publications, annual meetings, and training seminars.

In addition to constantly monitoring the potential security risks that may target their business or organization, information security analysts must also stay informed of legislation and political developments related to digital security, particularly those that affect the rights of business clients and the civil liberties of individuals.

Duties and Responsibilities

- Monitoring the use of data files to protect information from unauthorized access and security violations
- Performing regular systems tests to ensure that all security measures are functioning properly
- Educating users about security issues
- Updating virus protection programs as necessary to combat new threats
- Encrypting data and erecting firewalls to keep information confidential
- Keeping documentation regarding security policies and procedures current
- Keeping abreast of new developments in the field

WORK ENVIRONMENT

Relevant Skills and Abilities

Analytical Skills
- Analyzing data

Communication Skills
- Speaking effectively
- Writing concisely

Organization & Management Skills
- Paying attention to and handling details
- Managing time
- Managing equipment/materials
- Coordinating tasks
- Making decisions
- Handling challenging situations

Research & Planning Skills
- Identifying problems
- Determining alternatives
- Gathering information
- Solving problems
- Defining needs
- Developing evaluation strategies

Technical Skills
- Performing scientific, mathematical, and technical work
- Using technology to process information

Physical Environment

Information security analysts predominantly work in office settings with occasional off-site work. They work in almost every industry, from business and finance to education, government, transportation, communications, and the military.

Human Environment

Many of the tasks of information security analysts are conducted individually. However, the explanation of different security systems to coworkers and clients requires group and one-on-one interactions.

Technological Environment

Information security analysts are highly trained in information technology. They utilize a variety of computer science technologies, including software, hardware, and network technology. They must also be adept at computer programming languages and web communication.

EDUCATION, TRAINING, AND ADVANCEMENT

High School/Secondary

High school students can best prepare for a career as an information security analyst by completing courses in algebra, calculus, geometry, trigonometry, and computer courses such as introductory programming. Exposure to computer systems via internships or volunteer work can also build an important foundation for students interested in being employed in computer science.

Suggested High School Subjects
- Algebra
- Applied Communication
- Applied Math
- Business & Computer Technology
- Business Data Processing
- Calculus
- College Preparatory
- Computer Programming
- Computer Science
- English
- Geometry
- Keyboarding
- Mathematics
- Statistics
- Trigonometry

Famous First

The first convicted computer hacker was a former director of computer security at a Texas insurance firm. In 1985 the man was fired from his job, and three days later company officials discovered that thousands of sales records had been erased from the firm's computer system. The man had used a computer virus of the "worm" type (also known as a "logic bomb") to destroy the files. He was later convicted on third-degree felony charges and sentenced to seven years' probation and a $12,000 fine.

College/Postsecondary

A bachelor's degree is a standard requirement for nearly all employment vacancies in the information security profession. Most candidates arrive to the field after academic training in general computer science, programming or software development, while others prepare for the role by completing degree programs dedicated specifically to computer and network security. Postsecondary students who study information security complete coursework in such topics as network design, intrusion detection, wireless security, system administration, and cryptography. Additional related coursework also includes system administration and architecture and firewall construction.

Related College Majors
- Computer Installation & Repair
- Computer Maintenance Technology
- Computer Programming
- Computer Science
- Data Processing Technology
- Information Sciences & Systems
- Information Security
- Management Information Systems

Adult Job Seekers

The field of information security requires extensive academic and professional training. Individuals with no background in a related field should enroll in a college or a technical or vocational school that offers a program in computer security. Technical schools are also a great place for job seekers to network. Communication technologies and standards are always changing, so information security analysts should be willing to continue learning throughout their career.

Professional Certification and Licensure

There are numerous professional certifications available for information security professionals, each of which expands their frame of reference while making them attractive candidates for professional vacancies. They include Certified Information Systems Security Professional (CISSP), Certified Ethical Hacker (CEH), Certified Information Security Manager (CISM), and Global Information Assurance Certification (GIAC).

Additional Requirements

Information security is a constantly evolving field. Those interested in a career as an information security analyst must possess the patience and professionalism to stay up to date on rapidly emerging developments in a variety of technical disciplines, notably mobile communications, network diagnostics, software development, and hardware design.

EARNINGS AND ADVANCEMENT

Mean annual earnings of information security analysts were $89,290 in 2012. The lowest ten percent earned less than $49,960, and the highest ten percent earned more than $135,600.

Information security analysts may receive paid vacations, holidays and sick days; life and health insurance; and retirement benefits. These are usually paid by the employer.

Metropolitan Areas with the Highest
Employment Level in this Occupation

Metropolitan area	Employment[1]	Employment per thousand jobs	Hourly mean wage
Washington-Arlington-Alexandria, DC-VA-MD-WV	9,400	4.01	$49.35
New York-White Plains-Wayne, NY-NJ	3,860	0.75	$56.67
Dallas-Plano-Irving, TX	2,450	1.17	$40.52
Boston-Cambridge-Quincy, MA	2,010	1.18	$48.28
Seattle-Bellevue-Everett, WA	1,930	1.37	$46.42
Atlanta-Sandy Springs-Marietta, GA	1,780	0.79	$40.33
Baltimore-Towson, MD	1,670	1.32	$47.87
Houston-Sugar Land-Baytown, TX	1,550	0.59	$45.60

[1]Does not include self-employed. Source: Bureau of Labor Statistics

Fun Facts

Women represent just 11 percent of the information security profession globally.
Source: Agents of Change: Women in the Information Security Profession, The (ISC)2 Global Information Security Workforce

EMPLOYMENT AND OUTLOOK

Information security analysts held about 75,000 jobs nationally in 2012. Employment is expected to grow much faster than the average for all occupations through the year 2022, which means employment is projected to increase 30 percent or more. Almost every organization in today's workforce needs to keep a computer network running smoothly and secure from hackers, viruses and other attacks. The growth of security as a main concern for organizations will help to fuel the growth of information security analysts.

Employment Trend, Projected 2012–22

Information Security Analysts: 37%

Computer Occupations: 18%

Total, All Occupations: 11%

Note: "All Occupations" includes all occupations in the U.S. Economy. Source: U.S. Bureau of Labor Statistics, Employment Projections Program

Related Occupations
- Computer & Information Systems Manager
- Computer Engineer
- Computer Network Architect
- Computer Programmer
- Computer Support Specialist
- Computer Systems Analyst
- Information Technology Project Manager
- Software Developer

Related Military Occupations
- Computer Programmer
- Computer Systems Officer
- Computer Systems Specialist

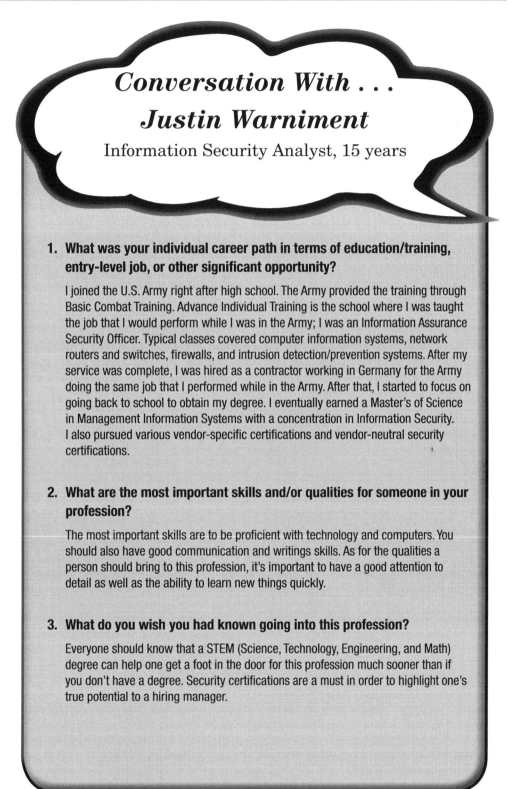

Conversation With . . .
Justin Warniment
Information Security Analyst, 15 years

1. What was your individual career path in terms of education/training, entry-level job, or other significant opportunity?

I joined the U.S. Army right after high school. The Army provided the training through Basic Combat Training. Advance Individual Training is the school where I was taught the job that I would perform while I was in the Army; I was an Information Assurance Security Officer. Typical classes covered computer information systems, network routers and switches, firewalls, and intrusion detection/prevention systems. After my service was complete, I was hired as a contractor working in Germany for the Army doing the same job that I performed while in the Army. After that, I started to focus on going back to school to obtain my degree. I eventually earned a Master's of Science in Management Information Systems with a concentration in Information Security. I also pursued various vendor-specific certifications and vendor-neutral security certifications.

2. What are the most important skills and/or qualities for someone in your profession?

The most important skills are to be proficient with technology and computers. You should also have good communication and writings skills. As for the qualities a person should bring to this profession, it's important to have a good attention to detail as well as the ability to learn new things quickly.

3. What do you wish you had known going into this profession?

Everyone should know that a STEM (Science, Technology, Engineering, and Math) degree can help one get a foot in the door for this profession much sooner than if you don't have a degree. Security certifications are a must in order to highlight one's true potential to a hiring manager.

4. Are there many job opportunities in your profession? In what specific areas?

According to the 2013 (ISC)2 Global Information Security Workforce Study, the number of professionals in this industry is expected to grow steady globally by more than 11 percent annually over the next five years. Also, of the 39 job categories used in the survey questionnaire, security analysts were identified as the top need in terms of shortages by job title. Companies cannot fill their vacancies fast enough. Application and software security is huge and understanding how systems and applications interact with each other is essential. With all of the recent breaches in computer systems, information security is a really big concern for most organizations.

5. How do you see your profession changing in the next five years? What role will technology play in those changes, and what skills will be required?

This is one of the fastest growing professions due to the rapid pace at which technology evolves. It is very important that one stays up to date on all of the latest industry trends and attacks. That skill set is very valuable to organizations across every industry.

6. Do you have any general advice or additional professional insights to share with someone in your profession? What is the most fulfilling part of your job, and what is the most frustrating?

This profession is very rewarding, both personally and professionally. Again, with all of the data breaches that are occurring today, knowing that your daily actions help to keep your organization's or clients' information secure is very rewarding. The most frustrating part is the constant battle of trying to outthink your opponent. You have to adjust your tactics to the latest trends within a fast-paced environment.

7. Can you suggest a valuable "try this" for students considering a career in your profession?

Yes, look for cyber competition programs available for high school students. One is the Air Force Association's US Cyber Patriot, a national youth cyber education program. You can find more information about it at www.uscyberpatriot.org. This is a hands-on competition that would be the closest to real-world experience of the profession.

There's also a national public-private partnership that was formed to address the shortage in the cybersecurity workforce. It's called U.S. Cyber Challenge (www.uscyberchallenge.org) and its holds "cyber camps" for high school and college students. At these camps, the students get specialized cybersecurity training as well as other opportunities to enhance their skills. My organization, (ISC)2 has supported this program in the past by providing college scholarships and vouchers for our SSCP exam to the winners.

SELECTED SCHOOLS

Programs in information security are available at numerous four-year colleges and universities. The student may also gain initial training at a technical or community college. The website of the U.S. National Security Agency's Central Security Service (see below) provides a state-by-state listing of recognized school programs. Below are listed some of the more prominent institutions in this field.

DePaul University
College of Computing and Digital Media
243 S. Wabash Avenue
Chicago, IL 60604
312.362.8381
www.cdm.depaul.edu

George Mason University
Department of Applied Information Technology
5400 Nguyen Engineering Building, MS1G8
Fairfax, VA 22030
703.993.4871
ait.gmu.edu

Indiana University, Bloomington School of Informatics and Computing
901 E. 10thStreet
Bloomington, IN 47408
812.856.5754
www.soic.indiana.ed

Johns Hopkins University
Department of Computer Science
224 Croft Hall
3400 N. Charles Street
Baltimore, MD 21218
410.516.6134
www.cs.jhu.edu

Northeastern University
College of Computer and Information Science
440 Huntington Avenue
202 W. Village H
Boston, MA 02115
617.373.2462
www.ccs.neu.edu

University of Pittsburgh
School of Information Sciences
135 N. Bellefield Avenue
Pittsburgh, PA 15260
412.624.5230
www.ischool.pitt.edu

University of Maryland, College Park
Department of Computer Science
A.V. Williams Building
College Park, MD 20742
301.405.2662
www.cs.umd.edu

University of Southern California
Computer Science Department
941 Bloom Walk, SAL 300
Los Angeles, CA 90089
213.740.4494
www.cs.usc.edu

University of Texas, San Antonia
Department of Computer Science
One UTSA Circle
San Antonio, TX 78249
210.458.4436
www.cs.utsa.edu

University of Washington
Information School
Mary Gates Hall, Suite 370
P.O. Box 352840
Seattle, WA 98195
206.685.9937
Ischool.uw.edu

MORE INFORMATION

Applied Computer Security Associates
2906 Covington Road
Silver Spring, MD 20910
www.acsac.org

Computer Security Resource Center
National Institute of Standards and Technology
100 Bureau Drive
Mail Stop 8930
Gaithersburg, MD 20899-8930
301.975.6478
csrc.nist.gov

Information Systems Security Association
9220 SW Barbour Boulevard
#119-333
Portland, OR 97219
866.349.5818
www.issa.org

National Security Agency Central Security Service
9800 Savage Road
Fort Meade, MD 20755
301.688.6524
www.nsa.gov

John Pritchard/Editor

Inspector and Compliance Officer

Snapshot

Career Cluster(s): Government & Public Administration; Law & Criminal Justice; Public Safety & Security

Interests: Laws and regulations, accident prevention and safety, detail work

Earnings (Yearly Average): $65,392

Employment & Outlook: Average Growth Expected

OVERVIEW

Sphere of Work

Inspectors and compliance officers investigate and assess various goods, services, buildings, businesses, and other regulated activities to ensure that they meet government standards. They operate on behalf of state and federal government in such fields as agriculture, buildings and construction, health, animal management, and banks and finance. Inspectors and compliance officers travel frequently within their jurisdictions to visit businesses and sites. They verify that certification and licenses are current, waste is managed

appropriately, the proper reports are filed, and systems are operating safely.

Work Environment

Compliance officers and inspectors spend a great deal of their time visiting regulated sites and businesses. They may work in extreme weather or in challenging environmental conditions, such as waste management facilities or factory floors. Much of their time is also spent in offices, interviewing workers and reviewing paperwork to ensure that it is current. The work environments vary based on the area with which the agency has oversight. Construction inspectors, for example, may assess building sites, dams, bridges, and sewer systems, while agricultural inspectors may work on farms and in meat processing facilities.

Profile

Working Conditions: Work both Indoors and Outdoors
Physical Strength: Light Work
Education Needs: Bachelor's Degree
Licensure/Certification: Required
Physical Abilities Not Required: No Heavy Labor
Opportunities For Experience: Apprenticeship, Military Service
Holland Interest Score*: ERS

* See Appendix A

Occupation Interest

Inspectors and compliance officers are responsible for ensuring that businesses and property owners are engaged in legal and ethical behavior. These professionals enforce government regulations designed to protect people, animals, and the economy. Crises such as oil spills, financial collapses, structure fires, and outbreaks of salmonella are often caused by lack of compliance with government laws and regulations; therefore, inspectors and compliance officers are extremely important to the prevention of natural, health, and financial emergencies.

A Day in the Life—Duties and Responsibilities

Compliance officers and inspectors monitor and enforce existing regulations among businesses and property owners. They draft and maintain inspection records for each group they oversee; these records include license information, applications, and any other relevant information. Compliance officers and inspectors use current information on regulations in order to conduct proper inspections and analyze how those regulations must be applied to each specific group under their watch.

With the most up-to-date regulatory information and a thorough assessment of a target group's liability, an inspector visits those businesses to investigate their level of compliance. In the case of agricultural, environmental, and occupational health inspectors, this investigation often includes taking soil, water, and air samples. Building inspectors and compliance officers check to see if fire sprinklers, exits, and alarms are properly functioning; electrical systems are up to code; and foundations, roofs, and chimneys are sound. In most cases, the inspector also confirms that the organization's license and certification are current and posted publicly, as required by law.

Upon completing an inspection, the compliance officer writes his or her report, noting any violations and recommending fines and/ or corrective action regarding those issues. He or she then files this report with his or her agency and notifies the business owner of the violations (including providing information about how to rectify those problems). A construction inspector may issue a "stop work" order preventing a developer from proceeding with a project until the violations are corrected.

Duties and Responsibilities

- Examining work and/or production facilities for conformance to applicable laws and regulations
- Collecting material samples for analysis
- Examining records and documents to identify any discrepancies
- Informing individuals of specific regulations affecting their establishment
- Assuring that required licenses and permits have been obtained and are displayed
- Assembling evidence of any violations of laws
- Submitting findings to appropriate government authorities

OCCUPATION SPECIALTIES

Building Inspectors

Building Inspectors ensure that construction meets local and national building codes and ordinances, zoning regulations, and contract specifications.

Field Health Officers

Field Health Officers check the safety of foods produced in dairies and processing plants or foods served in restaurants, schools, and other institutions.

Immigration Inspectors

Immigration Inspectors are law enforcement agents who check business establishments to ensure their compliance with federal immigration laws.

Health Care Facilities Inspectors

Health Care Facilities Inspectors inspect facilities such as hospitals, nursing homes, sheltered care homes, and day care centers to enforce public health laws and to investigate any complaints.

Occupational Safety and Health Inspectors

Occupational Safety and Health Inspectors inspect places of employment to detect unsafe or unhealthy working conditions.

Customs Inspectors

Customs Inspectors examine exports and imports for admissibility and tariff and inspect goods carried by travelers in order to intercept contraband and clear those crossing the border.

Food & Drug Inspectors

Food & Drug Inspectors inspect establishments where food, drugs, cosmetics, and similar consumer items are manufactured, handled, stored, or sold to enforce legal standards of sanitation, purity, and grading.

Postal Inspectors

Postal Inspectors observe and recommend improvements to the postal system and investigate criminal activities in cooperation with other agencies.

Agricultural Commodity Graders

Agricultural Commodity Graders examine food products for quality and grade, and may also inspect processing plants and equipment for sanitation.

Environmental Compliance Inspectors

Environmental Compliance Inspectors investigate pollution sources to protect the public and the environment.

WORK ENVIRONMENT

Physical Environment

Inspectors and compliance officers usually have offices in state or local government buildings. They conduct inspections in a wide range of locations, depending on the agency for which they work. For example, agriculture inspectors analyze farms and slaughterhouses, while home inspectors visit private residences. In some situations, the inspector may be exposed to dangerous substances and systems, such as toxic chemicals, faulty wiring, or mold.

Human Environment

Inspectors and compliance officers generally work alone during the course of their investigations. However, they interact frequently with government officials and the public, in addition to the individuals whom they are investigating. On complex inspections, they may work with other compliance officers who focus on complementary systems within the building or business.

Relevant Skills and Abilities

Communication Skills
- Speaking and writing effectively

Interpersonal/Social Skills
- Cooperating with others
- Working both independently and as a member of a team

Organization & Management Skills
- Demonstrating leadership
- Making decisions
- Identifying problems
- Paying attention to and handling details

Research & Planning Skills
- Using logical reasoning

Technical Skills
- Performing technical work

Technological Environment

Compliance officers and inspectors must be familiar with the relevant tools and technologies that help reveal whether a business or structure meets regulatory requirements. Although many violations are visually apparent, inspectors may use tape measures, concrete strength measurers, cameras, soil sampling equipment, Geiger counters, and other technologies to assess compliance on-site. They use computer systems and other laboratory equipment to analyze samples.

EDUCATION, TRAINING, AND ADVANCEMENT

High School/Secondary

High school students interested in becoming compliance officers and inspectors are encouraged to take courses in the fields in which they seek to work. Such courses include shop classes, such as building trades or engineering. Because writing and communication are essential to these jobs, English and writing courses are recommended as well.

Suggested High School Subjects
- Business
- Driver Training
- English

- Health
- Home Economics
- Horticulture
- Photography
- Psychology
- Shop

Famous First

The first pure food and drug law was New York State's 1881 law "to prevent the adulteration of food or drugs." Violators were guilty of a misdemeanor, subject to a $50 fine for the first offense and a $100 fine for each subsequent offense. A full 25 years later President Theodore Roosevelt signed into law the federal Pure Food and Drug Act along with the Federal Meat Inspection Act.

Library of Congress

College/Postsecondary

Although experience in the field is important, most government employers expect a postsecondary degree in a related field, such as a bachelor's degree in agriculture, public health, architecture, or engineering. Many junior and community colleges offer associate's degrees in inspection technology.

Related College Majors
- Agricultural & Food Products Processing
- Agronomy & Crop Science
- Building Design & Construction
- Food Sciences & Technology
- Occupational Safety & Health Technology
- Occupational Health & Industrial Hygiene
- Plant Sciences
- Public Health
- Public Safety & Security

Adult Job Seekers

Aspiring compliance officers and inspectors may find employment through first working as an apprentice. Because most inspectors and compliance officers are fully versed in the fields in which they work, adult job seekers may use a current occupation as a plumber, electrician, or environmental engineer to qualify for open positions with the local or state government.

Professional Certification and Licensure

Many state and local governments require inspectors to obtain professional licensure or certification. Such requirements usually involve a combination of on-the-job experience, formal education, and satisfactory completion of an examination. Some inspector certification programs also include a requirement that the individual purchase liability insurance. Interested individuals should research the requirements of their state or local government.

Additional Requirements

Because inspectors and compliance officers conduct so many field investigations, they need a valid driver's license and physical stamina. They should have an extensive knowledge of the field they monitor as well as its regulatory environment. Finally, these professionals should have strong written and verbal communication skills.

EARNINGS AND ADVANCEMENT

Earnings of inspectors and compliance officers depend on the type of position and the qualifications of the applicant. Inspectors and compliance officers are employed in a wide variety of industries. Mean annual earnings of various specialties in 2012 were agricultural inspectors, $42,460; construction and building inspectors, $55,230; fire inspectors and investigators, $57,400; forest fire inspectors and prevention specialists, $41,860; and transportation (vehicle and railroad) inspectors, $66,470. Other areas include aviation safety inspectors, $102,817; highway safety inspectors, $99,834; internal revenue agents, $86,679; environmental protection specialists, $82,337; safety and occupational health managers, $80,143; customs inspectors, $62,246; immigration inspectors, $54,453; consumer safety inspectors, $53,465; and food inspectors, $51,124.

Inspectors and compliance officers may receive paid vacations, holidays, and sick days; life and health insurance; and retirement benefits. These are usually paid by the employer.

Metropolitan Areas with the Highest Employment Level in this Occupation (Building Inspector)

Metropolitan area	Employment[1]	Employment per thousand jobs	Hourly mean wage
New York-White Plains-Wayne, NY-NJ	3,380	0.66	$31.13
Chicago-Joliet-Naperville, IL	2,770	0.76	$26.57
Washington-Arlington-Alexandria, DC-VA-MD-WV	2,060	0.88	$32.45
Phoenix-Mesa-Glendale, AZ	1,900	1.10	$26.12
Dallas-Plano-Irving, TX	1,800	0.86	$27.20
Houston-Sugar Land-Baytown, TX	1,690	0.64	$30.04
Los Angeles-Long Beach-Glendale, CA	1,680	0.44	$36.97
Pittsburgh, PA	1,390	1.23	$23.87

[1]Does not include self-employed. Source: Bureau of Labor Statistics

EMPLOYMENT AND OUTLOOK

Nationally, about 275,000 inspectors and compliance officers were employed in 2012. While the majority of jobs were spread throughout the private sector, almost half worked for federal, state and local government agencies. Within the federal government, most jobs are as Occupational Safety and Health Administration (OSHA) inspectors, who enforce U.S. Department of Labor regulations that ensure adequate safety principles, practices and techniques are applied in workplaces.

Employment is expected to grow about as fast as the average for all occupations through the year 2022, which means employment is projected to increase 10 percent to 15 percent. This reflects a balance of continuing public demand for a safe and healthy work environment and quality products against the desire for smaller government and fewer regulations.

Employment Trend, Projected 2012–22

Public Safety and Security Occupations: 12%

Inspectors and Compliance Officers: 12%

Total, All Occupations: 11%

Note: "All Occupations" includes all occupations in the U.S. Economy. Source: U.S. Bureau of Labor Statistics, Employment Projections Program

Related Occupations
- Customs Inspector
- Federal Law Enforcement Agent
- Police Officer

Related Military Occupations
- Environmental Health & Safety Officer
- Environmental Health & Safety Specialist
- Food Service Manager
- Law Enforcement & Security Specialist

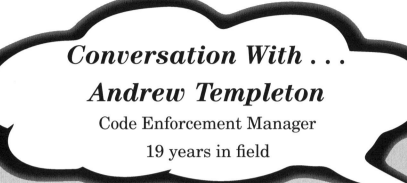

Conversation With . . .
Andrew Templeton
Code Enforcement Manager
19 years in field

1. **What was your individual career path in terms of education/training, entry-level job, or other significant opportunity?**

   I hold a journalism degree with an area of specialization in political science. After nine years in newspaper work, I entered employment with the City of Sand Springs as Solid Waste (trash) superintendent. I was assigned to code enforcement upon the city's initiation of a full-time code enforcement program. It was not something I sought out, but it ended up being a good employment fit.

2. **What are the most important skills and/or qualities for someone in your profession?**

   Common sense, good judgment and rationality, excellent verbal and written communication skills, self-motivated, ability to work independently, substantial trustworthiness, organizational skills to track cases and meet very specific deadlines.

3. **What do you wish you had known going into this profession?**

   I had written news articles on code enforcement efforts, so I had a general understanding of the profession. I would have welcomed the very specific training that is now available when I first entered the profession.

4. **Are there many job opportunities in your profession? In what specific areas?**

   Yes. Code enforcement is a growing profession as cities and towns market themselves as offering safe and healthy environments. Small cities and towns that would never have endeavored to do code enforcement are now getting involved. Well-regulated regions of the country have cities with significant code enforcement programs. However, there are opportunities in most any city of any size.

5. How do you see your profession changing in the next five years? What role will technology play in those changes, and what skills will be required?

As people expect more services and protections from their communities in the next five years, the number and complexity of code cases will increase. Technology will continue to make field work more safe and efficient. Prospective officers will need to be able to comprehend and effectively use specialized municipal software programs designed for code work as well as general office software programs.

6. Do you have any general advice or additional professional insights to share with someone in your profession? What is the most fulfilling part of your job, and what is the most frustrating?

Code officers are similar to law officers, with the difference being that police deal primarily with people issues and code officers primarily deal with property issues. Code officers get to learn and use both civil and criminal processes in their profession. In addition to being a stable career, it is an excellent opportunity to learn about other careers, such as government administration, law enforcement, construction code administration, and legal work.

Code officers can make a very visible difference in the communities where they work and can take great pride in seeing properties and neighborhoods once left for dead come alive again due in significant part to their efforts. As corny as it may sound, making a difference is a key component in job satisfaction.

One has to be able to handle the inevitable confrontation that can occur when telling someone they can no longer do something they've done for years and perhaps decades. Code enforcement can also be very political, and the job can become very frustrating if one does not have a grasp of the community's political will.

7. Can you suggest a valuable "try this" for students considering a career in your profession?

Spend time with a code officer. That will allow you to experience first-hand what the profession entails and why it matters to a community's current and future health, safety and prosperity.

You may not get a job as a code officer straight out of high school, but a good basis is to take a municipal job and work toward a code officer's position. Most of the training is available upon hiring, so the primary requirements are a demonstrated track record of working independently, making good judgment calls and following through on assignments.

SELECTED SCHOOLS

Programs in academic subjects relevant to becoming an inspector and compliance officer are available at many colleges and universities. The student may also gain initial training at a community college. Interested students are advised to consult with a school guidance counselor.

MORE INFORMATION

American Society of Home Inspectors, Inc.
932 Lee Street, Suite 101
Des Plaines, IL 60016
847.759.2820
www.homeinspector.org

Board of Certified Safety Professionals
206 W. Bradley Avenue
Champaign, IL 61821
217.359.9263
www.bcsp.org

Consumer Product Safety Commission
4330 East West Highway
Bethesda, MD 20814
800.638.2772
www.cpsc.gov

International Code Council
500 New Jersey Avenue NW
6th Floor
Washington, DC 20001
888.422.7233
www.iccsafe.org

National Academy of Building Inspection Engineers
P.O. Box 860
Shelter Island, NY 11964
800.294.7729
www.nabie.org

National Association of Safety Professionals
501 Forest Hill Drive
P.O. Box 167
Shelby, NC 28150
800.922.2219
www.naspweb.com

National Highway Traffic Safety Administration
1200 New Jersey Avenue, SE
West Building
Washington, DC 20590
888.327.4236
www.nhtsa.gov

National Institute of Standards and Technology
100 Bureau Drive
Gaithersburg, MD 20899
301.975.6478
www.nist.gov

North American Transportation Association
9120 Double Diamond Parkway
Suite 346
Reno, NV 89521
800.805.0040
www.ntassoc.com

Occupational Safety and Health Administration
200 Constitution Avenue, NW
Washington, DC 20210
800.321.6742
www.osha.gov

U.S. Environmental Protection Agency
Office of Inspector General
1200 Pennsylvania Avenue, NW
Washington, DC 20460
202.566.2391
www.epa.gov

U.S. Food and Drug Administration
10903 New Hampshire Avenue
Silver Spring, MD 20993
888.463.6332
www.fda.gov

Michael Auerbach/Editor

Judge

Snapshot

Career Cluster: Law & Criminal Justice; Public Safety & Security

Interests: Law, research, writing, dealing with conflict, solving problems

Earnings (Yearly Average): $102,470

Employment & Outlook: Slower Than Average Growth Expected

OVERVIEW

Sphere of Work

A judge is a public official who oversees the legal process in the courtroom. The judge serves as the chief administrator of a court proceeding. He or she sets the tone of the proceeding by advising attorneys, plaintiffs, and defendants on the rules and procedures of the hearing or trial, ruling on the relevance of testimony, determining whether evidence is admissible, and settling disputes between opposing attorneys during the proceedings. A judge also meets with litigants outside of the courtroom to determine whether a trial or hearing is necessary at all. Once a jury has ruled on a defendant's

liability or guilt, the judge will apply the sentence or award damages based on the law.

Work Environment

Judges work in office settings (known as "chambers"), where they meet with attorneys and other legal professionals, study evidence and legal precedents, write opinions, and organize the procedures for court cases. They also work in the courtroom, overseeing proceedings in civil and criminal courts. Judges may be found in a wide range of courts, such as municipal and superior courts, appellate courts, state supreme courts, federal district courts and the highest court in the country, the U.S. Supreme Court. Judges work with a large and diverse number of people, including lawyers, accused criminals, security and law enforcement professionals, victims of crime, and the general public.

Profile

Working Conditions: Work Indoors
Physical Strength: Light Work
Education Needs: Law Degree
Licensure/Certification: Required
Physical Abilities Not Required: No Heavy Labor
Opportunities For Experience: Military Service, Volunteer Work, Part-Time Work
Holland Interest Score*: ESA

* See Appendix A

Occupation Interest

A judge is a leading figure in the application and interpretation of laws. The judge is the highest authority in a courtroom, setting the rules, allowing or excluding evidence, ruling on objections and courtroom conduct, and controlling other important aspects of the courtroom proceedings. A judge is the individual who works to ensure that the hearing proceeds in such a way that it is truly fair and equitable for both defendants and plaintiffs.

Outside of the courtroom, a judge is also an expert on the law. He or she may offer statements regarding new laws, pending lawsuits, and even the tenets of the Constitution. A judge's legal opinion may answer pivotal questions about whether a business or government policy is compliant with the law and concurrent with the best interests of society.

A Day in the Life—Duties and Responsibilities

Most judges spend much of their work day in chambers, hearing attorney arguments and either arbitrating a legal dispute or determining whether a case should go to trial. Their discussions also cover issues such as the admissibility of evidence, witnesses, and other elements of a case. Judges write legal opinions and organize trial and hearing rules while in their chambers or locating information in law libraries. They also supervise their staff members, including administrative and clerical personnel. When they are called into court, judges work to ensure that the proceeding is fair, including instructing the jurors on which information to retain, disciplining unruly parties in the courtroom, and monitoring evidence to ensure that no inadmissible material is introduced that could bias jury members.

Federal judges share many of the responsibilities of municipal and regional judges, but they focus on issues that have more broad-reaching or national implications. Appellate court judges and Supreme Court justices will often hear arguments regarding cases on which other judges at a more local level have already ruled—it is the responsibility of these judges to weigh whether the previous ruling was legal and/or constitutional.

Duties and Responsibilities

- Establishing rules of procedure
- Researching legal matters
- Reading or listening to statements
- Listening to case presentations by lawyers
- Settling disputes
- Instructing jury members on applicable law and proper procedures
- Sentencing defendants in criminal cases according to law

OCCUPATION SPECIALTIES

Appellate-Court Judges

Appellate-Court Judges review cases handled by the lower courts and administrative agencies, and if they determine that errors were made in a case and if legal precedent does not support the judgment of the lower court, they may overturn the verdict of that court.

Juvenile Court Judges

Juvenile Court Judges arbitrate, advise, and administer justice in matters dealing with youth and young adults.

Municipal Court Judges

Municipal Court Judges preside over cases within a city. Traffic violations, misdemeanors, small claims cases, and pretrial hearings constitute the bulk of their work.

Probate Judges

Probate Judges arbitrate, advise, and administer justice in estate (inheritance) matters and the registration and certification of official documents such as last wills and testaments.

Justices of the Peace

Justices of the Peace are magistrates with jurisdiction over a small district or part of a county that decides cases, holds pretrial hearings, and can perform marriages.

Magistrates

Magistrates are state court judges that preside over cases only within a certain jurisdiction with limited judicial powers.

Hearing Officers

Hearing Officers are employed by government agencies to make decisions about ap0peals of agency administrative decisions, such as eligibility for social assistance benefits.

WORK ENVIRONMENT

Physical Environment

Judges spend the majority of their time working in their chambers or in a courtroom or hearing room, both of which are typically located in secure government buildings and/or courthouses. The office setting is professional and orderly, with administrative staff researching laws, preparing opinions, and drafting court documents. The courtroom is highly organized and orderly: each individual present is tasked with specific duties, and the jury is legally bound to follow the rules and instructions of the judge.

Relevant Skills and Abilities

Communication Skills
- Expressing thoughts and ideas clearly
- Speaking and writing effectively

Interpersonal/Social Skills
- Cooperating with others
- Counseling others
- Providing support to others
- Working as a member of a team

Organization & Management Skills
- Displaying leadership
- Making decisions

Research & Planning Skills
- Developing evaluation strategies
- Using logical reasoning

Human Environment

Judges work with a wide variety of people, such as litigants (the plaintiff and defendant), legal counsel for each side, court reporters, witnesses, security personnel, the public in attendance and, of course, the members of the jury. Supreme Court (state and federal) justices and appeals court judges (who may sit on three-judge panels or en banc) also collaborate to formulate collective opinions on legal and constitutional issues.

Technological Environment

Judges often use computers to write opinions and organize court procedures for each case. Courtrooms tend to employ simple technology, including microphones and television monitors used for the presentation of evidence.

EDUCATION, TRAINING, AND ADVANCEMENT

High School/Secondary

High school students who aspire to become judges should study political science and government, social studies, history, and philosophy. English and communications courses are also extremely useful to build research, writing, analysis, and public speaking skills. An awareness of current events on a local and national level is of benefit as well. Students should also pursue activities that allow them to gain experience outside the classroom, such as involvement in Student Council and other leadership organizations.

Suggested High School Subjects
- Algebra
- College Preparatory
- Composition
- Economics
- English
- Government
- History
- Humanities
- Literature
- Political Science
- Psychology
- Sociology
- Speech

Fun Facts

President George Washington appointed the most federal justices of the U.S. Supreme Court: eleven.

Source: "Kid's Court," U.S. District Court, Western District of North Carolina

Famous First

The first state supreme court composed entirely of women was the Special Supreme Court of Texas, appointed by Governor Pat M. Neff in 1925. The women's appointment came about after the three male sitting judges had to recuse themselves because of conflicts of interest. Governor Neff, finding it difficult to find suitable male replacements, appointed Hortense Ward of Houston as special chief justice and Hattie Henenberg of Dallas and Ruth Brazzil of Galveston as special associate judges. The new judges ultimately upheld the lower court's decision in favor of the fraternal organization. While they were engaged in the case, moreover, the state's first woman governor, Miriam A. Ferguson, took office. Yet, it would be another 30 years before women were permitted to sit on juries in Texas.

Library of Congress

College/Postsecondary

Aspiring judges must have an undergraduate degree in a related field (with a pre-law focus), such as political science, English, or history. In addition to undergraduate training, most judges are required to have a degree in law, such as an LLB or a JD. This training gives students exposure to a wide range of significant legal rulings and helps them become fully versed in the law, its application, and interpretation.

Related College Majors
- Law (L.L.B., J.D.)

Adult Job Seekers

State and federal judges are usually appointed by senior government officials, such as governors or, in the case of federal judges, the president. Municipal and regional judges are elected by the public. Those having hopes for a judicial appointment or election should practice law for several years, building a positive reputation within the legal community and the community in which they live. Since politicians and the voting public determine who will become a judge, prospective judges must be self-promoters and knowledgeable about how to use the media to their advantage.

Professional Certification and Licensure

In addition to earning his or her law degree, a judge must pass the bar examination of the state in which he or she works. Judges may also join a professional legal association, such as the American Bar Association.

Additional Requirements

Judges should have prior experience as lawyers, as well as an exceptional understanding of the law and the U.S. Constitution. They should have strong analytical and communication skills, which help them apply the law or the tenets of the Constitution to the issues brought before them by the litigants. Ideally, judges should be even-handed and decisive, especially in light of the strong emotions that can arise during arbitration and court proceedings.

EARNINGS AND ADVANCEMENT

Earnings of judges depend on the judicial level and geographic location of the court which they serve. Mean annual earnings of judges were $102,470 in 2012. The lowest ten percent earned less than $30,060, and the highest ten percent earned more than $166,880. Judges at the state government level had mean annual earnings of $118,910 in 2012.

In federal government courts in 2012, the Chief Justice of the United States Supreme Court earned around $236,910, and the Associate Justices earned around $226,734. Federal circuit judges earned $195,570 annually, while district court judges had median annual earnings of $184,440 in 2012.

Judges may receive paid vacations, holidays, and sick days; life and health insurance; and retirement benefits. These are usually paid by the employer. Judges may also receive a cost-of-living allowance, travel and library allowances and payment of state bar or other association dues.

Metropolitan Areas with the Highest Employment Level in this Occupation

Metropolitan area	Employment	Employment per thousand jobs	Hourly mean wage
New York-White Plains-Wayne, NY-NJ	790	0.15	$62.50
Atlanta-Sandy Springs-Marietta, GA	650	0.29	$43.12
Los Angeles-Long Beach-Glendale, CA	440	0.11	$80.81
Houston-Sugar Land-Baytown, TX	410	0.16	$42.07
Phoenix-Mesa-Glendale, AZ	390	0.23	$53.97
Charleston, WV	370	2.55	n/a
Columbus, OH	300	0.33	$34.22
Minneapolis-St. Paul-Bloomington, MN-WI	290	0.16	$55.91

Source: Bureau of Labor Statistics

EMPLOYMENT AND OUTLOOK

Judges held about 45,000 jobs nationally in 2012. All worked for federal, state, or local governments. Employment is expected to grow slower than the average for all occupations through the year 2022, which means employment is projected to increase 0 percent to 5 percent. As in the past, most job openings will result from the retirement of judges. However, public concerns about crime and safety, as well as a public willingness to go to court to settle disputes, should spur demand for judges. Both the quantity and the complexity of the work have increased because of developments in information technology, medical science, electronic commerce, and globalization. The prestige associated with serving on the bench will ensure continued competition for judge positions.

Employment Trend, Projected 2012–22

Total, All Occupations: 11%

IJudges, Magistrate Judges, and Magistrates: 2%

Judges and Hearing Officers: 1%

Administrative Law Judges, Adjudicators, and Hearing Officers: -2%

Note: "All Occupations" includes all occupations in the U.S. Economy. Source: U.S. Bureau of Labor Statistics, Employment Projections Program

Related Occupations
- Lawyer

Related Military Occupations
- Lawyer

Conversation With . . .
The Hon. Jerry A. Brown
Bankruptcy Judge, 22 years

1. What was your individual career path in terms of education/training, entry-level job, or other significant opportunity?

I always wanted to be a lawyer, and I had a couple of uncles who encouraged me to be a lawyer. I went to Murray State College in Western Kentucky; there wasn't a pre-law program but I majored in history and social sciences and was on the debate team. Tulane University Law School, back in the early '50s, offered regional scholarships and I received one. I wanted to go in the Army first and fulfill my military obligation and Tulane was very clear: you go do your military duty and we'll hold the scholarship.

When I graduated, I was a law clerk for Judge John Minor Wisdom. He was an outstanding judge on the U.S. Fifth Circuit Court of Appeals, a wonderful person to work for, a great writer. He was a legal giant, well known for his influential votes during the Civil Rights era. That's when I first got the urge to be a judge.

I was in private practice with one of the fine old law firms, Monroe and Lemann, for 30 years. I did commercial law, business law, defense work, and some reorganization work, which is a specialized portion of bankruptcy. I left in 1990 and went with a boutique bankruptcy firm, Bronfin and Heller. Not quite two years later, I applied and was appointed to the Bankruptcy Court of the Eastern District of Louisiana by the Fifth U.S. Circuit Court of Appeals. I served one 14-year-term, another five-year abbreviated term, then retired but was recalled twice for a total of six years. I will finish my current three year recall term in September, 2017, and if my good health continues I plan to ask for another three year recall.

2. What are the most important skills and/or qualities for someone in your profession?

Being able to write well and being able to analyze and solve problems in writing. So much of legal problems is decided on the written word. Oral argument has been curtailed a great deal. For a judge, writing and a command of the English language is all-important.

3. What do you wish you had known going into this profession?

I wish I'd known how to write better. I was assistant editor at Tulane Law Review and did a lot of legal writing as a lawyer, but it's a different style and a different approach when you're a judge. As a lawyer you advocate your point. As a judge, you've got to weigh both sides and come to a just decision.

4. Are there many job opportunities in your profession? In what specific areas?

Judgeships open up from time to time. Some people retire, and some people don't get reappointed for various reasons. There are always openings in the judiciary but they come at odd times.

5. How do you see your profession changing in the next five years? What role will technology play in those changes, and what skills will be required?

It's changing dramatically, primarily because of electronic filing and computers. In 2002, we in the bankruptcy court were one of the first in this area to make electronic filing compulsory. Almost all federal courts now have electronic filing and case management, and state courts are going that way. Some judges are proficient enough to listen to an argument or witness testimony and at the same time be pulling cases or other research up on the computer. The big problem is the temptation of judges and law clerks to get on the computer and get information that is not in evidence.

6. What do you enjoy most about your job? What do you enjoy least?

I enjoy being in court. Some judges want to do everything through briefs or the written word but I enjoy the interchange with lawyers. I still enjoy trying cases and doing research. The thing I enjoy most is solving problems and reaching a just and fair solution that helps people that is permitted by the law involved.

The thing I enjoy least is probably arguments about attorney's fees. I also don't like a lying witness or fraud. Fortunately, we don't have too much of that.

7. Can you suggest a valuable "try this" for students considering a career in your profession?

Most judges will welcome students into their courtroom, and maybe into their chambers. Find out if there's an interesting trial or hearing going on and go in and listen. I also suggest that a young person try to get a lawyer or judge to mentor them, perhaps through a college or law school program.

The other thing is you should concentrate on learning English. It's a sad story that many lawyers do not write well enough and cannot formulate a logical English sentence.

SELECTED SCHOOLS

There are many good law schools available, including many top-rated ones. Below are listed some of the more prominent institutions in this field.

Duke University School of Law
210 Science Drive
Durham, NC27708
919.613.7006
law.duke.edu

Harvard Law School
1563 Massachusetts Avenue
Cambridge, MA 02138
617.495.3109
www.law.harvard.edu

New York University School of Law
40 Washington Square S
New York, NY 10012
212.998.0606
www.law.nyu.edu

Stanford Law School
559 Nathan Abbott Way
Stanford, CA 94305
650.723.2465
www.law.stanford.edu

University of California,Berkeley School of Law
215 Boalt Hall
Berkeley, CA 94720
510.642.1741
www.law.berkeley.edu

University of Michigan Law School
625 S. State Street
Ann Arbor, MI 48109
734.764.1358
www.law.umich.edu

University of Pennsylvania Law School
3501 Sansom Street
Philadelphia, PA 19104
215.898.7483
www.law.upenn.edu

University of Virginia School of Law
580 Massie Road
Charlottesville, VA 22903
434.924.7354
www.law.virginia.edu

Vanderbilt Law School
131 21st Avenue S
Nashville, TN 37203
615.322.2615
law.vanderbilt.edu

Yale Law School
127 Wall Street
New Haven, CT 06511
203.432.4992
www.law.yale.edu

MORE INFORMATION

American Bar Association
321 N. Clark Street
Chicago, IL 60654-7598
800.285.2221
www.americanbar.org

American Judges Association
300 Newport Avenue
Williamsburg, VA 23185-4147
757.259.1841
aja.ncsc.dni.us

**Association of American Law
Schools**
1201 Connecticut Avenue, NW
Suite 800
Washington, DC 20036-2717
202.296.8851
www.aals.org

Federal Bar Association
1220 N. Fillmore Street, Suite 444
Arlington, VA 22201
571.481.9100
www.fedbar.org

Law School Admission Council
662 Penn Street
Newtown, PA 18940
215.968.1101
www.lsac.org

U.S. Supreme Court
1 1st Street NE
Washington, DC 20543
202.479.3211
www.supremecourt.gov

Michael Auerbach/Editor

Lawyer

Snapshot

Career Cluster: Government & Public Administration; Law & Criminal Justice; Public Safety & Security

Interests: Law, business, writing, research, resolving conflict, helping others

Earnings (Yearly Average): $130,880

Employment & Outlook: Average Growth Expected

OVERVIEW

Sphere of Work

Lawyers (also called attorneys) work within the legal system. They represent the rights and interests of individuals, corporations, and other entities under federal, state, and even international law.

Lawyers work in a wide array of areas, such as regulatory compliance, criminal law, lobbying, business and industries, probate (wills), and human rights. Attorneys work in law offices, business offices, government agencies, and courtrooms. Over one-quarter of attorneys are self-employed, either working in their own practices or as partners in a law firm. To some, attorneys act as counsels, providing advice on everyday business and personal

activities. For others, lawyers act as an advocate, speaking on their behalf in court during criminal or civil proceedings.

Work Environment

Lawyers typically work in office environments. Large law firms are often fast-paced, with lawyers meeting with clients, preparing and filing paperwork, conducting research, and performing other legal tasks. Attorneys at smaller firms or practices must often perform more tasks than their counterparts at larger firms or practices. Government agencies and major business corporations typically retain or employ attorneys who perform research, write position papers, and issue recommendations for changes in action based on new law and regulations.

Lawyers usually work long and sometimes erratic hours, including late nights and weekends. They should expect to work within a highly competitive environment, both during and after their job search. Private law firms and government law offices may be strikingly different in terms of financial resources, and tend to offer different rates of compensation. Different lawyers may also specialize in different areas of the law, such as corporate law, environmental law, or malpractice cases.

Profile

Working Conditions: Work Indoors
Physical Strength: Light Work
Education Needs: Law Degree
Licensure/Certification: Required
Physical Abilities Not Required: No Heavy Labor
Opportunities For Experience: Military Service, Part-Time Work
Holland Interest Score*: ESA

* See Appendix A

Occupation Interest

Although the work of an attorney is often very challenging, it can also be exciting and rewarding. Lawyers are considered experts in the field of law, and use this expertise to help others conduct business, deal with legal troubles, protect the environment, and write legislation. Many attorneys become judges or politicians, while others use their knowledge to help a business grow and profit in the marketplace.

A Day in the Life—Duties and Responsibilities

An attorney's daily responsibilities vary based on the type of law in which the individual works or specializes in. A staff attorney or legal counsel for a major business corporation spends much of his or her day analyzing regulations and legislation, researching legal precedents, studying tax codes, meeting with government officials, writing legal correspondence, attending negotiations, and drafting contracts and other legal documents. Private lawyers may perform these activities as well, although in the absence of large numbers of co-workers, they may also perform administrative tasks, including billing and office management.

Lawyers who work as advocates in the court system perform many of the tasks as other attorneys, but also focus on proceedings in the courts. They research previous judicial decisions, interview witnesses and litigants, meet with judges and opposing attorneys, prepare courtroom questions and comments, review testimony, file motions, select juries and, during hearings and trials, present evidence on their clients' behalf.

In addition to their work on behalf of clients, many attorneys perform a number of other activities. For example, they often perform academic work, teaching at law schools and other universities, and write scholarly papers for law journals and similar periodicals. Many attorneys work with the poor or impoverished, assist in disputes between clients and landlords, and provide advice on personal financial decisions.

Duties and Responsibilities

- **Interviewing clients and witnesses**
- **Advising clients as to legal rights and responsibilities**
- **Gathering evidence to commence legal action or form a defense**
- **Examining and cross-examining witnesses**
- **Summarizing cases to juries**
- **Writing reports and legal briefs**
- **Representing clients in court and before other agencies of government**
- **Preparing various documents such as wills, property titles, and mortgages**
- **Acting as trustee, guardian, or executor**

OCCUPATION SPECIALTIES

Criminal Lawyers or Defense Attorneys

Criminal Lawyers, or Defense Attorneys, specialize in legal cases dealing with offenses against society or the state, such as theft, murder, and arson. They are responsible for the legal defense of their client, preparing the case for trial, examining and cross-examining witnesses, and summarizing the case to the jury.

District Attorneys or Prosecutors

District Attorneys, also known as Prosecutors, are criminal law specialists who conduct prosecution in court proceedings for a city, county, state, or the federal government.

Corporate Lawyers

Corporate Lawyers advise corporations on legal rights, obligations, and privileges in accordance with the constitution, statutes, prior legal decisions, and ordinances.

Legal Aid Lawyers

Legal Aid Lawyers work for private, nonprofit organizations for disadvantaged people. They generally handle civil cases, such as those about leases, job discrimination, and wage disputes, rather than criminal cases.

Family Lawyers

Family Lawyers handle a variety of legal issues that pertain to the family. They may advise clients regarding divorce, child custody, and adoption proceedings.

Patent Lawyers

Patent Lawyers specialize in patent law and advise clients such as inventors, investors, and manufacturers whether an invention can be patented, and on other issues such as infringement on patents, validity of patents, and similar items.

Environmental Lawyers

Environmental Lawyers specialize in the policies of environmental law and help their clients to follow those statutes. They may help clients to properly prepare and file for licenses and applications and represent parties such as interest groups and construction firms in their dealings with the U.S. Environmental Protection Agency.

WORK ENVIRONMENT

Physical Environment

Lawyers work primarily in office settings, such as law firms, government agencies, corporate headquarters, and similar business environments and home offices. They also attend hearings and trials in courtrooms, conduct research in law libraries, and meet with clients and other individuals at their homes or at other locations, including prisons.

Relevant Skills and Abilities

Communication Skills
- Persuading others
- Speaking and writing effectively

Interpersonal/Social Skills
- Cooperating with others
- Providing support to others
- Working as a member of a team

Organization & Management Skills
- Organizing information or materials
- Paying attention to and handling details
- Performing duties that change frequently

Research & Planning Skills
- Analyzing information
- Developing evaluation strategies
- Gathering information
- Using logical reasoning

Human Environment

Lawyers work with a wide variety of other people. During legal and civil cases, these individuals interact with clients and opposing litigants, judges, witnesses, law enforcement officials, and courtroom professionals. Outside the courtroom, lawyers interact with business executives, elected and government officials, paralegals, labor representatives, and administrative personnel.

Technological Environment

Lawyers rely on office computer systems and related software to prepare cases, draft motions, and write correspondence. They may use presentation equipment, such as laptop projectors, video units, and similar equipment, for presenting courtroom evidence and for offsite presentations.

EDUCATION, TRAINING, AND ADVANCEMENT

High School/Secondary

High school students who plan to become lawyers are encouraged to take courses that help build their understanding of the law, such as history, political science, social studies, business, and economics. They would also benefit from taking courses that build communication and writing skills, such as composition and public speaking classes.

Suggested High School Subjects
- Algebra
- Business Law
- College Preparatory
- Composition
- Economics
- English
- Foreign Languages
- Government
- History
- Literature
- Political Science
- Psychology
- Social Studies
- Sociology
- Speech

Famous First

The first public defender was Walton J. Wood of Los Angeles County, in 1914. The office resulted from the lobbying efforts of California's first woman attorney, Clara S. Folz, who witnessed the harm done in court to defendants who either had no lawyer or were assigned a novice lawyer pro bono. In 1921 California enacted a law mandating the assignment of public defenders to all of its state courts. More than 40 years later, in the wake of the landmark U.S. Supreme Court decision Gideon v. Wainwright (1963), public defenders were required for all defendants who could not afford an attorney of their own.

College/Postsecondary

Aspiring attorneys need a bachelor's degree in a related field, such as history, political science, government, or public safety, with a focus on pre-law studies. After they receive their undergraduate degree, they must enter an accredited law school, where they will pursue their juris doctorate (JD) degree.

Related College Majors
- Law (L.L.B., J.D.)
- Pre-Law Studies

Adult Job Seekers

Many adults find employment as a lawyer through their law school's placement office. Attorneys who seek employment positions with the government may apply through government websites. Professional associations such as the American Bar Association (ABA) also offer resources on how to pursue a job in the legal field.

Professional Certification and Licensure

In addition to their law degrees, lawyers must pass the bar examination of the state or states in which they work. They may also join a professional legal association such as the ABA or similar state organizations.

Additional Requirements

Lawyers must have excellent analytical, research, and communications skills. They must have strong understanding of the law (particularly in the areas in which they work) and the U.S. Constitution, and tend to be both driven and highly organized. Lawyers often work long hours, and should be comfortable dealing with conflict. Furthermore, lawyers must often work with accused criminals, which can lead to tension and confrontations with such people if the case is not proceeding as desired. Because they are legally bound to protect clients' privacy regardless of guilt or innocence, lawyers must sometimes be willing to subordinate personal ethical feelings to the demands of their job.

EARNINGS AND ADVANCEMENT

Earnings depend on lawyers' area of expertise and whether they are in private practice or employed by law firms or governmental agencies. Lawyers who practice alone usually earn less than those who are partners in law firms.

Mean annual earnings of lawyers were $130,880 in 2012. The lowest ten percent earned less than $54,310, and those in the 75th percentile earned more than $168,010. (Figures are not available for the highest ten percent.)

Lawyers may receive paid vacations, holidays, and sick days; life and health insurance; and retirement benefits. These are usually paid by the employer.

Metropolitan Areas with the Highest Employment Level in this Occupation

Metropolitan area	Employment[1]	Employment per thousand jobs	Hourly mean wage
New York-White Plains-Wayne, NY-NJ	51,850	10.05	$79.65
Washington-Arlington-Alexandria, DC-VA-MD-WV	40,390	17.23	$76.82
Chicago-Joliet-Naperville, IL	23,380	6.42	$69.79
Los Angeles-Long Beach-Glendale, CA	23,130	5.97	$77.99
Boston-Cambridge-Quincy, MA	13,980	8.17	$66.94
Philadelphia, PA	13,640	7.48	$68.13
Atlanta-Sandy Springs-Marietta, GA	12,130	5.36	$69.71
Houston-Sugar Land-Baytown, TX	10,910	4.13	$78.79

[1]Does not include self-employed. Source: Bureau of Labor Statistics

EMPLOYMENT AND OUTLOOK

There were approximately 760,000 lawyers employed nationally in 2012. About one-fourth of lawyers practiced privately, either in law firms or in solo practices. Most of the remaining lawyers held positions in government, the greatest number at the local level. Employment of lawyers is expected to grow about as fast as the average for all occupations through the year 2022, which means employment is projected to increase 8 percent to 15 percent. This is due to an ever increasing population and growing business activity that will result in more legal transactions, and civil and criminal cases. Demand will also be strong because of the growth of legal action in areas such as healthcare, intellectual property, environmental law, and bankruptcy. Due to intense competition for jobs, willingness to relocate may be an advantage in securing a job. In addition, employers increasingly seek graduates who have advanced law degrees and experience in a particular field such as tax, patent or other types of law.

Employment Trend, Projected 2012–22

Total, All Occupations: 11%

Legal Occupations: 11%

Lawyers: 10%

Note: "All Occupations" includes all occupations in the U.S. Economy. Source: U.S. Bureau of Labor Statistics, Employment Projections Program

Related Occupations
- Judge
- Paralegal

Related Military Occupations
- Lawyer

Conversation With . . .
Joshua T. Gillelan II
Lawyer, 41 years

1. What was your individual career path in terms of education/training, entry-level job, or other significant opportunity?

I didn't decide I wanted to be a lawyer until after college. At the time I was teaching in the Baltimore City Public Schools and quickly despaired of making the difference I had wanted to make in that role. I began to consider a career as a public official and thought I needed to go to law school to do that, so I took the LSAT. I scored in the 98th percentile, which helped make my decision to apply to law school. In the first year appellate moot court competition, I realized that I had found my niche and should be an appellate litigator. Upon graduation, although offered other opportunities for more money – one a clerkship for a judge and one a non-appellate government position – I found a job with the U.S. Dept. of Labor that had me arguing my first case in a federal court of appeals about six weeks after I was sworn into the bar. My career at the Labor Department lasted 31 years, and I retired as a senior appellate attorney having briefed and argued over 200 cases in the U.S. courts of appeals. I also did a substantial amount of work in U.S. Supreme Court cases. In 2004, I opened my own practice and continue to advocate on behalf of injured maritime, offshore oil, and overseas defense contractor employees.

2. What are the most important skills and/or qualities for someone in your profession?

As an appellate specialist, you must possess the ability to articulate a reasoned analysis of existing precedents and argue persuasively that they compel the result you seek. Any attorney who sets foot in any courtroom needs the ability to step back from his or her own understanding of the case and hear where the judge is coming from and provide the best response to that point of view.

3. What do you wish you had known going into this profession?

I wish I'd known the extent to which court-imposed deadlines can interfere with family and personal life. For instance, I recently had a case at the Supreme Court with deadlines that meant I worked virtually throughout the holiday season and even through New Year's Eve and Day.

4. Are there many job opportunities in your profession? In what specific areas?

This is a booming profession – total receipts of the law profession continue to grow -- but law schools are cranking out a surplus of applicants for the available legal jobs. Try very hard to avoid graduating in the bottom half of your law school class.

5. How do you see your profession changing in the next five years? What role will technology play in those changes, and what skills will be required?

Already a great deal of legal work has been transferred from lawyers to paralegals and now some document analysis is being outsourced to South Asia – India, mostly. In addition, technology has changed the face of legal research, which used to involve moldy old books and now is online. The law office, in general, is going paperless and cases are now digitized. Most of the federal courts require only e-filing a digital copy of most documents.

The way things are moving, the future may hold more and more binding arbitration of disputes that may not go to court. My own view is that this is a terrible thing because the public pays for impartial adjudicators. Whether I think it's gotten them or not, I trust that process more than the selection of a corporate arbitrator.

6. What is the most fulfilling part of your job, and what is the most frustrating?

What I find most fulfilling is to receive a favorable decision from an appellate court that establishes precedent that will govern – and thereby produce the same favorable outcome -- in thousands of other cases. The greatest challenge is appearing before judges who have a philosophical disagreement with the purposes of the applicable statute.

7. Can you suggest a valuable "try this" for students considering a career in your profession?

To see if you're interested in becoming an appellate lawyer, go online and find a federal court of appeals decision on a subject that interests you and read the briefs to which the court's decision responded. See if you think you'll be able to think and write that way, because that's what's required. It's not like any other kind of writing. It's formal and it tends toward the abstract. You need to formulate general principles that the courts' previous reported results are consistent with and that produce the result you're after.

If you're wondering if you possess a mind that is suitable for the legal profession, get one of the LSAT practice books. Don't pay attention to how you do the first time you try it but do check the right answers and figure out what it is they're looking for. Then try again. If you don't get it after two or three practice tests, you may have an uphill battle.

Fun Facts

In 1980, 81 percent of law firms were made up of 2-5 lawyers; in 2005, this percentage dropped to 76 percent.
Source: The Lawyer Statistical Report, American Bar Foundation 1985, 1994, 2004 and 2012.

In 2011, there were 1,245,205 licensed lawyers in the US.
Source: American Bar Association Market Research Dept., 4/2012

SELECTED SCHOOLS

There are many good law schools available, including many top-rated ones. Below are listed some of the more prominent institutions in this field.

Columbia Law School
435 W. 116th Street
New York, NY 10025
212.854.2640
www.law.columbia.edu

Harvard Law School
1563 Massachusetts Avenue
Cambridge, MA 02138
617.495.3109
www.law.harvard.edu

New York University School of Law
40 Washington Square S
New York, NY 10012
212.998.0606
www.law.nyu.edu

Stanford Law School
559 Nathan Abbott Way
Stanford, CA 94305
650.723.2465
www.law.stanford.edu

University of California, Berkeley
School of Law
215 Boalt Hall
Berkeley, CA 94720
510.642.1741
www.law.berkeley.edu

University of Chicago Law School
1111 E. 60th Street
Chicago, IL 60637
773.702.9494
www.law.uchicago.edu

University of Michigan Law School
625 S. State Street
Ann Arbor, MI 48109
734.764.1358
www.law.umich.edu

University of Pennsylvania Law School
3501 Sansom Street
Philadelphia, PA 19104
215.898.7483
www.law.upenn.edu

University of Virginia School of Law
580 Massie Road
Charlottesville, VA 22903
434.924.7354
www.law.virginia.edu

Yale Law School
127 Wall Street
New Haven, CT 06511
203.432.4992
www.law.yale.edu

MORE INFORMATION

American Bar Association
740 15th Street, NW
Washington, DC 20005-1019
202.662.1000
www.americanbar.org

**Association of American Law
Schools**
1201 Connecticut Avenue, NW
Suite 800
Washington, DC 20036-2717
202.296.8851
www.aals.org

Association of Corporate Counsel
1025 Connecticut Avenue NW
Suite 200
Washington, DC 20036
202.293.4103
www.acc.com

**Commercial Law League of
America**
205 N. Michigan Avenue
Suite 2212
Chicago, IL 60601
312.240.1400
www.clla.org

Federal Bar Association
1220 N. Fillmore Street, Suite 444
Arlington, VA 22201
571.481.9100
www.fedbar.org

Law School Admission Council
662 Penn Street
Newtown, PA 18940
215.968.1101
www.lsac.org

**National District Attorneys
Association**
44 Canal Center Plaza, Suite 110
Alexandria, VA 22314
703.549.9222
www.ndaa.org

Michael Auerbach/Editor

Legal Secretary

Snapshot

Career Cluster: Business Administration; Law & Criminal Justice

Interests: Business, law, office technology, organizing information, detail analysis

Earnings (Yearly Average): $44,380

Employment & Outlook: Average Growth Expected

OVERVIEW

Sphere of Work

Legal secretaries have specialized skills and knowledge specific to the legal profession, and do much more than just perform general administrative duties. They typically work in law offices drafting common legal documents, recording trial dates, conducting research, and billing clients. As information technology has evolved over the past twenty years, legal secretaries increasingly are taking on tasks that many attorneys may not have the time to address. A key responsibility of legal secretaries is doing preparatory work to save time for lawyers, such as research prior to legal proceedings.

Work Environment

Legal secretaries generally work in small or large law firms. Some work from home as "virtual" legal secretaries. Because legal secretaries work in close proximity to lawyers or teams of lawyers, their work environment is typically fast-paced, and involves a significant amount of interaction with others. The legal profession tends to attract assertive individuals, so legal secretaries should be able to respond to challenges, meet expectations, and be flexible enough to respond to a variety of requests throughout the day.

Profile

Working Conditions: Work Indoors
Physical Strength: Light Work
Education Needs: High School Diploma Or G.E.D., Technical/Community College
Licensure/Certification: Recommended
Physical Abilities Not Required: No Heavy Labor
Opportunities For Experience: Part-Time Work
Holland Interest Score*: CSE

* See Appendix A

Occupation Interest

Because of recent advances in information technology, legal secretaries are performing a wider range of duties than in the past. As a result, legal secretaries are helping run law offices more efficiently, and are increasingly accorded the respect due to roles integral to the success of an organization. Individuals attracted to this profession tend to be well organized and detail oriented. They are versatile, demonstrate strong interpersonal skills, and are proficient in the use of common office technology tools. Legal secretaries find satisfaction in helping attorneys be successful in their jobs.

A Day in the Life—Duties and Responsibilities

A legal secretary's typical work day includes preparation of legal documents such as correspondences, complaints, motions, and subpoenas, usually under the supervision of a paralegal or attorney. Legal secretaries often review legal journals in order to fact-check information used in documents. They understand technical legal terminology and procedures well enough to be able to assist lawyers in completing some of the more routine legal paperwork, research, and other tasks. They conduct Internet research for a variety of projects, such as gathering client information, learning about the opposing counsel, and locating expert witnesses.

Tasks specific to their role include completing forms and reports for clients; taking dictation; managing files at courthouses and large legal firms; knowing legal procedures, and helping with legal proceedings. New legal secretaries can gain experience working under the guidance of more experienced legal secretaries or paralegals, and eventually work more independently on handling files and legal procedures.

Duties and Responsibilities

- Taking dictation
- Maintaining files
- Performing other clerical duties
- Creating initial drafts of common legal documents
- Handling the payment of bills
- Recording trial dates
- Scheduling appearances of witnesses
- Preparing evidence for trial
- Delivering subpoenas
- Keyboarding
- Fact checking

WORK ENVIRONMENT

Physical Environment

Legal secretaries usually work in comfortable office environments where they may sit for long periods of time. They typically work a standard forty-hour week, some part time, and some on a temporary basis. Some are self-employed and work from home. Sometimes legal secretaries conduct work at courthouses or work extra hours as needed to support lawyers or meet case deadlines.

Human Environment

Regardless of the size of the law firm, legal secretaries are usually surrounded by attorneys who need secretarial support. Excellent interpersonal skills are useful in this job, since legal secretaries work with many different types of people. Self-employed legal secretaries may work more independently from home, where it is essential to be highly motivated. Legal secretaries interact not only with attorneys, but with clients, other employees, and colleagues.

Relevant Skills and Abilities

Communication Skills
- Editing written information
- Speaking and writing effectively

Interpersonal/Social Skills
- Cooperating with others
- Working as a member of a team

Organization & Management Skills
- Making decisions
- Organizing information or materials
- Performing duties that change frequently

Technical Skills
- Keyboarding
- Working with data, numbers, or information

Technological Environment

A legal secretary's technological environment includes computers, word processing and spreadsheet software, and legal transcription software. These are used to create documents and spreadsheets, prepare presentations, track deadlines, maintain calendars, enter data, and draw up bill and invoices. Legal secretaries should be familiar with document management and desktop publishing programs, as well as videoconferencing.

EDUCATION, TRAINING, AND ADVANCEMENT

High School/Secondary

Legal secretaries must have at least a high school diploma and some office training. High school students interested in pursuing a career as a legal secretary should prepare themselves by building good study habits and learning technology skills such as computer word processing, accounting, filing, and record keeping. Correct spelling, punctuation, and grammar are essential. They should also try to learn about the legal field through research, part-time work, volunteering, or internships.

Suggested High School Subjects
- Applied Communication
- Business
- Business & Computer Technology
- Business Data Processing
- Business Law
- Composition
- English
- Keyboarding
- Shorthand

Famous First

The first dictionary of American law was John Bouvier's *A Law Dictionary Adapted to the Constitution* and *Laws of the United States of American and of the Several States of the American Union with References to the Civil and Other Systems of Foreign Law*. Published in two volumes in Philadelphia in 1839, it became widely used and was undergoing its fourth major revision when its author died in 1851. Although subsequent editions continued to be popular, the work was eventually supplanted by *Black's Law Dictionary*, which first came out in 1891 and continues to be published today.

College/Postsecondary

Students can pursue formal training to become legal secretaries through one- or two-year college programs that focus on legal topics such as family law, criminal law, civil litigation, intellectual property, or wills and probate. Relevant degrees would be in business or industries in which students are interested, as legal help and advice crosses all fields. Because writing is an integral part of a legal secretary's job, student coursework should focus on developing strong skills in reading, writing, proofreading, and use of legal terminology. Typing and computer software skills are considered equally valuable. Colleges can train students to understand the minutiae of legal practices, and how to create and format pleadings and transactional documents.

Related College Majors
- Administrative Assistant/Secretarial Science
- Legal Administrative Assistant/Secretarial Science

Adult Job Seekers

Adults seeking legal secretary jobs have generally earned a high school diploma or associate's degree. Adult job seekers can advance through temporary work or part-time or full-time clerical positions in law offices, and may also benefit from joining legal secretary associations as a means of professional networking. In some work environments and professional societies, supervisors and mentors advise aspiring legal secretaries on how to advance their careers.

Professional Certification and Licensure

As legal secretaries gain experience, they can earn various certifications: general certifications include Certified Professional Secretary (CPS) and Certified Administrative Professional (CAP), while legal certifications, offered by the National Association for Legal Professionals (NALS), include Accredited Legal Secretary (ALS) and Professional Legal Secretary (PLS). These advanced certifications demonstrate proficiency in specialty areas such as civil litigation, intellectual property and criminal law, and core competencies of legal secretaries.

Additional Requirements

Legal secretaries should demonstrate good judgment and discretion, good time management and attention to detail, and willingness to continue learning new skills and take on new responsibilities. It is also important for legal secretaries to maintain and improve skill sets through continuing education and by finding out the latest trends through professional associations.

EARNINGS AND ADVANCEMENT

Mean annual earnings of legal secretaries were $44,380 in 2012. The lowest ten percent earned less than $26,250, and the highest ten percent earned more than $67,790.

Legal secretaries may receive paid vacations, holidays, and sick days; life and health insurance; and retirement benefits. These are usually paid by the employer.

Metropolitan Areas with the Highest Employment Level in this Occupation

Metropolitan area	Employment[1]	Employment per thousand jobs	Hourly mean wage
New York-White Plains-Wayne, NY-NJ	12,620	2.45	$28.09
Los Angeles-Long Beach-Glendale, CA	9,500	2.46	$25.29
Chicago-Joliet-Naperville, IL	7,810	2.15	$22.20
Philadelphia, PA	5,890	3.23	$23.13
Washington-Arlington-Alexandria, DC-VA-MD-WV	5,840	2.49	$30.77
Newark-Union, NJ-PA	4,500	4.73	$22.84
Dallas-Plano-Irving, TX	3,980	1.90	$20.30
Boston-Cambridge-Quincy, MA	3,810	2.22	$26.09

[1]Does not include self-employed. Source: Bureau of Labor Statistics

EMPLOYMENT AND OUTLOOK

Legal secretaries held about 230,000 jobs nationally in 2012. Employment is expected to grow about the same as the average for all occupations through the year 2022, which means employment is projected to increase 7 percent to 14 percent. This is due to overall slow but steady growth of the legal services industry.

Employment Trend, Projected 2012–22

Secretaries and Administrative Assistants: 12%

Total, All Occupations: 11%

Office and Administrative Support Occupations: 7%

Note: "All Occupations" includes all occupations in the U.S. Economy. Source: U.S. Bureau of Labor Statistics, Employment Projections Program

Related Occupations
- Court Clerk
- Court Reporter

Conversation With . . .
Hannah Tillis

Legal Assistant, 3 years

7 years in industry

1. What was your individual career path in terms of education/training, entry-level job, or other significant opportunity?

I received my bachelor's degree in public relations and graduated in 2009. The job market wasn't great, so I did a long internship in PR but realized I wasn't in love with it. So, when this opportunity came up -- part-time, digitizing files dating back to 1985 -- I went to work for this office. Eventually my boss asked if I would be interested in training to become a legal assistant. In our firm, which mostly handles divorce, legal assistants also do the office work a legal secretary typically handles -- such as answering phones, scheduling, and filing -- but secretaries are not as independent. As a legal assistant, I have clients that I'm assigned. We are the intermediary between the client and the firm.

2. What are the most important skills and/or qualities for someone in your profession?

You need to be organized and keep all case files together. For example, let's say a husband is paying a wife alimony. It's my job to have a record of what he makes and what she makes and spends. If he says he can't afford it but I have bank records showing he's been on vacation in Florida or New York, I have this information condensed on a list so the attorney has the records she needs.

You need to be familiar with all MS Office applications, and the more you know, the better off you are. You need to know how to find out things you don't know. Also, patience is huge. There are things you deal with every day that your clients don't understand. The divorce process can be very confusing for clients. They don't know what's going on, or even worse, they think they know the process from TV. You have to balance their expectations.

3. What do you wish you had known going into this profession?

Developing my organizational system and what works for me took some time. I keep a binder of clients that includes what's going on and I update it when something new comes in. There are a lot of little details in the law and it's easy to overlook things when you're very busy.

4. **Are there many job opportunities in your profession? In what specific areas?**

Yes. The larger law firms tend to hire more legal secretaries and assistants; there are a lot more attorneys and they need more day-to-day help.

5. **How do you see your profession changing in the next five years? What role will technology play in those changes, and what skills will be required?**

That's a big question. A lot of things that a firm would once have hired out -- like the files I digitized -- are coming into the firm and we do them on our computers. That goes for websites, and filing court documents. It means you have to be even more meticulous with what you are doing. Also most people now have access to a smartphone. So, for instance, if we are sitting in a mediation and we're splitting up a bank account and we need a bank record, boom, there it is. Everything can happen faster.

6. **What do you enjoy most about your job? What do you enjoy least?**

Being in divorce, it's nice to be able to help people out. You get to see people through what is usually the roughest time of their life. Nobody likes being in the court system; it's scary and you don't know what's going to happen. Selfishly, I like my job because I work regular hours most of the time. It's not the same for attorneys, who tend to work longer hours.

The hard part is, things don't always go your way. Even when you do your best, it can feel like a personal failure. In divorce, you see a lot of awful things going on. How can I not go home and worry about this person?

7. **Can you suggest a valuable "try this" for students considering a career in your profession?**

Internships are a possibility but typically for those you get the job I started with -- filing and faxing and copying. I would definitely recommend asking if you could do an interview with a firm for an entry-level job.

SELECTED SCHOOLS

Programs in secretarial studies are available at many technical and community colleges and vocational schools; many of these schools also have programs in legal secretarial studies. Interested students are advised to check with a school guidance counselor.

MORE INFORMATION

Association of Executive and Administrative Professionals
900 S. Washington Street
Suite G-13
Falls Church, VA 22046
703.237.8616
http://theaeap.com

International Association of Administrative Professionals
P.O. Box 20404
Kansas City, MO 64195-0404
www.iaap-hq.org

International Virtual Assistants Association
2360 Corporate Circle
Suite 400
Henderson, NV 89074
877.440.2750
www.ivaa.org

Legal Secretaries International
2302 Fannin Street
Suite 500
Houston, TX 77002-9136
www.legalsecretaries.org

National Association for Legal Professionals
8159 East 41st Street
Tulsa, OK 74145
918.582.5188
www.nals.org

Office & Professional Employees International Union
265 W. 14th Street, 20th Floor
New York, NY 10011
800.346.7348
www.opeiu.org

Susan Williams/Editor

Paralegal

Snapshot

Career Cluster: Law & Criminal Justice
Interests: Law, legal system, research, political science, investigation, administrative tasks
Earnings (Yearly Average): $50,220
Employment & Outlook: Faster Than Average Growth Expected

OVERVIEW

Sphere of Work

Paralegals are professionals who provide background research and other forms of assistance to attorneys. Paralegals help attorneys prepare for judicial hearings, trials, and corporate or client meetings, in addition to other legal tasks. Much of their preparatory work involves researching laws and legal decisions, preparing briefs, contracts, and agreements, and assembling other documents, legal or otherwise, for use during the trial process or other function (such as a real estate transaction). Paralegals generally begin their careers performing basic research and administrative tasks. As they become more experienced, their responsibilities expand significantly to the point where they may assist attorneys in

determining the best course of action, attend trials and hearings, and help to prepare arguments.

Work Environment

Paralegals typically work a standard forty-hour week as employees of private law firms, government agency offices, and corporations. During their workdays, paralegals often manage multiple tasks, as the caseload requires. In addition to their work in an office setting, paralegals may spend a great deal of time in law libraries, researching judicial decisions, statutes, and other legal information. As they become more experienced, paralegals may be drawn into more time-consuming and high-profile casework. Such work may require that they travel for business, conduct client interviews, and attend hearings and off-site meetings.

Profile

Working Conditions: Work Indoors
Physical Strength: Light Work
Education Needs: Technical/ Community College
Licensure/Certification: Recommended
Physical Abilities Not Required: No Heavy Labor
Opportunities For Experience: Military Service, Part-Time Work
Holland Interest Score*: SEC

* See Appendix A

Occupation Interest

Paralegals are seen as important contributors to the legal field. Although paralegals are prohibited from practicing law, much of their work is viewed as similar to the work that attorneys perform. Paralegals are, therefore, part of the dynamic world of law without the requirement of a law degree. Individuals who are interested in becoming paralegals typically enjoy research, studying and working within the legal system, and helping others.

A Day in the Life—Duties and Responsibilities

Depending on the field of law in which they work, paralegals may have a very diverse set of responsibilities. As they help attorneys prepare for trials, paralegals collect and organize all of the case facts, locate relevant case laws and past court decisions, assist with depositions, and obtain affidavits (or sworn testimony). Paralegals often prepare this information in the form of detailed reports for the attorneys' use. They also draft litigation documents and notes for arguments. More experienced paralegals may join the attorney in the courtroom, keeping his or her documentation readily available.

Outside of the courtroom, paralegals assist in creating a wide range of legal documents, including patent papers, mortgages, contracts, and divorce settlement or separation papers. In corporate settings, paralegals are responsible for compiling employee benefits, shareholder agreements, and other packages of relevance to the business. A paralegal who works in a government office or in a legal services office that provides legal assistance to the poor may prepare law guides, provide non-legal guidance to clients, and file legal documents.

Because paralegals are not required to pass the bar exam, they are not permitted to provide legal guidance directly to clients, provide arguments in the courtroom, or authorize any legal tasks. However, many consider the work of the paralegal to be just as demanding and important as a practicing attorney. In fact, many paralegals eventually use their knowledge of the law and the legal system to enter law school and become practicing attorneys. Other paralegals continue on to managerial-level positions within their organizations.

Duties and Responsibilities

- Organizing and indexing documents and files
- Performing research using a variety of sources
- Summarizing depositions
- Interviewing clients
- Investigating the facts of a case
- Drafting organizational documents for corporations
- Drafting minutes of meetings of corporate directors
- Drafting deeds of trust, leases, and contracts of purchase and sale
- Preparing histories of cases
- Obtaining affidavits for a lawyer

OCCUPATION SPECIALTIES

Corporate Paralegals

Corporate Paralegals help lawyers prepare employee contracts, shareholder agreements, stock-option plans, and companies' annual financial reports. They may also monitor and review government regulations to ensure that the corporation is aware of new legal requirements.

Litigation Paralegals

Litigation Paralegals maintain documents received from clients, conduct case research for lawyers, and retrieve and organize evidence for use at depositions and trials.

Legal Investigators

Legal investigators are licensed private investigators or law firm staff investigators who specialize in preparing cases for trial for attorneys. Their job is to gather information and evidence that advance legal theories to benefit the client's case.

WORK ENVIRONMENT

Physical Environment

Paralegals typically work in an office environment. These locations are generally very active, with multiple meetings, projects, and activities occurring independent of one another. The environment can be fast-paced and often hectic. Paralegals also often perform research in law libraries, which are considerably quieter. Paralegals are rarely exposed to dangerous substances or situations, although confrontations between disputing parties can be contentious.

Relevant Skills and Abilities

Communication Skills
- Speaking and writing effectively

Interpersonal/Social Skills
- Cooperating with others
- Working as part of a team

Organization & Management Skills
- Organizing information or materials
- Paying attention to and handling details
- Performing duties that may change frequently
- Performing routine work

Research & Planning Skills
- Analyzing information
- Gathering information
- Using logical reasoning

Human Environment

As part of a law office, government agency, or corporation, paralegals must work with many different professionals. They work most closely with attorneys, and often support several attorneys at once. They also interact with witnesses, clients, legal experts, interns, and administrative professionals.

Technological Environment

Paralegals are expected to have familiarity with basic office technology and computer systems in particular. They need to learn a number of software programs used for writing projects, spreadsheets, document storage (such as those used for scanning hard copies), and presentations.

EDUCATION, TRAINING, AND ADVANCEMENT

High School/Secondary

High school students who are interested in pursuing a career as a paralegal are encouraged to take courses that develop their writing skills, such as journalism. They will also need to study many fundamentals areas of law, such as political science, sociology, philosophy, economics, and history. They may also take business classes, which will help them apply their skills as a paralegal in a corporate environment.

Suggested High School Subjects
- Applied Communication
- Business English

- Business Law
- College Preparatory
- Composition
- Economics
- English
- Foreign Languages
- Government
- History
- Humanities
- Journalism
- Keyboarding
- Mathematics
- Philosophy
- Political Science
- Psychology
- Social Studies
- Sociology
- Speech

Famous First

The first law code adopted by a state was the Louisiana Code of 1825, *A System of Penal Law, Divided into Code of Crimes and Punishments, Code of Procedure, Code of Evidence* [etc.]. To this day Louisiana remains the only state whose legal system is founded on civil law, or extensive legal codes (laws), rather than on common law, or case law based on legal precedent (earlier cases). Louisiana inherited its system of civil law from its French colonial past. Civil law is used in France and elsewhere in Europe, whereas common law prevails in England and America outside of Louisiana.

College/Postsecondary

The majority of paralegal professionals receive an associate's degree in paralegal studies. Those individuals who receive a degree through a four-year college can also obtain certificates in paralegal studies from a number of educational institutions. A large number of law schools, universities, and other schools offer formal training programs as well.

Related College Majors
- Paralegal/Legal Assistant Training
- Pre-Law

Adult Job Seekers

Adults who are interested in becoming paralegals may obtain jobs through career placement services and temporary employment companies. Some are able to learn about paralegal jobs while they attend a paralegal training or certification program. Still others first join a law firm as an intern and, based on their performance, may be hired as a full-time paralegal.

Professional Certification and Licensure

Paralegals are not necessarily required to receive certification as a professional paralegal. However, becoming certified can enhance a paralegal's qualifications. Certification demonstrates commitment to the field and underscores the individual's research, writing, and communications skills.

Several professional organizations offer certifications to experienced paralegals who complete an examination. Most certifications must be renewed through continuing education. The National Association of Legal Assistants, American Alliance of Paralegals, Inc., and National Federation of Paralegal Associations each have different requirements for certification. Consult credible professional associations within the field, such as the American Bar Association, and follow professional debate as to the relevancy and value of any certification program.

Additional Requirements

Paralegals are expected to have exceptional research skills, as they may be called upon to provide the full complement of facts, history, and other information relevant to the case or project assigned to them. They should have strong communications abilities and excellent organizational skills.

EARNINGS AND ADVANCEMENT

Earnings of paralegals depend on the type and geographic location of the employer and the employee's education, training and experience. Generally, those who work for large law firms or in large metropolitan areas earn more than those who work for smaller firms or in less populated regions. In addition to a salary, many paralegals receive bonuses.

Mean annual earnings of paralegals were $50,220 in 2012. The lowest ten percent earned less than $29,420, and the highest ten percent earned more than $75,410.

Paralegals may receive paid vacations, holidays, and sick days; life and health insurance; and retirement benefits. These are usually paid by the employer.

Metropolitan Areas with the Highest
Employment Level in this Occupation

Metropolitan area	Employment[1]	Employment per thousand jobs	Hourly mean wage
New York-White Plains-Wayne, NY-NJ	18,470	3.58	$27.14
Washington-Arlington-Alexandria, DC-VA-MD-WV	10,850	4.63	$31.76
Chicago-Joliet-Naperville, IL	9,700	2.66	$25.47
Los Angeles-Long Beach-Glendale, CA	8,000	2.07	$28.66
Atlanta-Sandy Springs-Marietta, GA	7,010	3.10	$24.82
Houston-Sugar Land-Baytown, TX	5,630	2.13	$26.84
Philadelphia, PA	4,780	2.62	$28.43
Dallas-Plano-Irving, TX	4,680	2.23	$27.12

[1]Does not include self-employed. Source: Bureau of Labor Statistics

EMPLOYMENT AND OUTLOOK

In 2012, there were approximately 277,000 paralegals employed nationally. Nearly three-fourths were employed by private law firms. Employment of paralegals is expected to grow faster than the average for all occupations through the year 2022, which means employment is projected to increase 10 percent to 19 percent. Private law firms will continue to be the largest employers of paralegals, but a growing array of other organizations, such as corporate legal departments, insurance companies, real estate and title insurance firms, and banks hire paralegals. Demand for paralegals also is expected to grow as an expanding population increasingly requires legal services, especially in areas such as intellectual property, health care, international law, elder issues, criminal law, and environmental law. Competition for jobs should increase as the number of graduates from training programs rises. Still, job prospects are expected to be good for highly skilled graduates.

Employment Trend, Projected 2012–22

Paralegals and Legal Assistants: 17%

Total, All Occupations: 11%

Legal Occupations: 11%

Note: "All Occupations" includes all occupations in the U.S. Economy. Source: U.S. Bureau of Labor Statistics, Employment Projections Program

Related Occupations
- Lawyer
- Research Assistant

Related Military Occupations
- Legal Specialist & Court Reporter

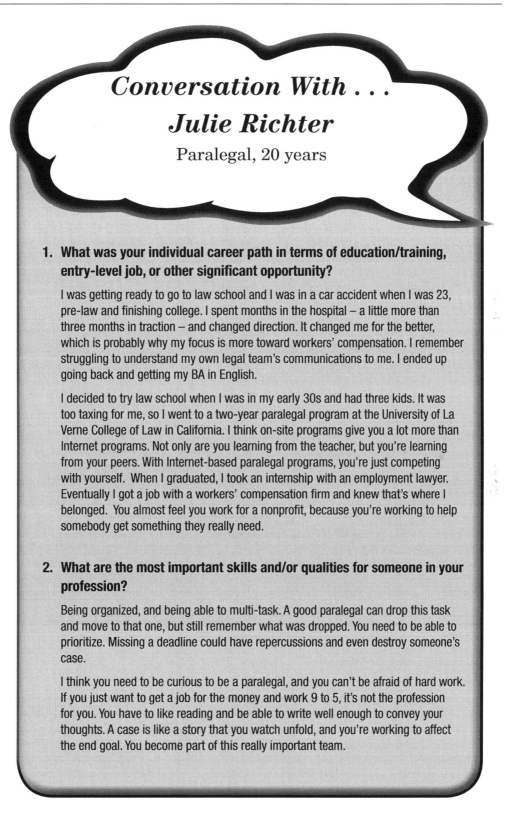

Conversation With . . . Julie Richter

Paralegal, 20 years

1. What was your individual career path in terms of education/training, entry-level job, or other significant opportunity?

I was getting ready to go to law school and I was in a car accident when I was 23, pre-law and finishing college. I spent months in the hospital – a little more than three months in traction – and changed direction. It changed me for the better, which is probably why my focus is more toward workers' compensation. I remember struggling to understand my own legal team's communications to me. I ended up going back and getting my BA in English.

I decided to try law school when I was in my early 30s and had three kids. It was too taxing for me, so I went to a two-year paralegal program at the University of La Verne College of Law in California. I think on-site programs give you a lot more than Internet programs. Not only are you learning from the teacher, but you're learning from your peers. With Internet-based paralegal programs, you're just competing with yourself. When I graduated, I took an internship with an employment lawyer. Eventually I got a job with a workers' compensation firm and knew that's where I belonged. You almost feel you work for a nonprofit, because you're working to help somebody get something they really need.

2. What are the most important skills and/or qualities for someone in your profession?

Being organized, and being able to multi-task. A good paralegal can drop this task and move to that one, but still remember what was dropped. You need to be able to prioritize. Missing a deadline could have repercussions and even destroy someone's case.

I think you need to be curious to be a paralegal, and you can't be afraid of hard work. If you just want to get a job for the money and work 9 to 5, it's not the profession for you. You have to like reading and be able to write well enough to convey your thoughts. A case is like a story that you watch unfold, and you're working to affect the end goal. You become part of this really important team.

3. What do you wish you had known going into this profession?

I wish I'd known more about the rules of the particular courts, jurisdictional-type things. For example, when they say something is due 10 days before trial and I get the letter today, when does the 10 days start?

4. Are there many job opportunities in your profession? In what specific areas?

I think there are a lot of job opportunities for broad-range paralegals who have a lot of experience. Even though you have all the knowledge to be a paralegal when you finish school, you almost have to complete an apprenticeship to be fully competent. Start at a law firm as an intern.

5. How do you see your profession changing in the next five years? What role will technology play in those changes, and what skills will be required?

Computer skills are very, very important. It seems to me that the law is becoming paperless, which is pretty difficult from the law office perspective because it's still a paper-driven profession for judges. It will be easier for newer paralegals when the profession is less paper-driven and there are software programs to help them be organized.

6. What do you enjoy most about your job? What do you enjoy least?

I love knowing that I have someone's trust in my hands. If I do a good job, I can help somebody get something more than they would have gotten if I'd done a bad job. That's where I get more than 50 percent of my job satisfaction. What I enjoy least about my job are the mundane but necessary tasks. Every piece of paper that comes into the office for a client comes to me; sometimes a client will give you a note or a receipt for something. I have to keep track of all that stuff. We work on the plaintiffs' – or claimants' – side, and the only way we get paid is by keeping good records of the work that's been done, which is a bookkeeping task that can take two to four hours of your day.

7. Can you suggest a valuable "try this" for students considering a career in your profession?

The best thing a student can do in high school is get an unpaid or minimal wage internship. Write to attorneys in the area, tell them you think you might be interested in the law. I would think a good number of attorneys would be happy to have workers; there are a lot of little things that could be done. The other thing you can do is read a deposition or a trial transcript. Sometimes you need to summarize those as a paralegal.

SELECTED SCHOOLS

Many community colleges and four-year schools offer programs in paralegal training. The website of the American Association for Paralegal Education (see below) provides a search tool for locating schools in your area.

MORE INFORMATION

American Association for Paralegal Education
19 Mantua Road
Mount Royal, NJ 08061
856.423.2829
www.aafpe.org

American Bar Association Standing Committee on Paralegals
321 N. Clark Street
Chicago, IL 60654-7598
312.988.5522
www.americanbar.org/groups/
paralegals

International Paralegal Management Association
P.O. Box 659
Avondale Estates, GA 30002-0659
404.292.4762
www.paralegalmanagement.org

National Association of Legal Assistants
1516 S. Boston, Suite 200
Tulsa, OK 74119
918.587.6828
www.nala.org

National Association of Legal Investigators
235 N. Pine Street
Lansing, MI 48933
517-202-9835
www.nalionline.org

National Federation of Paralegal Associations, Inc.
P.O. Box 2016
Edmonds, WA 98020
425.967.0045
info@paralegals.org
www.paralegals.org

Michael Auerbach/Editor

Park Ranger

Snapshot

Career Cluster: Government & Public Administration; Hospitality & Tourism; Law & Criminal Justice; Public Safety & Security

Interests: Public safety, law enforcement, wildlife, natural resources, conservation, history

Earnings (Yearly Average): $58,311

Employment & Outlook: Slower Than Average Growth Expected

OVERVIEW

Sphere of Work

Park rangers are professionals who enforce laws, regulations, and rules in parks, historic sites, and other sites. In this capacity, rangers investigate illegal activity in the parks and patrol the areas using a variety of vehicles. Rangers also work to protect natural resources and wildlife at these sites. They teach the public about how to enjoy the parks in ways that minimize negative impacts to the region's wildlife and resources. Furthermore, park rangers act as public safety officers. As such, they hunt animals that pose a danger to the public, rescue endangered campers, and administer first aid as needed. Park rangers often work with police, fire, and other personnel in addressing emergency situations and other special circumstances.

Work Environment

Park rangers generally work outdoors at parks, historical sites, recreation areas, and similar venues. Rangers often work in rugged, heavily forested environments and in all weather conditions. Many rangers spend days and even weeks stationed in remote locations within these areas. Because they typically serve as law enforcement officer as well as protectors of the area's wildlife and natural resources, they may face dangerous situations involving park visitors as well as animals and terrain. Park rangers also work in offices, where they perform managerial and administrative duties. Experienced park rangers can expect to perform more work indoors over time.

Profile

Working Conditions: Work both Indoors and Outdoors
Physical Strength: Medium Work
Education Needs: Bachelor's Degree
Licensure/Certification: RecommendedHeavy
Opportunities For Experience: Apprenticeship,Volunteer Work, Part-Time Work
Holland Interest Score*: ESR

* See Appendix A

Occupation Interest

Park rangers play an important role in protecting parks, recreational areas, historical sites, and similar locations. Those who enjoy working outdoors in rugged natural environments may be drawn to the position of a park ranger, as these individuals spend the majority of their workdays in the field. In addition, park rangers tend to like working with people. They also have the responsibility of teaching others about these natural and historical locations and demonstrating conservation principles. Although the job of a park ranger is challenging and often dangerous, those who work in this field demonstrate a great deal of personal satisfaction in their work.

A Day in the Life—Duties and Responsibilities

The day-to-day responsibilities of a park ranger often vary greatly based on where he or she works. A ranger who works at a historical site focuses primarily on teaching others about the significance of the building or area, providing to the general public presentations on and tours of the venue, answering questions, and protecting displays from damage. Meanwhile, a ranger who works in a national park such as Yosemite or the Grand Canyon spends a great deal of time on patrol in the field. Patrol tasks may include monitoring and protecting against forest fires, performing campground safety checks, and taking scientific samples for analysis.

Although a ranger's job responsibilities vary based on the type of recreational venue at which he or she works, all rangers perform certain duties. A park ranger works closely with the public. He or she shares information about conservation and history. The park ranger acts as the park's law enforcement and public safety officer, maintaining security, ensuring that the site is protected and safe, patrolling the trails or hallways, arresting or ejecting unruly visitors, and spotting dangers like forest fires. A park ranger is seen as the steward of a park, protecting it and encouraging others to do so as well.

Duties and Responsibilities

- Enforcing park regulations
- Maintaining park grounds
- Assisting visitors
- Offering conservation and recreation activities
- Patrolling park areas to check for fires or dangerous situations

WORK ENVIRONMENT

Physical Environment

Park rangers work mostly outdoors at natural and historical sites. They may work in parks, national forests, seashores, mountain ranges, battlefields, capitol buildings, and wildlife preserves, often in extreme weather conditions, in locations throughout the country. They also occasionally work in office environments, where they coordinate with other rangers and conduct the administrative business of the site.

Relevant Skills and Abilities

Communication Skills
- Speaking effectively

Interpersonal/Social Skills
- Working both independently and as part of a team

Organization & Management Skills
- Performing duties that may change
- Performing routine work

Technical Skills
- Working with your hands

Other Skills
- Being physically active
- Working outdoors
- Working with plants or animals

Human Environment

Park rangers work with a wide range of individuals. These parties include park visitors, law enforcement and fire officers, elected and appointment government officials, and scientists. They may travel extensively from site to site throughout the country to work with different groups of rangers and the public.

Technological Environment

Park rangers must be able to use the tools they will need to patrol and operate in the recreational sites at which they work. In mountain areas, for example, they will need to know how to use ski and snow equipment. Other equipment includes radios, computer mapping equipment, binoculars, fire control devices, and, where necessary, weapons.

EDUCATION, TRAINING, AND ADVANCEMENT

High School/Secondary

High school students who seek to become park rangers are encouraged to take courses that focus on interpersonal skills, public safety, and surveillance. Such training includes English, geography, math, and the natural sciences (such as biology, chemistry, physics, and ecology). Students may also benefit from activities in which public speaking is emphasized, such as debate club and oral presentations in class. Interested students should consider pursuing volunteer opportunities and part-time or seasonal work at parks or with environmental groups.

Suggested High School Subjects
- Agricultural Education
- Algebra
- American History
- Applied Biology/Chemistry
- Biology
- Business
- English
- First Aid Training
- Geography
- Geometry
- Psychology
- Sociology
- Speech

Famous First

The first national park was Yellowstone National Park, in Wyoming, authorized in 1872. The first park ranger, hired in 1880, was Harry Yount, a Civil War veteran and all-around mountain man who bore the nickname "Rocky Mountain Harry." In one of his annual reports Yount noted that it was impossible for one man to patrol the park, and so he urged the creation of a professional ranger force within the National Park Service. Today, that force consists of commissioned law enforcement Rangers along with Special Agents who conduct criminal investigations.

Library of Congress

College/Postsecondary

Park rangers usually have a bachelor's degree in a related field, such as zoology, geology, forestry, criminal justice, social science, or botany. Park ranger jobs are highly competitive. Individuals with an advanced degree in these disciplines have an advantage in the application process.

Related College Majors
- Geography
- Law Enforcement/Police Science

- Natural Resources Law Enforcement & Protective Services
- Parks and Recreation Management
- Public History

Adult Job Seekers

Park ranger jobs are highly competitive. Some adults may gain access to such jobs by obtaining short seasonal positions or serving as park volunteers, which will give them exposure to the field. The National Park Service holds on-the-job training programs for rangers in Harper's Ferry, West Virginia, in Brunswick, Georgia, and at the Grand Canyon. Because these positions are usually government jobs, aspiring rangers should research and apply directly to these agencies through their websites and job boards.

Advancement in the field depends on the ranger's education level and the size of the site. Park rangers may advance to supervisory positions at large sites, transfer between sites, or specialize in one aspect of the position.

Professional Certification and Licensure

Most park ranger positions require passing a civil service exam. Park rangers may also need licenses or permits to operate the equipment and vehicles used on the job.

Professional certification may be helpful but is not typically required. The National Recreation and Park Association is responsible for conducting Certified Park and Recreation Professional (CPRP) certification. Candidates must have a bachelor's degree, meet experience requirements, and obtain a passing score on the written CPRP exam. Continuing education is required for certification renewal. Consult credible professional associations within the field and follow professional debate as to the relevancy and value of any certification program.

Additional Requirements

Park rangers should be physically fit, able to spend a great deal of time on their feet and in rugged terrain. They should also have excellent communication and public speaking skills. Experience in the geographic area in which they seek to become a ranger is also useful. Employers may require a prospective park ranger to be a US citizen and pass a background check.

EARNINGS AND ADVANCEMENT

Park rangers may advance to district or park manager levels or site superintendents. Administrative positions at various levels of park headquarters are also another advancement possibility. Entry-level annual salaries for park rangers with the National Park Service were between $26,433 and $37,967 in 2012. Park rangers who worked in state and local parks received a higher salary, starting between $36,361 and $42,935 in 2012. Median annual earnings for all park rangers were $58,311 in 2012.

Park rangers may receive paid vacations, holidays, and sick days; life and health insurance; and retirement benefits. These are usually paid by the employer. In most Federal and State parks, park rangers are supplied housing on the park premises and senior park rangers are usually given a vehicle.

EMPLOYMENT AND OUTLOOK

Police and detectives, of which park rangers are a part, held about 780,000 jobs nationally in 2012. Employment is expected to grow slower than the average for all occupations through the year 2022, which means employment is projected to increase 3 percent to 9 percent. The number of job openings will still increase because the last wave of entry-level park rangers hired in the 1970s will be retiring. Competition in the National Park Service is stiff, with one-hundred qualified applicants for every one park ranger hired. Budgets of Federal and State government also limit the number of open positions.

Related Occupations
• Fish and Game Warden

Conversation With . . .
Jessica Conley
Park Ranger, 9 years

1. What was your individual career path in terms of education/training, entry-level job, or other significant opportunity?

I first became interested in environmental education through internships and programs I did growing up in middle school and high school, such as through the Chesapeake Bay Foundation. I knew I wanted to be in the environmental ed field, I just wasn't sure how. I earned a B.A. in environmental science from Messiah College in Pennsylvania, and had a number of jobs -- from research biologist to managing a fish farm – when I was trying to decide what I wanted to do with my career. Then I started a family and earned a Master's of Education from American Intercontinental University. While I was working on my master's, I took a seasonal position as a naturalist. I worked for one year as a naturalist, then was hired as a civilian park ranger.

2. What are the most important skills and/or qualities for someone in your profession?

First and foremost, being clearheaded and calm in the face of emergency and crisis. We can literally be showing a 5-year-old leaves and how a tree grows and get a call for a medical emergency like heatstroke, then an hour later be telling someone to put dog on a leash. You also need to be flexible. You can't predict what will happen: a tree coming down, someone getting lost, or someone walking in and wanting information. Finally, it's important to be well-spoken and to have public speaking skills. You're interfacing with the public every single day.

3. What do you wish you had known going into this profession?

I wish I had realized it's more a way of life than a job. I'm on call a lot, and willing to jump in and help my co-workers. That's been a big adjustment for my family; they have to be the family of a park ranger.

4. Are there many job opportunities in your profession? In what specific areas?

I see turnover with retirement, for one, so while there are always positions coming open, they tend to come in waves. Also, I don't think everyone in the field realizes they are cut out for this before they begin. They usually figure out very quickly if it doesn't work out. There's not a lot of middle ground – you either love this, or figure it out quickly and leave.

5. How do you see your profession changing in the next five years? What role will technology play in those changes, and what skills will be required?

We're continually challenged with the resources necessary to manage the various needs of the park including operations, maintenance and programming. We must be creative with the funds we are given. Regarding technology, I think it can help us deliver services at lower cost. For example, we are offering trail maps online. Or, through the Dept. of Natural Resources app, you can make a reservation or learn to learn what's going on at a park at any given moment. Technology's important to get the word out to our visitors and help us do our job more effectively.

6. What do you enjoy most about your job? What do you enjoy least?

I love the unpredictable aspect of it. I love that if it's a gorgeous day I get to be outside. I get to work in place that people come to play, and be in one of Maryland's most beautiful places. What I like least is a harder question to answer. My family would certainly like it if I made more money; we don't get into this for the pay at all. I think a lot of people would complain about that. I don't have a lot of challenges to say about job; I love my job.

7. Can you suggest a valuable "try this" for students considering a career in your profession?

I think the best thing for someone to try would be a seasonal position. That gives you such a good idea of what goes on day in and day out in a park. Also, we recruit heavily from the Maryland Conservation Corps; its part of Americorps, a national program, so anyone should be able to access the program.

SELECTED SCHOOLS

Programs in parks and recreation management are available at many four-year colleges and universities. The student may also gain initial training at a community college. A degree in police science is especially useful for those seeking to become certified law enforcement rangers. Interested students are advised to consult with a school guidance counselor.

MORE INFORMATION

Association of National Park Rangers
25958 Genesee Trail Road
PMB 222
Golden, CO 80401
www.anpr.org

National Recreation and Park Association
22377 Belmont Ridge Road
Ashburn, VA 20148-4501
800.626.6772
www.nrpa.org

Park Law Enforcement Association
4397 McCullough Street
Port Charlotte, FL 33948
www.myparkranger.org

U.S. Forest Service
1400 Independence Avenue, SW
Washington, DC 20250-0002
800.832.1355
www.fs.fed.us

Michael Shally-Jensen

Fun Facts

More than 280 million people visit U.S. National Parks each year.
Source: NPS

Parole and Probation Officer

Snapshot

Career Cluster: Law & Criminal Justice; Public Safety & Security
Interests: Criminal justice system, public safety, law enforcement, legal system, psychology, counseling
Earnings (Yearly Average): $52,380
Employment & Outlook: Slower Than Average Growth Expected

OVERVIEW

Sphere of Work

Probation and parole officers personally monitor criminal offenders' compliance with court orders and conditions of parole. Probation and parole officers work within federal and state justice systems. They are responsible for working with those individuals convicted for criminal acts but who are allowed to remain in society (probation), or are being released back into society from prison under certain conditions (parole). The function of probation and parole officers is to monitor and assist those convicted of crimes as they work to become productive members of society.

Work Environment

Parole and probation officers spend most of their time working in offices. They are also responsible for testifying in court cases and at parole hearings, visiting clients in their homes, therapy offices, or places of work, and meeting with incarcerated clients. Traveling to meet clients is a necessity of the job, since many people on probation or parole must adhere to travel or other restrictions ordered by the courts. Parole and probation officers are required to provide periodic reports about each client to the courts and parole boards.

Profile

Working Conditions: Work Indoors
Physical Strength: Light Work
Education Needs: Bachelor's Degree, Master's Degree
Licensure/Certification: Sometimes Required
Physical Abilities Not Required: No Heavy Labor
Opportunities For Experience: Internship, Apprenticeship, Volunteer Work
Holland Interest Score*: SEC

* See Appendix A

Occupation Interest

As officers in the justice system, probation and parole officers must have a comprehensive understanding of state and federal laws pertaining to the legal system, both of which they have sworn to uphold, as well as those portions of the Constitution related to prisoners' legal rights. Parole and probation officers are also expected to know the procedural and administrative duties of the legal system and its various components, so they should be interested in the criminal justice system and how it works. Parole and probation officers must be at least twenty-one years of age and in good physical and emotional health. Federal court systems restrict individuals older than thirty-seven years of age from applying for parole or probation officer positions.

A Day in the Life—Duties and Responsibilities

While parole officers and probation officers have similar job responsibilities, they work with different groups of people. Probation officers work with individuals who are given the opportunity to avoid incarceration through compliance with court-ordered probation. Each jurisdiction treats juvenile offenders separately from adult offenders (juvenile probation is referred to as "aftercare").

Parole allows a convicted person to transition into regular society for the remainder of their sentence, and is considered suitable for those individuals who have exhibited non-violent and cooperative behavior while incarcerated. Parole officers monitor these individuals to ensure compliance with the rules of their parole.

Because probation and parole officers work directly with criminal offenders to monitor these individuals' compliance with court orders and conditions of parole, they need to develop strong interpersonal and communication skills. They generally meet with clients on a monthly or bi-weekly basis, depending on the client's risk assessment analysis. When an officer has clients spread over a large area, probation and parole officers sometimes use other government and law enforcement facilities to conduct these meetings and interviews. Parole and probation officers must also attend departmental staff meetings and ongoing training on policies and procedures.

A typical work day for a parole and probation officer might be frequently stressful due to the nature of their job responsibilities, which include interacting with angry or upset families and potentially violent offenders, constantly meeting deadlines, working a heavy caseload, being subject to random drug testing required by the government, making themselves available outside of regular work hours as emergencies and unexpected events arise, and possibly carrying a firearm for personal protection. However, the potential for job satisfaction is high when a parole or probation officer is able to successfully help a former criminal turn his or her life around.

Duties and Responsibilities

- Handling probation and parole cases
- Meeting with clients on a regular basis
- Monitoring the progress of clients
- Counseling clients or referring them to other helpful agencies
- Conducting pre-sentence investigations for the court
- Interacting with other law enforcement personnel
- Investigating the clients' homes
- Appearing at hearings and giving testimony
- Preparing reports and performing other administrative tasks

OCCUPATION SPECIALTIES

Parole Officers

Parole Officers work with people who have been released from jail and are serving parole, to help them re-enter society. Parole officers monitor post-release offenders and provide them with information on various resources, such as substance-abuse counseling or job training, to aid in their rehabilitation.

Probation Officers

Probation Officers supervise people who have been placed on probation by a court or judge, instead of being sent to prison. They work to ensure that the offender is not a danger to the community and to help in his or her rehabilitation.

Pretrial Services Officers

Pretrial Services Officers investigate an offender's background to determine if the offender can be safely allowed back into the community before his or her trial date. Officers must assess the risk and make a recommendation to a judge who decides on the appropriate sentencing or bond amount.

Correctional Treatment Specialists

Correctional Treatment Specialists, also known as case managers or correctional counselors, advise offenders and develop rehabilitation plans for them to follow when they are no longer in prison or on parole. They also work with inmates, probation officers, and staff of other agencies to develop parole and release plans.

WORK ENVIRONMENT

Physical Environment

Probation and parole officers work with various law enforcement and court officials in offices, courtrooms, law enforcement agencies, correctional facilities, client's homes, and treatment facilities. Since these officers work with people convicted of a wide range of criminal offenses, sometimes violent, they must assess new work situations with personal safety in mind. They may analyze the area where client appointments will occur to identify safety and security concerns, such as possible weapons, and conceive a possible escape plan if doing so seems advisable.

Relevant Skills and Abilities

Communication Skills
- Speaking effectively

Interpersonal/Social Skills
- Cooperating with others
- Working as a member of a team

Organization & Management Skills
- Coordinating tasks
- Managing people/groups
- Managing time
- Organizing information or materials
- Paying attention to and handling details

Other Skills
- Knowledge of or familiarity with criminal justice system

Human Environment

Probation and parole officers work directly with criminal offenders to monitor these individuals' compliance with court orders and parole conditions. Officers must be conscious of the surrounding environment and any potential risks, as well as remain aware of who is in the general vicinity and determine the safest location for their interactions with their clients. Probation and parole officers work with a variety of support staff within their respective departments and interact with law enforcement personnel such as judges, prosecutors, defense attorneys, police, and prison and jail officers. These officers also interact with a variety of social service personnel, such as psychiatrists, psychologists, and counselors, in order to monitor compliance with orders of the court and conditions of the parole board.

Officers assess risk on a case-by-case basis by analyzing each client's behavioral history, employment and family history, criminal history, peer associations, and mental health and substance abuse history.

Technological Environment

Probation and parole officers should have an understanding of and familiarity with computer technology and software (such as word processing programs to write reports). They also use cell phones and Internet communication tools to perform their work. Because they may carry a concealed weapon, weapons training may be required as well.

EDUCATION, TRAINING, AND ADVANCEMENT

High School/Secondary

High school students can best prepare for a career as a probation and parole officer by focusing on social sciences, government, and psychology. In addition, students will benefit from taking courses in communications. Communication and problem-solving skills are vital for success in this occupation. High school students should also consider working in law enforcement or volunteering with judicial, public safety, or legal aid organizations, which allow the student to gain knowledge and understanding of the judicial system.

Suggested High School Subjects
- Applied Communication
- English
- Government
- Psychology
- Social Studies
- Sociology

Famous First

The first probation system was established for juveniles in Massachusetts in 1869. The new law was designed to address the problem of juvenile delinquency. Under it, the governor appointed an officer to work for the welfare and redemption of delinquents, rather than for their punishment. The officer or his deputies were required to visit youths assigned to the system at least once every three months. In 1880 the system was expanded to include adult offenders.

Library of Congress

College/Postsecondary

Students interested in this profession should pursue a bachelor's degree in sociology, criminal justice, psychology, or a related field for an entry level position. A master's degree is recommended for those considering career advancement.

College and university programs often offer co-op study programs and internships with local, state, and federal probation and parole agencies. These opportunities allow students to develop valuable experience while completing their remaining academic coursework for graduation. Internships also give students an opportunity to make valuable professional contacts for their future in the profession.

Related College Majors
- Criminal Justice/Law Enforcement Administration
- Social Work

Adult Job Seekers

Courts and departments of corrections frequently reevaluate sentencing and parole issues as a means of coping with periodic or diminished funding for correctional institutions. As the use of probation and parole options increases, there will be excellent job growth prospects for parole and probation officers.

Professional Certification and Licensure

Depending on the state in which they seek employment, probation and parole officers may be required to undertake a state-sponsored or federally sponsored training program and certification test, or possibly a psychological test. A juvenile parole and probation officer may require separate training and certification.

Additional Requirements

Local, state, and federal agencies may have their own training programs required for new employees. Some may provide training and certification programs in self defense, hostility de-escalation, and client assessment. Parole and probation officers should be poised, intelligent, and physically and emotionally hardy individuals who gain satisfaction from helping others from a wide variety of backgrounds and situations. They must be comfortable interacting with those who have broken the law, as well as people whose lives are in transition, and thus may be chaotic or disruptive.

EARNINGS AND ADVANCEMENT

Those with both a graduate degree and a great deal of work experience may be candidates for an administrative or supervisory position. Higher wages tend to be found in urban areas. Mean annual earnings of parole and probation officers were $52,380 in 2012. The lowest ten percent earned less than $31,590, and the highest ten percent earned more than $83,410.

Parole and probation officers may receive paid vacations, holidays, and sick days; life and health insurance; and retirement benefits. These are usually paid by the employer.

Metropolitan Areas with the Highest Employment Level in this Occupation

Metropolitan area	Employment[1]	Employment per thousand jobs	Hourly mean wage
Los Angeles-Long Beach-Glendale, CA	4,020	1.04	$34.06
New York-White Plains-Wayne, NY-NJ	2,120	0.41	$34.12
Atlanta-Sandy Springs-Marietta, GA	1,610	0.71	$17.72
Houston-Sugar Land-Baytown, TX	1,530	0.58	$19.46
Philadelphia, PA	1,300	0.71	$24.75
Riverside-San Bernardino-Ontario, CA	1,170	1.01	$38.13
Washington-Arlington-Alexandria, DC-VA-MD-WV	1,130	0.48	$25.71
Baltimore-Towson, MD	1,100	0.88	$25.58

[1]Does not include self-employed. Source: Bureau of Labor Statistics

Fun Facts

Boston bootmaker and teetoler, John Augustus, is credited with creating "probation," believing that, rather than serving jail sentences, alcoholics could be rehabilitated through understanding and kindness. In 1841, he bailed out a "common drunkard," returning him to court three weeks later a newly sober man. He was a volunteer "probation" officer (his term) for 18-years. The nation's first probation law was enacted in Massachusetts in 1859 soon after his death.

EMPLOYMENT AND OUTLOOK

Parole and probation officers held about 90,000 jobs nationally in 2012. Most worked for state or local governments. Employment is expected to grow slower than the average for all occupations through the year 2022, which means that the employment rate will remain essentially unchanged (0 percent growth). Even though overcrowding in prisons has increased the number of persons on probation, many states face severe funding limitations, including the amounts allocated to corrections.

Employment Trend, Projected 2012–22

Counselors, Social Workers, and Related Occupations: 19%

Total, All Occupations: 11%

Parole and Probation Officers: -1%

Note: "All Occupations" includes all occupations in the U.S. Economy. Source: U.S. Bureau of Labor Statistics, Employment Projections Program

Related Occupations
- Correctional Officer
- Federal Law Enforcement Agent
- Police Officer & Detective
- Social Worker

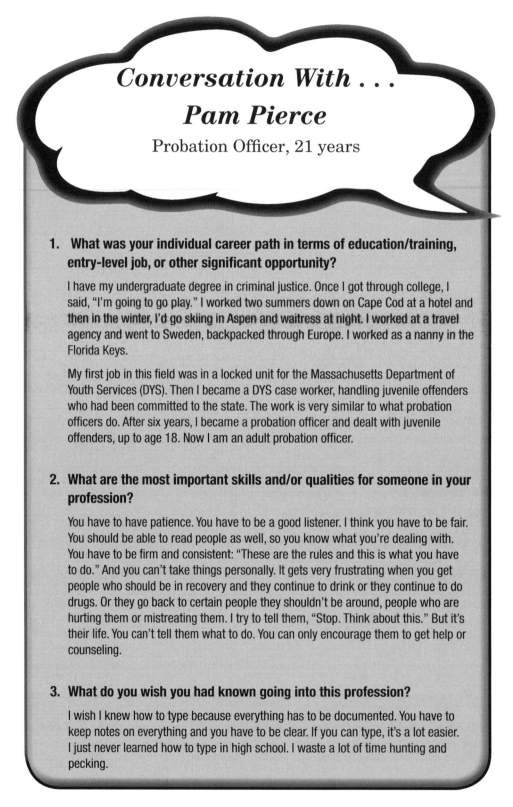

Conversation With . . .
Pam Pierce
Probation Officer, 21 years

1. **What was your individual career path in terms of education/training, entry-level job, or other significant opportunity?**

I have my undergraduate degree in criminal justice. Once I got through college, I said, "I'm going to go play." I worked two summers down on Cape Cod at a hotel and then in the winter, I'd go skiing in Aspen and waitress at night. I worked at a travel agency and went to Sweden, backpacked through Europe. I worked as a nanny in the Florida Keys.

My first job in this field was in a locked unit for the Massachusetts Department of Youth Services (DYS). Then I became a DYS case worker, handling juvenile offenders who had been committed to the state. The work is very similar to what probation officers do. After six years, I became a probation officer and dealt with juvenile offenders, up to age 18. Now I am an adult probation officer.

2. **What are the most important skills and/or qualities for someone in your profession?**

You have to have patience. You have to be a good listener. I think you have to be fair. You should be able to read people as well, so you know what you're dealing with. You have to be firm and consistent: "These are the rules and this is what you have to do." And you can't take things personally. It gets very frustrating when you get people who should be in recovery and they continue to drink or they continue to do drugs. Or they go back to certain people they shouldn't be around, people who are hurting them or mistreating them. I try to tell them, "Stop. Think about this." But it's their life. You can't tell them what to do. You can only encourage them to get help or counseling.

3. **What do you wish you had known going into this profession?**

I wish I knew how to type because everything has to be documented. You have to keep notes on everything and you have to be clear. If you can type, it's a lot easier. I just never learned how to type in high school. I waste a lot of time hunting and pecking.

4. Are there many job opportunities in your profession? In what specific areas?

I don't think so. We need more people, but there's a hiring freeze. It's a very difficult job to get now in Massachusetts. It's a very popular job. That's one reason they're looking at people with master's degrees now.

We used to be the second highest paid probation department in the country. The benefits are very good. People pretty much don't leave this job once they get it.

5. How do you see your profession changing in the next five years? What role will technology play in those changes, and what skills will be required?

The big focus now is trying to track and reduce the rate of recidivism. One of the keys to doing that, I think, is jobs. If you get kids good jobs, they wouldn't be back out on the street.

GPS is a major technological advance that's helping. People are on the ankle bracelet and we're able to track and monitor them. There's also a new computer system where anyone in the state (with the right clearance) can read someone else's notes (on a given client.) And because of the National Crime Information Center, we have access to more information about offenders. But the crux of the job won't change. Probation involves a lot of human interaction, building a rapport with the defendants and their families. It involves trying to get people to think about how they can improve their lives.

6. What do you enjoy most about your job? What do you enjoy least?

I enjoy trying to make a difference in people's lives and help them turn their lives around. When it happens, it's really quite a joyous thing. It's nice when you see someone in court and find out they're not there for themselves. I tell them, "Hey, life's not so bad being Mr. Average and just kind of going along, is it?"

What I like least is the paperwork. It cuts into the amount of time you can spend with people. Also, worrying and staying on top of the caseload.

7. Can you suggest a valuable "try this" for students considering a career in your profession?

I would suggest what I did years ago. I went in and sat in the courtroom and watched what went on. I watched what the judge did. I watched what everyone's role was. Also, try to do an internship through the court with a probation officer, not just the front desk, so you can sit in on their interviews and office visits.

SELECTED SCHOOLS

Programs in criminal justice, social work, and related fields are available in many colleges and universities. The student may also gain initial training at a community college. Interested students are advised to consult with their school guidance counselor.

MORE INFORMATION

American Correctional Association
206 N. Washington Street
Suite 200
Alexandria, VA 22314
800.222.5646
www.aca.org

American Jail Association
1135 Professional Court
Hagerstown, MD 21740-5853
301.790.3930
www.aja.org

American Probation and Parole Association
P.O. Box 11910
Lexington, KY 40578-1910
859.244.8203
www.appa-net.org/eweb

Federal Probation and Pretrial Officers Association
400 S. Virginia Street, Room 103
Reno, NV 89501-2193
fppoa.org

Chuck Goodwin/Editor

Police Officer & Detective

Snapshot

Career Cluster: Law & Criminal Justice; Public Safety & Security

Interests: Public safety, law enforcement, criminal justice, security, psychology, sociology, investigation

Earnings (Yearly Average): $57,770 (officer); $77,860 (detective)

Employment & Outlook: Average Growth Expected

OVERVIEW

Sphere of Work

Police officers and detectives enforce federal, state, and local laws. They investigate criminal activity, arrest suspects, interview witnesses, redirect the flow of traffic around accidents, construction and crime scenes, and intervene in public disturbances. Police patrol and monitor the streets and other designated areas. They are trained to use both non-lethal and lethal force in subduing criminals. Some police are uniformed, using patrol cars and other marked vehicles, while others are detectives and investigators, who wear plain clothes while on duty. The

duties of police officers and detectives vary based on the size of the department and the community in which they serve.

Work Environment

All police officers (including detectives) are based in police stations, where they interview witnesses and suspects, detain suspects, conduct investigations, and perform administrative duties. On patrol and at the scenes of criminal activity, police officers face considerable dangers and stresses. The psychological impact on police officers comes not only from confrontations with suspects but from the trauma of witnessing crime and accident scenes. Police generally work forty- to sixty-hour workweeks, sometimes longer. Since police work is needed twenty-four hours a day, shifts may encompass late nights and holidays. Police are often on their feet while on duty and work in all types of weather.

Profile

Working Conditions: Work both Indoors and Outdoors
Physical Strength: Medium Work
Education Needs: Technical/ Community College
Licensure/Certification: Required
Opportunities For Experience: Apprenticeship, Military Service, Volunteer Work, Part-Time Work
Holland Interest Score*: REI, SCE, SCR, SEC, SER

* See Appendix A

Occupation Interest

Police officers protect people from crime and rescue people from emergency situations, such as vehicular accidents, muggings, and assaults. The work is rarely dull or routine – many aspiring police officers are attracted to the adrenaline rush of chasing down a suspect or otherwise capturing dangerous individuals. Police officers and detectives are often considered heroes in their communities, particularly in the wake of high-profile incidents. The demand for police officers continues to grow, even during periods of recession. Although police officers receive average compensation despite the dangers and stresses of their work, they also receive excellent benefits, including life insurance, health insurance, and retirement plans.

A Day in the Life—Duties and Responsibilities

Police officers and detectives maintain order and enforce federal, state, and local laws. Officers patrol designated areas on foot, horseback, motorcycle, and bicycle as well as in squad cars and other motor vehicles. Police respond to emergency calls or otherwise intervene when they see criminal activity. They interview witnesses, detain people of interest and suspects, and record information about the incident. Police also stop motor vehicle drivers for speeding and other safety violations, investigate accident scenes to assess whether a crime has been committed, and obtain warrants to search homes, offices, cars, and other personal property.

Police duties also include protecting and educating citizens. Police officers serve as first responders in the event of an accident or other medical emergency. They administer first aid, protect victims by keeping crowds away, and enable emergency vehicles to arrive, care for victims, and transport them to the hospital in a timely fashion. Additionally, police must testify in civil and criminal court cases when called upon by prosecutors and other attorneys. Police officers also educate both children and adults about the dangers of drugs, stranger abductions, child and spousal abuse, identity theft, terrorism, and other criminal activities.

Police officers' and detectives' responsibilities vary based on the size of the police force and community in which they serve. Large, urban police forces may have police officers, plainclothes detectives, and police patrolmen assigned to specific units, such as narcotics or robbery. Officers at smaller departments may perform multiple duties.

Duties and Responsibilities

- Patrolling an assigned area or beat
- Preventing crime and making arrests
- Investigating accidents and administering first aid to victims
- Controlling traffic and issuing tickets
- Writing and filing a variety of activity reports daily
- Investigating crimes and questioning witnesses
- Examining the scene of a crime for clues and evidence
- Preparing assigned cases for court
- Testifying before a court or grand jury

OCCUPATION SPECIALTIES

Uniformed Police Officers

Uniformed Police Officers have general law enforcement duties. They wear uniforms that allow the public to easily recognize them as police officers. They have regular patrols and also respond to emergency and non-emergency calls. Some police officers work only on a specific type of crime, such as narcotics. Others, especially those working in large departments, may work in special units, such as horseback, motorcycle, canine corps, and special weapons and tactics (SWAT) teams. Typically, officers must work as patrol officers for a certain number of years before they are appointed to one of these units.

State Highway Patrol Officers

State Highway Patrol Officers, or State Troopers, patrol state highways within an assigned area, in vehicles equipped with two-way radios, to enforce motor vehicle and criminal laws. State police officers have authority to work anywhere in the state and are frequently called on to help other law enforcement agencies, especially those in rural areas or small towns.

Transit Police

Transit Police patrol transit stations and railroad yards. They protect passengers and employees from crimes such as thefts and robberies. They remove trespassers from transit and railroad properties and check IDs of people who try to enter secure areas, to protect people and property.

Sheriffs and Deputy Sheriffs

Sheriffs and Deputy Sheriffs enforce the law on the county level. Sheriffs' departments tend to be relatively small. Sheriffs usually are elected by the public and do the same work as a local or county police chief. Some sheriffs' departments do the same work as officers in urban police departments. Others mainly operate the county jails and provide services in local courts. Police and sheriffs' deputies who provide security in city and county courts are sometimes called bailiffs.

Detectives and Criminal Investigators

Detectives and Criminal Investigators are uniformed or plainclothes investigators who gather facts and collect evidence for criminal cases. They conduct interviews, examine records, observe the activities of suspects, and participate in raids and arrests. Detectives usually specialize in investigating one type of crime, such as homicide or fraud. Detectives are typically assigned cases on a rotating basis and work on them until an arrest and trial are completed or until the case is dropped.

WORK ENVIRONMENT

Relevant Skills and Abilities

Communication Skills
- Speaking effectively

Interpersonal/Social Skills
- Being able to remain calm
- Cooperating with others
- Having good judgment
- Working as a member of a team

Organization & Management Skills
- Coordinating tasks
- Demonstrating leadership
- Handling challenging situations
- Making decisions
- Managing people/groups

Research & Planning Skills
- Solving problems
- Using logical reasoning

Other Skills
- Developing skill in the use and care of firearms

Physical Environment

Police officers and detectives are based in police stations, which tend to be well-organized, busy environments governed by strict procedures. Much of police officers' work is performed in locations throughout the community, including private residences, offices and businesses, and public roadways.

Human Environment

Police officers and detectives interact with all members of the general public, including victims of crime and suspects. Additionally, they work with attorneys, judges, and other public safety officials, such as firefighters, emergency medical technicians, and federal law enforcement officers. Depending on their area of specialization, police work as members of a local police force, at a state highway patrol facility, or in any number of federal departments and bureaus of law enforcement, such as the Federal Bureau of Investigation (FBI) or the Bureau of Indian Affairs (BIA).

Technological Environment

Police use different types of technology when on patrol or performing investigative work versus in the station. In addition to weapons of lethal force (including handguns and shotguns) and non-lethal force (such as Mace and Tasers), officers use laptop computers, radar guns, two-way radios, cellular and smart phones, and global positioning satellite systems (GPS). In the station, police officers use the Integrated Automated Fingerprint Identification System (AFIS), the National Crime Information Center (NCIC) database, ballistics information networks, photo-imaging and crime-mapping software, and basic office software systems.

EDUCATION, TRAINING, AND ADVANCEMENT

High School/Secondary

High school students are encouraged to take psychology, physical education, government, history, communications, speech, foreign languages, and social studies. Proficiency in a widely-used foreign language, such as Spanish or Chinese, can be a great advantage when applying for future jobs or pursuing career advancement.

Suggested High School Subjects
- Applied Communication
- Driver Training
- English
- First Aid Training
- Government
- History
- Physical Education
- Psychology
- Social Studies
- Sociology
- Speech

Famous First

The first state police were the Texas Rangers, authorized in 1835 when Texas was still a province of Mexico. (Texas was admitted to the Union in 1845.) The main task of the first three companies of Rangers was to protect the border. They took on wider law enforcement responsibilities when Texas became a state, and soon they were forever linked to the history of the Old West. Since 1935 they have officially been the Texas Ranger Division of the Texas Department of Public Safety. There is a museum dedicated to the Texas Rangers in Waco.

College/Postsecondary

Most police officers are expected to have some formal postsecondary education. Many attend junior and community colleges, receiving an associate's degree in law enforcement, security, or a related field. Many other police officers, including detectives, complete a bachelor's degree in law enforcement, criminal justice, and similar fields. Many departments, agencies, and states have programs that reimburse officers or pay for their tuition at these institutions. Before they can join the force, police candidates must enter a state or local police academy, where they receive twelve to fourteen weeks of relevant classroom and hands-on training.

Related College Majors
- Criminology
- Law Enforcement/Police Science
- Security

Adult Job Seekers

Qualified adults must apply directly to the agency, state, or municipality in which they seek to become officers. They may also network with peers through nationwide law enforcement organizations, such as the Fraternal Order of Police.

Professional Certification and Licensure

Police officers and detectives are subject to criminal background checks and must pass written, verbal, and physical examinations. Applying for a police job requires U.S. citizenship and a valid driver's license.

Additional Requirements

Police officers and detectives must be physically fit and of at least average physical strength, able to pass a number of physical tests. Officers must pass periodic drug and/or polygraph tests, as well as undergo extensive background checks, as a condition of continued employment.

Officers and detectives should be comfortable interacting with and providing assistance to the general public. Since police frequently deal with job-related tension and with unruly, violent, or uncooperative individuals, prospective police officers should be psychologically well-balanced and even-tempered; it is considered both professionally and ethically important to avoid escalating the level of violent conflict.

EARNINGS AND ADVANCEMENT

Earnings of police officers detectives depend on the individual's rank and years of service and the size and geographic location of the agency in which they are employed. Larger agencies usually pay more and provide a wider range of opportunities for advancement.

Mean annual earnings of police officers, sheriffs, and state troopers were $57,770 in 2012. The lowest ten percent earned less than $32,350, and the highest ten percent earned more than $89,310.

Mean annual earnings of police detectives and criminal investigators were $77,860 in 2012. The lowest ten percent earned less than $39,900, and the highest ten percent earned more than $122,099.

Police officers and detectives may receive paid vacations, holidays, and sick days; life and health insurance; and retirement benefits. These are usually paid by the employer.

Metropolitan Areas with the Highest Employment Level in this Occupation (Police, Sheriffs, Troopers)

Metropolitan area	Employment	Employment per thousand jobs	Hourly mean wage
New York-White Plains-Wayne, NY-NJ	36,180	7.02	$34.83
Los Angeles-Long Beach-Glendale, CA	24,590	6.35	$40.80
Chicago-Joliet-Naperville, IL	21,120	5.80	$34.93
Houston-Sugar Land-Baytown, TX	13,170	4.99	$25.87
Washington-Arlington-Alexandria, DC-VA-MD-WV	12,770	5.45	$30.50

Source: Bureau of Labor Statistics

Metropolitan Areas with the Highest Employment Level in this Occupation (Detectives & Investigators)

Metropolitan area	Employment[1]	Employment per thousand jobs	Hourly mean wage
New York-White Plains-Wayne, NY-NJ	6,600	1.28	$41.14
Washington-Arlington-Alexandria, DC-VA-MD-WV	4,230	1.80	$53.93
Los Angeles-Long Beach-Glendale, CA	3,090	0.80	$48.92
San Diego-Carlsbad-San Marcos, CA	3,070	2.43	$46.42
Atlanta-Sandy Springs-Marietta, GA	2,230	0.98	$28.51

[1]Does not include private detectives. Source: Bureau of Labor Statistics

EMPLOYMENT AND OUTLOOK

Police officers and police detectives held approximately 780,000 jobs in 2012. Most were employed by local governments, primarily in cities with a population of more than 25,000 people. State police agencies and various federal agencies also employed police officers.

Employment is expected to grow slower the average for all occupations through the year 2022, which means employment is projected to increase 3 percent to 9 percent. Concerns about security and drug-related crimes will contribute to the demand for police officers. Competition is expected to be strong for higher paying jobs with state and federal agencies and in larger police departments. Opportunities will be best for applicants with college training in police science or military police experience.

Employment Trend, Projected 2012–22

Total, All Occupations: 11%

Protective Service Occupations: 8%

Police and Detectives: 5%

Note: "All Occupations" includes all occupations in the U.S. Economy. Source: U.S. Bureau of Labor Statistics, Employment Projections Program

Related Occupations
- Correctional Officer
- Federal Law Enforcement Agent
- Inspector and Compliance Officer
- Parole and Probation Officer
- Private Detective
- Security Guard

Related Military Occupations
- Intelligence Officer
- Intelligence Specialist
- Law Enforcement & Security Officer
- Law Enforcement & Security Specialist
- Military Police

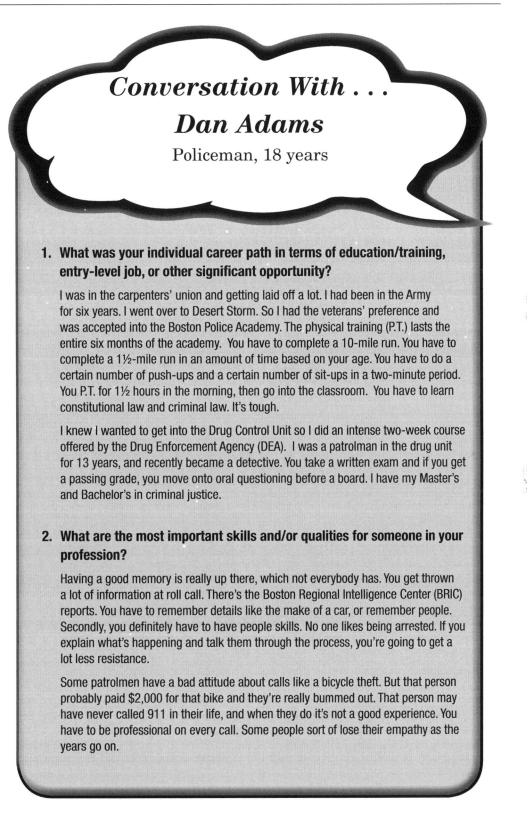

Conversation With . . .
Dan Adams
Policeman, 18 years

1. What was your individual career path in terms of education/training, entry-level job, or other significant opportunity?

I was in the carpenters' union and getting laid off a lot. I had been in the Army for six years. I went over to Desert Storm. So I had the veterans' preference and was accepted into the Boston Police Academy. The physical training (P.T.) lasts the entire six months of the academy. You have to complete a 10-mile run. You have to complete a 1½-mile run in an amount of time based on your age. You have to do a certain number of push-ups and a certain number of sit-ups in a two-minute period. You P.T. for 1½ hours in the morning, then go into the classroom. You have to learn constitutional law and criminal law. It's tough.

I knew I wanted to get into the Drug Control Unit so I did an intense two-week course offered by the Drug Enforcement Agency (DEA). I was a patrolman in the drug unit for 13 years, and recently became a detective. You take a written exam and if you get a passing grade, you move onto oral questioning before a board. I have my Master's and Bachelor's in criminal justice.

2. What are the most important skills and/or qualities for someone in your profession?

Having a good memory is really up there, which not everybody has. You get thrown a lot of information at roll call. There's the Boston Regional Intelligence Center (BRIC) reports. You have to remember details like the make of a car, or remember people. Secondly, you definitely have to have people skills. No one likes being arrested. If you explain what's happening and talk them through the process, you're going to get a lot less resistance.

Some patrolmen have a bad attitude about calls like a bicycle theft. But that person probably paid $2,000 for that bike and they're really bummed out. That person may have never called 911 in their life, and when they do it's not a good experience. You have to be professional on every call. Some people sort of lose their empathy as the years go on.

3. What do you wish you had known going into this profession?

Nothing, really. Now that I'm close to being a sergeant, I wish I had studied more so I could do well on that exam.

4. Are there many job opportunities in your profession? In what specific areas?

With mandatory retirement, there are always people retiring. Boston has 2,200 officers. We have a dive team. If you're into dogs, you can get on the canine unit. We have a bomb unit. I'm in the Drug Control Unit. We have community relations, a bank robbery task force, crimes against children … I could go on and on. You can do so many things in law enforcement. It's great.

5. How do you see your profession changing in the next five years? What role will technology play in those changes, and what skills will be required?

We're constantly getting upgrades and training. Finding people is so much easier; there's just so much of a paper trail. Just Google yourself–you'll be amazed. And the police have different search engines. In the old days, you would go out to location, asking, "Hey, have you seen Johnny?" Today, there are 81 cameras around the city. Within five years, that's going to be more like 800 cameras. I can be sitting at my desk manipulating a camera and watching.

6. What do you enjoy most about your job? What do you enjoy least?

We call it "hunting." It's going out and catching the bad guys. You might watch a kid in the freezing cold. For 45 minutes, he's standing around, he's checking his cell phone, he's watching the cars go by. Then a car pulls up and he goes around the block for one minute. It's what we call "a meaningless ride." Right now I'm working on a really big search warrant that we're going to execute tomorrow. I love that.

Because it's Civil Service–and I shouldn't complain about that, because I benefited from it–but it's so, so hard to get rid of the dead weight. People you would never want to work with. And then you have the people who are at the other end. A little power makes them goofy. Of course, there are plenty of really great guys that you love to work with, who have a really great work ethic and who are doing a lot to make Boston a better city.

7. Can you suggest a valuable "try this" for students considering a career in your profession?

Try to get a seasonal job in a tourist area that hires officers for the summer. People go for security guard jobs. An EMT position would also be good training.

SELECTED SCHOOLS

Programs in criminal justice, police science, security and related fields are available in many colleges and universities. The student may also gain solid training at a community college—and in many police departments an associate's degree or completion of some college is all that is required to become a candidate for police academy or similar basic training. For those seeking to become detectives or criminal investigators a bachelor's degree is necessary. Interested students are advised to consult with their school guidance counselor.

MORE INFORMATION

Federal Law Enforcement Training Center
1131 Chapel Crossing Road
Glynco, GA 31524
912.267.2100
www.fletc.gov

International Association of Chiefs of Police
515 N. Washington Street
Alexandria, VA 22314
703.836.6767
www.theiacp.org

National Association of Police Organizations
317 S. Patrick Street
Alexandria, VA 22314
703.549.0775
www.napo.org

National Fraternal Order of Police
Atnip-Orms Center
701 Marriott Drive
Nashville, TN 37214
615.399.0900
www.fop.net

Michael Auerbach/Editor

Fun Facts

The first "police officers" were medieval knights; their "badges" were their coats of arms. Today, police officers wear badges above their left chest pocket, over the heart, because officers pledge to protect, and because the left arm was used by medieval knights to hold up their shield, protecting their hearts and allowing them to fight with their dominant hand.

Source: symbolarts.com

Private Detective

Snapshot

Career Cluster: Law & Criminal Justice; Public Safety & Security
Interests: Security, surveillance, law, investigation, public safety, forensic technology
Earnings (Yearly Average): $50,780
Employment & Outlook: Average Growth Expected

OVERVIEW

Sphere of Work

Private detectives investigate people or data for individuals, families, lawyers, department stores, corporations, financial institutions, and many other businesses and organizations. Internal Revenue Service investigators, police detectives, and other public law enforcement agents perform similar work; private detectives (also known as private investigators), however, work for the private sector instead of the government or public sector. Private detectives can be generalists or specialize in

subjects such as computer crime, insurance fraud, loss prevention, or terrorism prevention.

Work Environment

Some private detectives work most anywhere. One might spend days and nights traversing a city to spy on a cheating spouse or locate a missing person, while another might debug corporate boardrooms. Other detectives conduct their work mostly at computers or otherwise remain on the premises of a singular business, such as a private detective for a hotel or retail outfit. Detectives may work alone or on a team of investigators. Their work typically requires much contact with other employees, customers, and authorities. Detectives may work regular day or night shifts, or they may need to work flexible hours, including nights, weekends, and holidays, as needed.

Profile

Working Conditions: Work both Indoors and Outdoors
Physical Strength: Light Work
Education Needs: On-The-Job Training, Technical/Community College, Bachelor's Degree
Licensure/Certification: Required
Physical Abilities Not Required: No Heavy Labor
Opportunities For Experience: Apprenticeship
Holland Interest Score*: ESA, ESC, SEC, SER, SRE

* See Appendix A

Occupation Interest

People who are attracted to private investigating are curious and enjoy analytical research and problem solving, and perhaps a thrill as well (though criminal apprehension is not within their jurisdiction or job scope). The glamour often associated with the job tends to be the creation of fiction writers, as most detective work is rather mundane. Other necessary qualities include resourcefulness, assertiveness, and an aptitude for quick problem solving, as well as communication skills, computer expertise, and business acumen. A commitment to upholding the law and maintaining confidentiality are also essential.

A Day in the Life—Duties and Responsibilities

The work of the private detective usually begins with a need, whether it's a family seeking to locate a long-missing member, a company requiring a background check on a potential new employee, or an environmental organization needing documentation of a manufacturer polluting the environment.

In most cases, the first step is to extract as much background information as possible from the client. After a thorough interview, the private detective or investigator determines what additional information is needed and how best to retrieve it. Additional research may involve searching online databases, public records, or social networking sites. He or she may need to visit government offices to search other files or request documentation from various agencies. In the case of a missing family member, the detective may decide to travel to past residences or workplaces to interview the person's former neighbors and coworkers. In the case of a manufacturer suspected of environmental pollution, the detective may decide to visit the site in question. If there are no useful vantage points from the ground, he or she may arrange to conduct aerial surveillance. For all cases, the private detective must keep careful records, obtain evidence, and create reports for the client.

A store detective, or loss prevention agent, may be responsible for managing the security system, inspecting merchandise stocks, and serving as an undercover shopper. The job entails confrontations with shoplifters and close collaboration with law enforcement. Private detectives in a corporate setting investigate worker's compensation fraud, embezzlement, and other illegal activities committed by employees. Some cases may require the detective to go undercover to gain information.

Detectives are also called upon to serve subpoenas and other legal documents in court cases and assist lawyers and law enforcement agents with interviews and evidence and, where the law permits, assist in evicting tenants (by, for example, serving an eviction notice). They often testify in court and, therefore, must be sure their investigations are conducted legally and documented fully.

Duties and Responsibilities

- **Conducting surveillance**
- **Interviewing people with material knowledge of a case**
- **Patrolling by auto or on foot**
- **Performing undercover operations to observe violation of company policy or the commission of illegal activity**
- **Managing detective projects or surveillance operations**
- **Tracking down and locating people**
- **Filing reports and doing paperwork**

OCCUPATION SPECIALTIES

Private Investigators

Private Investigators conduct investigations to locate missing persons, obtain needed information, and solve problems for clients.

Legal Investigators

Legal Investigators help prepare criminal cases, verify facts in civil law suits, locate witnesses, and serve legal documents. They often work for lawyers and law firms.

Corporate Investigators

Corporate Investigators conduct internal and external investigations for corporations. Internally, they may investigate drug use in the workplace or ensure that expense accounts are not abused. Externally, they may try to identify and stop criminal schemes, such as fraudulent billing by a supplier.

Financial Investigators

Financial Investigators may be hired to collect financial information on individuals and companies attempting to do large financial transactions. These investigators often are certified public accountants

(CPAs) who work closely with investment bankers and other accountants. Investigators might search for assets to recover damages awarded by a court in fraud and theft cases.

Computer Forensic Investigators

Computer Forensic Investigators specialize in recovering, analyzing, and presenting information from computers to be used as evidence. Many focus on recovering deleted emails and documents.

Store Detectives

Store Detectives, also known as loss prevention agents, catch people who try to steal merchandise or destroy store property.

WORK ENVIRONMENT

Relevant Skills and Abilities

Communication Skills
- Expressing thoughts and ideas
- Listening attentively
- Speaking effectively

Interpersonal/Social Skills
- Being able to work independently
- Cooperating with others

Organization & Management Skills
- Demonstrating leadership
- Performing routine work

Research & Planning Skills
- Analyzing information
- Using logical reasoning

Other Skills
- Being able to handle awkward or uncomfortable situations

Physical Environment

Private detectives are usually based in offices where they conduct much of their work on the phone and through the Internet. Fieldwork locations, however, can vary widely and include both indoor and outdoor sites. Some detectives handle most of their surveillance from their vehicles. Specialized detectives work in businesses such as department stores, law firms, and corporations. Others are employed in factories and industrial complexes to protect against theft of trade secrets, embezzlement, and other illegal employee behavior.

Human Environment

Most detectives interact with a variety of people. They meet with clients, conduct formal and informal interviews, and spend time observing people in the field. Some detectives communicate with people primarily through social networking sites or interact mostly with other employees. Entry-level detectives usually work closely with a supervisor until they acquire the experience to work independently.

Technological Environment

The tools used most often by private detectives are telecommunication-based, while instruments and devices such as binoculars are also common. Specialized equipment includes infrared cameras and bugging devices, where permitted by law. Some detectives also carry a firearm.

EDUCATION, TRAINING, AND ADVANCEMENT

High School/Secondary

A well-rounded college preparatory program that includes science, computer science, English, and political science or sociology is the best foundation for high school students interested in becoming private detectives.

Suggested High School Subjects
- Applied Communication
- Bookkeeping
- English
- First Aid Training
- Photography
- Physical Education
- Psychology
- Social Studies

Famous First

The first private detective agency in the United States was the Pinkerton Agency, founded in Chicago in 1850 by Allan Pinkerton. The agency's initial clients were Midwestern railroads, which sought to protect their property and maintain a closer watch over their employees. One of Pinkerton's early hires (1856) was Kate Warne, making her the first female private detective in America. Pinkerton later became famous when he allegedly foiled a plot to kill president-elect Abraham Lincoln in 1861. Afterward, Lincoln appointed Pinkerton to serve as the first head of the Army secret service.

Library of Congress

College/Postsecondary

On-the-job training—i.e., assisting an established professional—is the most common way for aspiring private detectives to gain skills and knowledge; however, job requirements vary by investigative specialty and may include the need for an undergraduate or advanced degree. For example, an investigator who specializes in computer crime may be required to have a bachelor's degree in computer science, while an insurance fraud investigator might need some courses in finance or business along with experience in the insurance industry. An associate's or bachelor's degree in criminal science is sometimes necessary. Degrees in related subjects, such as political science, communications, psychology, or forensic science, can also be useful. Individual courses in detective work and related subjects can help an applicant secure a job or learn new skills.

Related College Majors
- Corrections/Correctional Administration
- Criminal Justice/Criminology
- Forensic Technology
- Law Enforcement/Police Science
- Security & Loss Prevention Services

Adult Job Seekers

Adults often turn to private investigating after pursuing other careers as bodyguards, paralegals, and police officers. Almost any background can be put to good use, especially when a detective needs to go undercover. Some distance learning programs are available for adult job seekers. Drawbacks for those with family obligations include the long or odd hours and the potential danger associated with some types of detective work.

Adult job seekers may benefit from joining professional private investigation associations, including the Council of International Investigators (CII), World Association of Detectives (WAD), and ASIS International as a means of professional networking.

Advancement among private detectives depends on the size of the company and the type of investigating. An experienced detective can establish his or her own investigative firm or move into corporate positions with more sophisticated assignments and higher salaries.

Professional Certification and Licensure

Most states require a license for private detectives, a weapons permit, and a special business license for investigative firms. The private investigator (PI) license may involve a test and minimum education and experience requirements or both. Interested individuals should check the requirements of their home state.

Certification is offered through professional organizations, such as ASIS International, and may be required for some positions. ASIS International provides the Certified Protection Professional (CPP), Professional Certified Investigator (PCI), and Physical Security Professional (PSP) designations. Each has different experience and education requirements. Consult credible professional associations within the field and follow professional debate as to the relevancy and value of any certification program.

Additional Requirements

Most positions require the applicant to pass a background check, possess a driver's license, and be familiar with federal, state, and local laws pertaining to the type of investigating the company offers.

EARNINGS AND ADVANCEMENT

Earnings of private detectives depend on their employer, specialty and the geographic location in which they work.

Mean annual earnings of private detectives were $50,780 in 2012. The lowest ten percent earned less than $27,670, and the highest ten percent earned more than $79,790.

Most corporate private detectives receive paid vacations, holidays, and sick days; life and health insurance; and retirement benefits. These are usually paid by the employer.

Metropolitan Areas with the Highest Employment Level in this Occupation

Metropolitan area	Employment[1]	Employment per thousand jobs	Hourly mean wage
Washington-Arlington-Alexandria, DC-VA-MD-WV	1,080	0.46	$23.80
Philadelphia, PA	950	0.52	$23.39
Los Angeles-Long Beach-Glendale, CA	800	0.21	$30.44
Chicago-Joliet-Naperville, IL	690	0.19	$20.97
Dallas-Plano-Irving, TX	690	0.33	$30.73
Baltimore-Towson, MD	450	0.36	$24.67
Atlanta-Sandy Springs-Marietta, GA	440	0.19	$21.59
Pittsburgh, PA	390	0.35	$23.30

[1]Does not include self-employed. Source: Bureau of Labor Statistics

EMPLOYMENT AND OUTLOOK

Private detectives held about 35,000 jobs in 2012. About one-fourth were self-employed. Employment is expected to grow about as fast as the average for all occupations through the year 2022, which means employment is projected to increase 8 percent to 15 percent. Increased demand for private detectives will result from increased security concerns, an increase in cyber crimes and the need to protect confidential information and property of all kinds.

Employment Trend, Projected 2012–22

Total, All Occupations: 11%

Private Detectives and Investigators: 11%

Protective Service Occupations: 8%

Note: "All Occupations" includes all occupations in the U.S. Economy. Source: U.S. Bureau of Labor Statistics, Employment Projections Program

Related Occupations
- Federal Law Enforcement Agent
- Police Officer & Detective
- Security and Fire Alarm System Installer
- Security Guard

Conversation With . . .
Pamela Beason
Private Investigator, 6 years

1. What was your individual career path in terms of education/training, entry-level job, or other significant opportunity?

Before becoming a professional investigator, I worked as a technical writer/editor, mechanical/architectural drafter, college instructor and geological research technologist. I got two college degrees before completing a certification program in Investigation from the University of Washington, and then studying for the state exam for individual investigator. A few years later I met my business partner, Molly Monahan, and we both studied for the state agency exam and, after qualifying, set up our partnership at Sirius Investigations.

I also attended the Redmond Citizens Police and Fire Academy to learn the language and methodology employed by first responders, and I continue to attend educational seminars in specialized legal matters. My interests are pre-trial investigations and product liability issues.

2. What are the most important skills and/or qualities for someone in your profession?

There are very few employee jobs for investigators; most of us are independent contractors, so the ability to run your own business is paramount. As for the investigation work itself, you need to be able to think analytically without preconceived notions. You must be able to systematically sort through reams of data to find the important bits. You have to be able to communicate clearly in person and in writing; organize your time efficiently; and persuade all kinds of people to give you information. And every private investigator (PI) must have discretion, of course. It's our legal obligation to keep our clients' secrets.

3. What do you wish you had known going into this profession?

I wish I had known that most jobs would be only a few hours long, thus necessitating a lot of unpaid hours speaking to potential clients, as well as creating a major paperwork and bookkeeping hassle.

4. Are there many job opportunities in your profession? In what specific areas?

There are many more opportunities in large urban areas than in towns with smaller populations. Generally speaking, no matter where you live, you must set up and run your own business, because there are very few investigation agencies with employees. In some cities, public defender offices rely on private investigators for defense investigations, so that can be a big source of jobs, although they are usually not the best-paying contracts. There is always a need for surveillance—usually these jobs are to investigate insurance fraud (such as faking a disability) and document child custody issues (proving who is actually caring for the child and who is living in the home). Another fast-growing segment of investigative work involves computer analysis—recovering data from hard drives, tracking emails, and so forth. If you live in a large urban area, you can probably specialize. If you live in a smaller town such as Molly and I do, you have to handle all sorts of cases to make a living.

5. How do you see your profession changing in the next five years? What role will technology play in those changes, and what skills will be required?

I don't think the profession will change too much—there will always be a need for investigators to interview people, gather evidence, and file reports or testify in court. We already have to continually learn to use all sorts of new databases and interfaces to get information and we must adapt to all sorts of technology—computers, cameras, recorders, smart phones, etc. This need to constantly learn on the job will continue.

6. What do you enjoy most about your job? What do you enjoy least?

Because I'm a writer, too, I most enjoy interviewing witnesses and participants for upcoming court cases. I don't like surveillance work; it's very tedious, and my business partner (and almost every investigator I know) agrees with that. What Molly enjoys most is the joy of locating a "lost" loved one for a client, and the gratitude of clients when we get the results they want.

7. Can you suggest a valuable "try this" for students considering a career in your profession?

To test your interview skills, I'd suggest you interview someone and take notes (PIs often are not allowed to use recording devices), then write up that interview and share it with the interviewee to see how well you do. To test surveillance skills, spy on someone you know (warn them that you might do this so you won't scare them if they see you, but don't tell them when) and take time-stamped photos or video, then transform that into a package you could hand or email to a client.

I get asked so often what it's like to be an investigator that I wrote a little ebook to explain the job and the skills. It's called "So You Want to Be a PI?" by Pamela Beason.

SELECTED SCHOOLS

Programs in criminal justice, police science, security and related fields are available in many colleges and universities. The student may also gain solid training at a community college—and in many cases obtaining an associate's degree or completing some college is all that is needed to become a private investigator. For those seeking to work in specialized areas (e.g., computers, finance) a bachelor's degree is often necessary. Interested students are advised to consult with their school guidance counselor.

MORE INFORMATION

ASIS International
1625 Prince Street
Alexandria, VA 22314-2818
703.519.6200
www.asisonline.org

Council of International Investigators
2150 N. 107th Street, Suite 205
Seattle, WA 98133-9009
888.759.8884
www.cii2.org

World Association of Detectives
7501 Sparrows Point Boulevard
Baltimore, MD 21219
443.982.4586
www.wad.net

Sally Driscoll/Editor

Fun Facts

In the 1860s, the Pinkerton National Detective Agency had more agents than the US Army had soldiers. Its logo–an eye with the words "We Never Sleep"–is sometimes cited as the origin of the term "Private Eye," but most dictionaries say the term is a phonetic rendering of Private I., the abbreviation for "investigator."

Security & Fire Alarm System Installer

Snapshot

Career Cluster: Public Safety & Security

Interests: Electronics, technology, commercial wiring, safety and security systems

Earnings (Yearly Average): $43,210

Employment & Outlook: Average Growth Expected

OVERVIEW

Sphere of Work

Security and fire alarm system installers build and test residential, commercial, and industrial alarm systems. They also design systems using custom specifications to provide the adequate amount of security for a particular property or space. Security and fire alarm system installers traditionally possess both strong mathematical and technical aptitudes and familiarity with the latest alarm systems technology and software. They typically learn the skills of

their trade through specialized education and extensive on-the-job training.

Work Environment

Security and fire alarm system installers work in and around commercial, residential, and industrial complexes, installing alarm systems in both new buildings and established structures that need new or updated alarm equipment. Alarm installation requires both indoor and outdoor work and may entail climbing into small spaces and onto high places, such as roofs and protective fencing. Security and fire alarm system installers customarily work forty-hour weeks and have weekends off.

Profile

Working Conditions: Work both Indoors and Outdoors
Physical Strength: Light to Medium Work
Education Needs: On-The-Job Training, High School Diploma with Technical Education
Licensure/Certification: Required
Physical Abilities Not Required: No Heavy Labor
Opportunities For Experience: Apprenticeship, Part-Time Work
Holland Interest Score*: N/A

* See Appendix A

Occupation Interest

The field of alarm installation attracts professionals from a variety of different backgrounds. Many alarm professionals are skilled analytical problem solvers who may aspire to future careers as firefighters, police officers, or emergency medical personnel. Others are tech-savvy individuals who enjoy employing their knowledge of technology to the benefit and safety of others.

A Day in the Life—Duties and Responsibilities

Security and fire alarm system installers spend the workday consulting with customers in order to design, build, and install security systems that are best suited to their particular needs. The consulting and design phase of security and fire alarm installation involves one-on-one meetings with clients as well as research into the buildings involved, the clients' security history, and the criminal statistics surrounding their neighborhoods and regions. When designing or installing alarm systems, security and fire alarm system installers must take into account various aspects of the buildings in question, including the number of windows and doors, potential fire exits and prevalence of safes, and potentially hazardous materials or waste within the structures. Certain aspects of buildings require more security apparatuses than others.

Once installation of an alarm system is underway, security or fire alarm system installers must carry out a series of tests to ensure that the newly installed apparatus is functioning properly. During this testing phase, they may instruct property owners in how to operate, manipulate, and shut down the alarm system. State and local laws may require police or fire department officials to conduct final testing on equipment once installation is complete. After installation, security or fire alarm system installers may return to client locations to answer questions about alarm systems or troubleshoot potential problems.

Duties and Responsibilities

- Designing, building, and testing security and fire alarm systems
- Inspecting residential and commercial buildings to develop specifications
- Consulting with customers to determine their needs and preferences
- Ordering parts and equipment from a supplier
- Checking state building codes to ensure system compliance
- Making necessary system repairs and improvements as requested by customers

WORK ENVIRONMENT

Physical Environment

Security and fire alarm system installers work in residences, businesses, and industrial buildings as well as the surrounding areas. In addition to installing alarms in buildings under construction and those undergoing renovations, they may integrate systems into preexisting structures with antiquated or nonexistent alarm infrastructure. Installation of remote security systems may require work on outlying properties and structures.

Relevant Skills and Abilities

Communication Skills
- Speaking effectively

Interpersonal/Social Skills
- Being able to work independently
- Cooperating with others
- Working as a member of a team

Research & Planning Skills
- Solving problems
- Laying out a plan

Other Skills
- Working with your hands

Human Environment

Security and fire alarm system installers interact frequently with clients, supervisors, and fellow workers. As they must be able to explain complex systems to clients and instruct them in their proper use, strong communication, listening, and collaboration skills are essential.

Technological Environment

Security and fire alarm system installers use a bevy of technological devices and equipment, including cameras and imaging technology, sensors, and smoke and motion detectors. Sound knowledge of relevant machinery, electronics, and wiring is required. A complete electrician's toolbox is standard.

EDUCATION, TRAINING, AND ADVANCEMENT

High School/Secondary

High school students can prepare for careers in security and fire alarm system installation with courses in algebra, geometry, chemistry, physics, and computer science. Drafting and art classes can also teach skills relevant to future employment in systems design. Interpersonal communication and problem-solving skills are vital to success in the field, so English and writing courses are also beneficial.

Suggested High School Subjects
- Applied Math
- Composition
- Computers
- Electrical Shop
- English

- Government
- Social Studies

Famous First

The first fire alarm system operated by electricity was patented in 1857 by William F. Channing of Boston and Moses G. Farmer of Salem, Mass. The patent was for "a magnetic electric fire-alarm." A person witnessing a fire could run to an alarm box, trip the switch, and sound the alarm bell. The first city to adopt the system was Boston, which paid $10,000 for it (a very large sum at the time).Moses Farmer went on to develop a number of other notable electrical inventions, including an early lightbulb that was bought by Thomas Edison.

Library of Congress

Postsecondary

Postsecondary education is not traditionally a requirement for positions in the security and fire alarm system installation industry, and many professionals learn the trade through apprenticeships and on-the-job training. However, some employers may prefer candidates with some relevant postsecondary education. Certificate programs in security and fire alarm system installation are available nationwide. Such programs teach students the main functions and electronics involved in security system apparatuses and also cover the basics of system planning, commercial wiring, and sprinkler systems.

Individuals seeking supervisory, managerial, or ownership roles in the industry will benefit from collegiate-level work in entrepreneurship, computer science, business management, or a combination of the three. Knowledge of security systems is essential, and individuals must also be well versed in the parameters of business and employee management.

Related College Majors
- Commercial Wiring
- Electrical Equipment
- Security & Loss Prevention Services

Adult Job Seekers

Security and fire alarm system installation is a popular field for entry-level workers and transitioning professionals, largely because of the minimal amount of academic training required to enter the field and the extent of on-the-job training. Adult job seekers may benefit from enrolling in relevant certificate programs or pursuing hands-on training.

Professional Certification and Licensure

Certification and licensing requirements vary according to state and district regulations. To maintain certification, security and fire alarm system installers must often demonstrate their knowledge of the field's key concepts through annual tests.

Additional Requirements

Aspiring security and fire alarm system installers must be passionate about technology and able to learn new systems quickly. The extensive interaction with customers inherent to the position requires sound explanatory skills, patience, and amicability in interpersonal exchanges.

EARNINGS AND ADVANCEMENT

Earnings depend on the employee's training and experience. Experienced security and fire alarm system installers are often promoted to management positions, with an increase in salary, or may start their own firms.

Mean annual earnings of security and fire alarm system installers were around $43,210 in 2012. The lowest ten percent earned less than $26,370, and the highest ten percent earned more than $63,720. Many installers work on a project-by-project basis and are paid an hourly rate.

Security and fire alarm system installers may receive paid vacations, holidays, and sick days; life and health insurance; and retirement benefits. These are usually paid by the employer.

Metropolitan Areas with the Highest Employment Level in this Occupation

Metropolitan area	Employment[1]	Employment per thousand jobs	Hourly mean wage
New York-White Plains-Wayne, NY-NJ	2,020	0.39	$26.22
Los Angeles-Long Beach-Glendale, CA	1,850	0.48	$22.26
Washington-Arlington-Alexandria, DC-VA-MD-WV	1,700	0.72	$23.35
Philadelphia, PA	1,320	0.73	$25.73
Santa Ana-Anaheim-Irvine, CA	1,190	0.85	$23.28
Chicago-Joliet-Naperville, IL	1,110	0.30	$24.03
Tampa-St. Petersburg-Clearwater, FL	950	0.84	$19.52
Atlanta-Sandy Springs-Marietta, GA	820	0.36	$19.32

[1]Does not include self-employed. Source: Bureau of Labor Statistics

EMPLOYMENT AND OUTLOOK

Security and fire alarm system installers held about 65,000 jobs nationally in 2012. Employment is expected to grow about as fast as the average for all occupations through the year 2022, which means employment is projected to increase between 5 percent and 15 percent. Ongoing demand for these workers is expected to be generated by fear of crime, an increase in the use and cost of business equipment and computer technology and the need to protect confidential information and property of all kinds. Employment opportunities are best in large urban settings where large companies are located.

Employment Trend, Projected 2012–22

Electricians: 16%

Total, All Occupations: 11%

Electrical Equipment Installers: 5%

Note: "All Occupations" includes all occupations in the U.S. Economy. Source: U.S. Bureau of Labor Statistics, Employment Projections Program

Related Occupations
- Electrician
- Inspector & Compliance Officer

Conversation With . . .
Sam Splaine
Security and Fire Alarm Installer, 18 years

1. What was your individual career path in terms of education/training, entry-level job, or other significant opportunity?

The criminal justice/law enforcement program I was enrolled in at Montgomery College in Rockville, Md., included industrial and retail security. I had to do a paper on retail security so I went to Woodward and Lothrop, a department store, with a list of questions and interviewed a gentleman in their security department. By the time I got through, he had offered me a job. I finished my two-year degree and worked for the store as a store detective for about three years, then went to another store as security manager. Eventually, I wanted to move into something else. Dictograph Security was an electronic security and fire alarm company selling camera systems, access control, fire alarms, and security alarms. I was in their sales department for awhile and enjoyed it, but I had a tendency to hang out with the installers. I needed to know exactly how they used these products. I wasn't a salesman; I was a criminal justice major. I'd go in and educate customers on why they wanted a horn, a siren, a strobe light. I left Dictograph to open my own business in 1994.

2. What are the most important skills and/or qualities for someone in your profession?

You need to be able to communicate and present a professional appearance. When you meet with a homeowner or businessman, you have to focus on what his or her concerns are. For example, if a business owner says he wants a security system but his problems are in the parking lot, he doesn't need a burglar alarm. He needs lighting, a fence… something to control the parking area. So you need to know what product solves the problem. You have to be knowledgeable about what's on the market and keep up with new products.

3. What do you wish you had known going into this profession?

If you want to make money, you need to have an understanding of business. I've learned by trial and error, but it probably cost me money. For example, on really large jobs you have to estimate labor properly. As my company got bigger, I had to learn to delegate. We now have someone who handles bookkeeping and scheduling; I still try to keep track of ordering and inventory.

4. Are there many job opportunities in your profession? In what specific areas?

Cameras are really big. Their use has quadrupled in the last 10 years. You've also got access control–today you can go to the door, present a fob, and get into a business. This is not so much about burglaries but access to buildings. Then there are fire alarms, which is almost a field within itself. There are opportunities in the field with sales, installation, and central station opportunities, which is a bit like working for a police department as a dispatcher.

5. How do you see your profession changing in the next five years? What role will technology play in those changes, and what skills will be required?

For many years, you'd turn a system off and on with a keypad. Now it's off and on with a smartphone or tablet or laptop. There's also a focus on how much information you can get out of your system. If you have a child who comes home from school at 3 o'clock every day, you get an email when he comes through the front door. You can even get a photo to see if he's with friends, or followed by a stranger. This will continue to grow, as will the camera industry. I think that's going to be one of the biggest parts of the business.

6. What do you enjoy most about your job? What do you enjoy least?

I enjoy solving problems for people, I enjoy the independence of having my own business and watching it grow. There's a sense of accomplishment. The downside has been that it's a 24-hour business. I've gotten used to it, and my family has gotten used to it.

7. Can you suggest a valuable "try this" for students considering a career in your profession?

Instead of applying for a job, set up a list of questions and ask for an informational interview. Find out about their business. If you can go to college, take courses in fire science, criminal justice, physical security, electronic security, and industrial security. We do a lot of embassies in DC and they've got to have gates. How do you secure larger facilities? Talk to different business owners. And work on your communications skills.

SELECTED SCHOOLS

Training beyond high school is not necessarily expected of beginning security and fire alarm system installers . What matters more is some basic vocational instruction (e.g., electrical shop) at the high school level and on-the-job training. However, enrolling in a commercial vocational school or taking classes at a technical community college will put a candidate in a good position to advance. Interested students should consult with their school guidance counselor.

MORE INFORMATION

Electronic Security Association
6333 North State Highway 161
Suite 350
Irving, TX 75038
888.447.1689
www.esaweb.org

National Electrical Contractors Association
3 Bethesda Metro Center, Suite 1100
Bethesda, MD 20814
301.657.3110
www.neca.org

John Pritchard/Editor

Security Guard

Snapshot

Career Cluster: Law & Criminal Justice; Public Safety & Security

Interests: Public safety, safeguarding property, surveillance, patrolling, investigation, law

Earnings (Yearly Average): $27,240

Employment & Outlook: Average Growth Expected

OVERVIEW

Sphere of Work

Security guards protect property and people from a variety of threats, including theft, vandalism, assault, and other illegal activities. They supervise and control who enters company facilities and ensure the safety of individuals within the facility and grounds. They maintain surveillance of private or public property to prevent theft, especially at night. Security guards are responsible for communicating with emergency services, such as police or fire departments, as needed. Depending on their specific job duties, some may become licensed to carry firearms or other weapons.

Work Environment

Security guards work for private employers, government agencies, or security guard agencies. Some work primarily indoors, while others work outdoors in varying weather. Most security guards either maintain a stationary position, where they monitor one location directly or via closed-circuit television (CCTV), or conduct mobile patrols throughout their designated area during a shift. They spend long hours on their feet. Most security guards work forty to forty-eight hours per week, depending on whether they work for a security company or a company in another industry. Guards at security firms may work as many as sixty hours a week. Though a security guard's job may be tedious or routine at times, it can also be dangerous.

Profile

Working Conditions: Work both Indoors and Outdoors
Physical Strength: Light Work
Education Needs: On-The-Job Training, High School Diploma Or GED
Licensure/Certification: Required
Physical Abilities Not Required: No Heavy Labor
Opportunities For Experience: Apprenticeship, Military Service, Part-Time Work
Holland Interest Score*: ESR, SEC

* See Appendix A

Occupation Interest

People interested in pursuing a career as a security guard should possess a desire to safeguard property and people. They should respond to potential threats according to the training they have received. Prospective security guards should be physically fit and maintain a healthy lifestyle, as part of the success of the job depends on physical speed, dexterity, coordination, and strength. They should demonstrate good judgment and be able to make quick decisions, sometimes based on very little information. Being able to quickly assess possible threats and unusual situations, alert others to what they have observed, and safely investigate to gather more information are other desirable traits in this profession.

A Day in the Life—Duties and Responsibilities

Security guards are responsible for protecting private or public property, as well as ensuring the safety of people on those properties. They perform a wide range of duties to that end. Security guards are employed in many industries, and may work in such varied positions as gate tenders, merchant patrollers, or store detectives.

They keep track of visitors and employees who enter and exit the premises. They observe and record daily activities, especially any unusual occurrences, and submit those observations to their employers. Security guards are also responsible for making contact with law enforcement officials in the case of emergencies, such as fires, burglaries, medical emergencies, vandalism, terrorist attacks, and other incidents. They thoroughly investigate all areas of the property they oversee and attend to any disturbances or irregularities they encounter. They protect others from harm partly through their constant presence, which tends to discourage and prevent potential crime.

Security guards ensure that all entrances and exits of a structure, including windows, gates, and doors, are closed and properly secured. Occasionally, they may escort vehicles to specific destinations or provide individuals with personal protection. Some security guards operate detection equipment to screen people for weapons or other prohibited items. They may monitor alarms and electronic security systems.

Security guards must sometimes escort or bodily remove unauthorized personnel from the premises and explain security measures and rules to visitors and employees. They may also inspect incoming mail and packages for suspicious contents. Some security guards monitor and direct parking and traffic. Some are required to collect and verify the authenticity of various forms of identification from visitors or patrons, as well as conduct financial transactions.

Security Guards

Duties and Responsibilities

- Patrolling buildings and grounds at specific times
- Checking doors, windows, gates, locks, and lights
- Checking for proper identification at entrances
- Directing visitors and giving routine information
- Adjusting controls to maintain desired building temperatures or conditions
- Watching for and reporting fire hazards and property damage
- Monitoring video and other electronic security systems

OCCUPATION SPECIALTIES

Security Guards

Security Guards, also called Security Officers, protect property, enforce rules on the property, and deter criminal activity. Some guards are assigned a stationary position from which they monitor alarms or surveillance cameras. Other guards are assigned a patrol area where they conduct security checks.

Gaming Surveillance Officers

Gaming Surveillance Officers act as security agents for casinos. Using audio and video equipment in an observation room, they watch casino operations for suspicious activities, such as cheating and theft, and monitor compliance with rules, regulations, and laws. They maintain and organize recordings from security cameras, which are sometimes used as evidence in police investigations.

Armored Car Guards

Armored Car Guards protect money and valuables during transit. They pick up money and other valuables from businesses and transport them to another location. These guards usually wear bulletproof vests and carry firearms, because transporting money between the truck and the business is potentially dangerous.

Transportation Security Screeners

Transportation Security Screeners conduct screening of passengers, baggage, or cargo to ensure compliance with Transportation Security Administration (TSA) regulations. They may operate basic security equipment such as x-ray machines and hand wands (metal detectors) at screening checkpoints.

Bodyguards

Bodyguards ensure the safety of individual persons—for example, a political figure—or small groups in public spaces and elsewhere. They often are licensed to carry handguns and may also be trained in martial arts.

WORK ENVIRONMENT

Physical Environment

The immediate physical environment of security guards will vary based on the size and type of employer. Some security guards work indoors; others work outdoors in all kinds of weather. Some are stationed at small guard desks inside large buildings, while others work in outdoor guardhouses. Others patrol small stores, large shopping centers, nightclubs and bars (where they are called "bouncers"), museums, movie theaters, banks, hospitals, and office buildings. Some security guards work in airports or at rail terminals, while others are employed by universities, public parks, casinos, or sports stadiums.

Relevant Skills and Abilities

Interpersonal/Social Skills
- Being able to remain calm
- Cooperating with others
- Working as a member of a team

Organization & Management Skills
- Following instructions
- Handling challenging situations
- Meeting goals and deadlines
- Performing routine work
- Working quickly when necessary

Other Skills
- Staying alert

Human Environment

Security guards who work during the day usually interact often with members of the public as well as the staff of the property that they protect. Those who work at night often work alone and do not come into contact with many people. Many security guards also interact with law enforcement personnel, including police officers, firefighters, detectives, and other security officers as needed.

Technological Environment

Security guards may operate patrol cars, golf carts, automobiles, or other vehicles in the course of their work. They often carry cell phones, flashlights, two-way radios, and handcuffs, as well as a personal defense product such as pepper spray, Mace, or a Taser. Some security guards are licensed to carry handguns. Security guards also process documents, which may include witness reports, theft reports, and observation reports. They may use spreadsheet software, the Internet and email, and word processing software.

EDUCATION, TRAINING, AND ADVANCEMENT

High School/Secondary

High school students who are interested in becoming security guards can prepare themselves by taking courses in English, physical education, geography, sociology, and psychology. They should also participate in and maintain ongoing first aid training and certification. Outside of school, students can enroll in extracurricular self-defense courses or one-on-one physical training courses that allow them to understand the foundations of different self-defense techniques. Students can also tour local factories, office buildings, or shopping centers to learn more about the primary duties of a security guard.

Suggested High School Subjects
- English
- First Aid Training
- Physical Education
- Social Studies

Famous First

The first armored car robbery was staged in 1927 by the Flathead gang, a few miles outside of Pittsburgh, Penn. An armored vehicle carrying a $104,250 payroll of the Pittsburgh Terminal Coal Company blew up when it drove over a landmine planted under the roadbed by the bandits. Five guards were badly injured. The gang leader, Paul Jaworski, was later executed for a second payroll robbery that resulted in a murder.

Postsecondary

It is not necessary for security guards to obtain an undergraduate degree; many employers hire security guards who have earned a high school diploma or its equivalent. Other employers, however, may prefer to hire security guards who have some kind of postsecondary training in criminal justice or a related field. Since employer preferences vary widely, it is advisable to check the required education level and experience qualifications before applying for a job.

Employers usually require on-the-job training for newly hired security guards. Depending on a security guard's assignment, he or she may be trained in first aid, emergency procedures, interacting with potentially dangerous individuals, communications skills, and report writing. Security guards who carry weapons receive specific training in the use of force, practical applications of firearms, and weapons retention. The American Society for Industrial Security International provides employers with standard guidelines for the training of security guards, which include suggestions for a written examination covering emergency response techniques, crime prevention, legal issues, and other topics.

Related College Majors
- Corrections/Correctional Administration
- Security & Loss Prevention Services

Adult Job Seekers

Prospective security guards can enter the field by accepting part-time or summer work at local resorts, golf courses, amusement parks, or other seasonal employment venues. They may be able to participate in a job shadowing experience with a local security guard. Other prospective security guards may apply for positions through an employment agency, which then finds them appropriate work.

Professional Certification and Licensure

Security guards are usually required to be licensed by the state in which they seek employment. Licensing requirements vary by state but commonly include a background check, drug test, and practical training in such topics as emergency procedures, property rights, and criminal apprehension. Security guards must also be at least eighteen years of age and possess a valid driver's license. Armed security guards are legally required to obtain special certification in order to carry weapons.

Additional Requirements

Security guards must be able to pass an extensive screening process, including criminal background checks, drug tests, character references, and the demonstration of good physical health. They should possess a clean driving record and have no criminal or police record. Because security guards often work long shifts at night and frequently observe the same area, employers expect guards to be able to stay alert for the duration of a work shift, remain calm enough to follow proper procedures when incidents arise, and react swiftly in emergencies.

EARNINGS AND ADVANCEMENT

Earnings depend on the geographic location of the employer and the individual's level of experience. Mean annual earnings of security guards were $27,240 in 2012. The lowest ten percent earned less than $17,390, and the highest ten percent earned more than $42,490.

Security guards may receive paid vacations, holidays, and sick days; life and health insurance; and retirement benefits. These are usually paid by the employer.

Metropolitan Areas with the Highest Employment Level in this Occupation

Metropolitan area	Employment	Employment per thousand jobs	Hourly mean wage
New York-White Plains-Wayne, NY-NJ	78,120	15.15	$14.29
Los Angeles-Long Beach-Glendale, CA	51,950	13.42	$12.61
Chicago-Joliet-Naperville, IL	42,070	11.56	$12.13
Washington-Arlington-Alexandria, DC-VA-MD-WV	33,480	14.28	$17.89
Houston-Sugar Land-Baytown, TX	23,680	8.97	$11.06
Atlanta-Sandy Springs-Marietta, GA	20,590	9.10	$11.60
Dallas-Plano-Irving, TX	19,790	9.44	$12.68
Miami-Miami Beach-Kendall, FL	19,080	19.10	$11.29

Source: Bureau of Labor Statistics

EMPLOYMENT AND OUTLOOK

Security guards held over one million jobs nationally in 2012. Employment is expected to grow about as fast as the average for all occupations through the year 2022, which means employment is projected to increase 8 percent to 15 percent. Increased concern about crime, vandalism and terrorism will heighten the need for security in and around stores, offices, schools, hospitals and other areas. Many opportunities are expected for persons seeking full-time employment, as well as for those seeking part-time or second jobs at night or on weekends.

Employment Trend, Projected 2012–22

Security Guards: 12%

Total, All Occupations: 11%

Gaming Surveillance Officers: 7%

Note: "All Occupations" includes all occupations in the U.S. Economy. Source: U.S. Bureau of Labor Statistics, Employment Projections Program

Related Occupations
- Correctional Officer
- Police Officer
- Private Detective

Related Military Occupations
- Law Enforcement & Security Specialist
- Military Police

Conversation With . . .
Colin Vick, CPP
Security Officer, 14 years

1. What was your individual career path in terms of education/training, entry-level job, or other significant opportunity?

At one time I thought about becoming a law enforcement officer but police are often reactive. I wanted to be part of the solution that prevented incidents from occurring in the first place.

Initially I didn't have any formalized training and was hired on as a security officer, an entry-level position that allowed me to see the different types of security -- from mobile patrol service to providing security for retail stores, shopping malls, hotels, commercial buildings, and even some armed security jobs. That job really opened my eyes. I was in college so I left for awhile, but missed the operational aspects of security.

I started at Per Mar Security Services in November 2002, again as an entry-level security officer, and worked my way up. In that time, a greater emphasis has been placed on both security and emergency management due to a combination of heightened awareness since September 11, 2001 and the upgrades in technology we've seen. You almost need a background in electronics to know the inner workings of some of the technology. Many colleges and universities have added courses and offer degree programs in these fields since I started.

Different security organizations have certifications that enhance your credentials and your expertise. I took and passed a certification exam from ASIS International, a worldwide organization, to become a Certified Protection Professional in 2011. The certification is held in high esteem and, although the exam can be intimidating and exhausting, it is worth the effort.

2. What are the most important skills and/or qualities for someone in your profession?

I agree with the four values that guide our company: communication, so you have a solid foundation that is supported by a desire to communicate your expectations, your needs, your goals, or even simply what you witnessed; integrity, so your actions are guided by a set of moral or ethical principles; accountability, because you must answer for what you do and say, and, finally, excellent service.

3. What do you wish you had known going into this profession?

I wish I'd had a better understanding of what it means to have an integrated protection program. In addition to a security guard, such a program includes access control (entry devices, card readers, computer and verification systems); display and assessment (CCTV, workstations, fixed security posts and patrols); barriers (fences, gates, lighting, locking devices or clear zones), communications (radios, telephone equipment, intercoms, and data networks), identification (photos, fingerprints, signatures, ID cards, and vehicle decals), intrusion detection (exterior sensors, interior sensors, and duress sensors), and operations procedures, such as standards, training, policies, and crisis management.

4. Are there many job opportunities in your profession? In what specific areas?

Many, including supervisory and management positions. I work for a contract security company. We are hired to provide companies with contracted security officers. Some companies have their own proprietary security program and hire their own officers. The breakdown throughout the United States is close to 50% contract and 50% proprietary.

5. How do you see your profession changing in the next five years? What role will technology play in those changes, and what skills will be required?

Technology will play a huge role. The automation and biometrics fields have grown by leaps and bounds and this trend will continue. Leveraging greater security technological needs with security officers who can successfully navigate these systems will become a greater need. Many companies will have dedicated security operations centers -- a nerve center -- and security officers will need to know how to run access control systems, closed circuit television systems, building automation systems, central alarm monitoring, and communication systems, all from one console.

6. What do you enjoy most about your job? What do you enjoy least?

I enjoy doing physical security surveys for clients, which is an overview of vulnerability at a given facility or site. It allows me to take an objective look at an overall security program. This is often a puzzle that combines a mix of science and art to give the facility an upgraded security program that fits both their needs and their budget.

The thing I like least is dealing with people who don't take security seriously. While I believe this is rare, sometimes people work within this industry and just see it as a job.

7. **Can you suggest a valuable "try this" for students considering a career in your profession?**

Contact a security company and see if you can interview one of the managers about their day-to-day responsibilities. If that looks like something you might be interested in doing, perhaps an internship or a part-time job with the company might be an option. Also, many security organizations or magazines offer or sponsor free online webinars about various topics that are relevant within the security realm.

SELECTED SCHOOLS

Training beyond high school is not expected of security guards. However, taking classes in security operations at a vocational school or technical community college will put a candidate in good stead with an employer. Interested students should consult with their school guidance counselor.

MORE INFORMATION

American Society for Industrial Security International
1625 Prince Street
Alexandria, VA 22314-2818
703.519.6200
www.asisonline.org

International Union, Security, Police and Fire Professionals of America
25510 Kelly Road
Roseville, MI 48066
800.228.7492
www.spfpa.org

Service Employees International Union
1800 Massachusetts Avenue, NW
Washington, DC 20036
800.424.8592
www.seiu.org

United Government Security Officers of America
8670 Wolff Court, Suite 210
Westminster, CO 80031
800.572.6103
www.ugsoa.com

Briana Nadeau/Editor

What Are Your Career Interests?

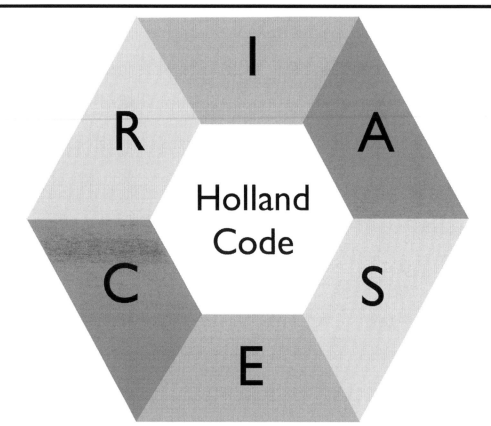

This is based on Dr. John Holland's theory that people and work environments can be loosely classified into six different groups. Each of the letters above corresponds to one of the six groups described in the following pages.

Different people's personalities may find different environments more to their liking. While you may have some interests in and similarities to several of the six groups, you may be attracted primarily to two or three of the areas. These two or three letters are your "Holland Code." For example, with a code of "RES" you would most resemble the Realistic type, somewhat less resemble the Enterprising type, and resemble the Social type even less. The types that are not in your code are the types you resemble least of all.

Most people, and most jobs, are best represented by some combination of two or three of the Holland interest areas. In addition, most people are most satisfied if there is some degree of fit between their personality and their work environment.

The rest of the pages in this booklet further explain each type and provide some examples of career possibilities, areas of study at MU, and co-curricular activities for each code. To take a more in-depth look at your Holland Code, take a self-assessment such as the SDS, Discover, or a card sort at the MU Career Center with a Career Specialist.

This hexagonal model of RIASEC occupations is the copyrighted work of Dr. John Holland, and is used with his permission. The Holland Game is adapted from Richard Bolles' "Quick Job Hunting Map." Copyright 1995, 1998 by the MU Career Center, University of Missouri-Columbia.

Realistic *(Doers)*

People who have athletic ability, prefer to work with objects, machines, tools, plants or animals, or to be outdoors.

Are you?		**Can you?**	**Like to?**
practical	independent	fix electrical things	tinker with machines/vehicles
straightforward/frank	ambitious	solve electrical problems	work outdoors
mechanically inclined	systematic	pitch a tent	be physically active
stable		play a sport	use your hands
concrete		read a blueprint	build things
reserved		plant a garden	tend/train animals
self-controlled		operate tools and machine	work on electronic equipment

Career Possibilities
(Holland Code):

Air Traffic Controller (SER)	Dental Technician (REI)	Laboratory Technician (RIE)	Property Manager (ESR)
Archaeologist (IRE)	Farm Manager (ESR)	Landscape Architect (AIR)	Recreation Manager (SER)
Athletic Trainer (SRE)	Fish and Game Warden (RES)	Mechanical Engineer (RIS)	Service Manager (ERS)
Cartographer (IRE)	Floral Designer (RAE)	Optician (REI)	Software Technician (RCI)
Commercial Airline Pilot (RIE)	Forester (RIS)	Petroleum Geologist (RIE)	Ultrasound Technologist (RSI)
Commercial Drafter (IRE)	Geodetic Surveyor (IRE)	Police Officer (SER)	Vocational Rehabilitation
Corrections Officer (SER)	Industrial Arts Teacher (IER)	Practical Nurse (SER)	Consultant (ESR)

Investigative *(Thinkers)*

People who like to observe, learn, investigate, analyze, evaluate, or solve problems.

Are you?		**Can you?**	**Like to?**
inquisitive	intellectually self-confident	think abstractly	explore a variety of ideas
analytical	Independent	solve math problems	work independently
scientific	logical	understand scientific theories	perform lab experiments
observant/precise	complex	do complex calculations	deal with abstractions
scholarly	Curious	use a microscope or computer	do research
cautious		interpret formulas	be challenged

Career Possibilities
(Holland Code):

Actuary (ISE)	Chemical Engineer (IRE)	Geologist (IRE)	Physician, General Practice (ISE)
Agronomist (IRS)	Chemist (IRE)	Horticulturist (IRS)	Psychologist (IES)
Anesthesiologist (IRS)	Computer Systems Analyst (IER)	Mathematician (IER)	Research Analyst (IRC)
Anthropologist (IRE)	Dentist (ISR)	Medical Technologist (ISA)	Statistician (IRE)
Archaeologist (IRE)	Ecologist (IRE)	Meteorologist (IRS)	Surgeon (IRA)
Biochemist (IRS)	Economist (IAS)	Nurse Practitioner (ISA)	Technical Writer (IRS)
Biologist (ISR)	Electrical Engineer (IRE)	Pharmacist (IES)	Veterinarian (IRS)

<u>A</u>rtistic *(Creators)*

People who have artistic, innovating, or intuitional abilities and like to work in unstructured situations using their imagination and creativity.

Are you?	original	Can you?	Like to?
creative	introspective	sketch, draw, paint	attend concerts, theatre, art
imaginative	impulsive	play a musical instrument	exhibits
innovative	sensitive	write stories, poetry, music	read fiction, plays, and poetry
unconventional	courageous	sing, act, dance	work on crafts
emotional	complicated	design fashions or interiors	take photography
independent	idealistic		express yourself creatively
Expressive	nonconforming		deal with ambiguous ideas

Career Possibilities
(Holland Code):

Actor (AES)
Advertising Art Director (AES)
Advertising Manager (ASE)
Architect (AIR)
Art Teacher (ASE)
Artist (ASI)

Copy Writer (ASI)
Dance Instructor (AER)
Drama Coach (ASE)
English Teacher (ASE)
Entertainer/Performer (AES)
Fashion Illustrator (ASR)

Interior Designer (AES)
Intelligence Research Specialist (AEI)
Journalist/Reporter (ASE)
Landscape Architect (AIR)
Librarian (SAI)

Medical Illustrator (AIE)
Museum Curator (AES)
Music Teacher (ASI)
Photographer (AES)
Writer (ASI)
Graphic Designer (AES)

<u>S</u>ocial *(Helpers)*

People who like to work with people to enlighten, inform, help, train, or cure them, or are skilled with words.

Are you?	cooperative	Can you?	Like to?
friendly	generous	teach/train others	work in groups
helpful	responsible	express yourself clearly	help people with problems
idealistic	forgiving	lead a group discussion	do volunteer work
insightful	patient	mediate disputes	work with young people
outgoing	kind	plan and supervise an activity	serve others
understanding		cooperate well with others	

Career Possibilities
(Holland Code):

City Manager (SEC)
Clinical Dietitian (SIE)
College/University Faculty (SEI)
Community Org. Director (SEA)
Consumer Affairs Director (SER)Counselor/Therapist (SAE)

Historian (SEI)
Hospital Administrator (SER)
Psychologist (SEI)
Insurance Claims Examiner (SIE)
Librarian (SAI)
Medical Assistant (SCR)
Minister/Priest/Rabbi (SAI)
Paralegal (SCE)

Park Naturalist (SEI)
Physical Therapist (SIE)
Police Officer (SER)
Probation and Parole Officer (SEC)
Real Estate Appraiser (SCE)
Recreation Director (SER)
Registered Nurse (SIA)

Teacher (SAE)
Social Worker (SEA)
Speech Pathologist (SAI)
Vocational-Rehab. Counselor (SEC)
Volunteer Services Director (SEC)

Enterprising *(Persuaders)*

People who like to work with people, influencing, persuading, leading or managing for organizational goals or economic gain.

Are you?	ambitious	**Can you?**	**Like to?**
self-confident	agreeable	initiate projects	make decisions
assertive	talkative	convince people to do things	be elected to office
persuasive	extroverted	your way	start your own business
energetic	spontaneous	sell things	campaign politically
adventurous	optimistic	give talks or speeches	meet important people
popular		organize activities	have power or status
		lead a group	
		persuade others	

**Career Possibilities
(Holland Code):**

Advertising Executive (ESA)
Advertising Sales Rep (ESR)
Banker/Financial Planner (ESR)
Branch Manager (ESA)
Business Manager (ESC)
Buyer (ESA)
Chamber of Commerce Exec
  (ESA)

Credit Analyst (EAS)
Customer Service Manager
  (ESA)
Education & Training Manager
  (EIS)
Emergency Medical Technician
  (ESI)
Entrepreneur (ESA)

Foreign Service Officer (ESA)
Funeral Director (ESR)
Insurance Manager (ESC)
Interpreter (ESA)
Lawyer/Attorney (ESA)
Lobbyist (ESA)
Office Manager (ESR)
Personnel Recruiter (ESR)

Politician (ESA)
Public Relations Rep (EAS)
Retail Store Manager (ESR)
Sales Manager (ESA)
Sales Representative (ERS)
Social Service Director (ESA)
Stockbroker (ESI)
Tax Accountant (ECS)

Conventional *(Organizers)*

People who like to work with data, have clerical or numerical ability, carry out tasks in detail, or follow through on others' instructions.

Are you?	practical	**Can you?**	**Like to?**
well-organized	thrifty	work well within a system	follow clearly defined
accurate	systematic	do a lot of paper work in a short	procedures
numerically inclined	structured	time	use data processing equipment
methodical	polite	keep accurate records	work with numbers
conscientious	ambitious	use a computer terminal	type or take shorthand
efficient	obedient	write effective business letters	be responsible for details
conforming	persistent		collect or organize things

**Career Possibilities
(Holland Code):**

Abstractor (CSI)
Accountant (CSE)
Administrative Assistant (ESC)
Budget Analyst (CER)
Business Manager (ESC)
Business Programmer (CRI)
Business Teacher (CSE)
Catalog Librarian (CSE)

Claims Adjuster (SEC)
Computer Operator (CSR)
Congressional-District Aide (CES)
Cost Accountant (CES)
Court Reporter (CSE)
Credit Manager (ESC)
Customs Inspector (CEI)
Editorial Assistant (CSI)

Elementary School Teacher
  (SEC)
Financial Analyst (CSI)
Insurance Manager (ESC)
Insurance Underwriter (CSE)
Internal Auditor (ICR)
Kindergarten Teacher (ESC)

Medical Records Technician
  (CSE)
Museum Registrar (CSE)
Paralegal (SCE)
Safety Inspector (RCS)
Tax Accountant (ECS)
Tax Consultant (CES)
Travel Agent (ECS)

BIBLIOGRAPHY

Police Work, Criminal Justice, and Federal Law Enforcement

Ackerman, Thomas H., *Federal Law Enforcement Careers: Profiles of 250 High-Powered Positions and Tactics for Getting Hired,* 2nd ed. St. Paul, MN: Jist Works, 2006.

ARCO, *Master the Probation Officer / Parole Officer Exam.* Lawrenceville, NJ: Thomson Peterson's, 2006.

Brezina, Corona, *Careers in Law Enforcement.* New York: Rosen Publishing Group, 2009.

Clear, Todd R., Michael D. Reisig, and George F. Cole, *American Corrections,* 10th ed. Belmont, CA: Wadsworth Cengage, 2012.

Harr, J. Scott, and Kären M. Hess, *Careers in Criminal Justice and Related Fields,* 6th ed. Boston: Cengage Learning, 2009.

Johnston, Coy H., *Careers in Criminal Justice.* Thousand Oaks, CA: SAGE, 2014.

Koletar, Joseph W., *The FBI Career Guide: Inside Information on Getting Chosen for and Succeeding in One of the Toughest, Most Prestigious Jobs in the World.* New York: AMACOM, 2006.

Lutze, Faith E., *Professional Lives of Community Corrections Officers: The Invisible Side of Reentry.* Thousand Oaks, CA: SAGE, 2012.

Moore, Steve, *Special Agent Man: My Life in the FBI as a Terrorist Hunter, Helicopter Pilot, and Certified Sniper.* Chicago: Chicago Review Books, 2012.

Prideaux, John, and Bob Kastama, *The Quiet Service II: Probation and Parole Officers in Action.* Spokane, WA: Gray Dog Press, 2010.

Sterngass, John, *Public Safety, Law, and Security (Great Careers with a High School Diploma).* New York: Facts on File, 2010.

Sutton, Randy, *A Cop's Life: True Stories from Behind the Badge.* New York: St. Martin's, 2006.

Forensics, Criminology, and Criminal Investigation

Briggs, Steven., *Criminology for Dummies.* Indianapolis: For Dummies, 2009.

Brown, Steven Kerry, *The Complete Idiot's Guide to Private Investigating,* 3rd ed. New York: Alpha, 2013.

Englert, Rod, *Blood Secrets: Chronicles of a Crime Scene Reconstructionist.* New York: Thomas Dunne Books, 2010.

Ferguson's, *Careers in Forensics.* New York: Ferguson's, 2010.

Fish, Jacqueline T., and Jonathan Fish, *Crime Scene Investigation Case Studies: Step by Step from the Crime Scene to the Courtroom.* Waltham, MA: Anderson, 2014.

Lyle, Douglas P., *Forensics for Dummies.* Indianapolis: For Dummies, 2004.

Siegel, Larry J., *Criminology: The Core,* 5th ed. Stamford, CT: Cengage Learning, 2013.

Stephens, Sheila L., *The Everything Private Investigation Book: Master the Techniques of the Pros.* Avon, MA: Adams Media, 2008.

Firefighting, Emergency Services, and Public Safety

Burau, Caroline, *Answering 911: Life in the Hot Seat.* St. Paul, MN: Borealis Books, 2007.

Giesler, Marsha P., *Fire and Safety Educator.* Boston: Cengage Learning, 2010.

Grubbs, John R., and Sean M. Nelson, *Safety Made Easy: A Checklist Approach to OSHA Compliance.* Lanham, MD: Government Institutes, 2007.

Harman, Daniel E., *Jobs in Environmental Cleanup and Emergency Hazmat Response.* New York: Rosen Publishing Group, 2010.

Lindsey, Jeffrey T., and Richard Patrick, *Emergency Vehicle Operations.* Upper Saddle River, NJ: Prentice Hall, 2006.

NFPA, *Fire and Life Safety Inspection Manual.* Sudbury, MA: Jones & Bartlett, 2012.

Shapiro, Larry, *Fighting Fire: Trucks, Tools, and Tactics.* Minneapolis, MN: Motorbooks, 2008.

Smith, Dennis, *Firefighters: Their Lives in their Own Words.* New York: Broadway Books, 2002.

Underwood, Lynn, *Building Code Compliance and Enforcement.* Carlsbad, CA: Craftsman Books, 2012.

Unger, Zac, *Working Fire: The Making of a Firefighter.* New York: Penguin, 2005.

Law and the Courts

Furi-Perry, Ursula, *50 Legal Careers for Non-Lawyers.* Chicago: American Bar Association, 2008.

Hatch, Scott, and Lisa Hatch, *Paralegal Career for Dummies.* Indianapolis: For Dummies, 2006.

Levine, Ann K., *The Law School Admissions Game: Play Like an Expert,* 2d ed. Santa Barbara, CA: Abraham Publishing, 2013.

Levit, Nancy, and Douglas O. Linder, *The Happy Lawyer: Making a Good Life in the Law.* New York: Oxford University Press, 2010.

McCormick, Robert W., Mary H. Knapp, and Melissa H. Blake, *The Complete Court Reporter's Handbook and Guide for Realtime Writers.* Upper Saddle River, NJ: Prentice Hall, 2011.

National Association for Law Placement, *The Official Guide to Legal Specialties.* Chicago: NALP, 2000.

Paschall, Cordy, *The Legal Secretary Guide.* Seattle: Amazon/PAS Publishing, 2012.

Peak, Kenneth, *Justice Administration: Police, Courts, and Corrections Management,* 7th ed. Upper Saddle River, NJ: Prentice Hall, 2011.

Prentzas, G. S., *Careers as a Paralegal and Legal Assistant.* New York: Rosen Publishing Group, 2014.

Schneider, Deborah, and Gary Belsky, *Should You Really Be a Lawyer? The Guide to Smart Career Choices Before, During, and After Law School.* Seattle: Lawyer Avenue, 2004.

Schneider, Steven, *The Everything Guide to Being a Paralegal: Winning Secrets to a Successful Career!* Avon, MA: Adams Media, 2006.

Schroeder, Donald, and Frank Lombardo, *Barron's Court Officer Exam,* 10th ed. Hauppauge, NY: Barron's Educational, 2013.

Park Ranger, Fish & Game Warden

Callan, Steven T., *Badges, Bears, and Eagles: The True Life Adventures of a California Fish and Game Warden.* Seattle: Coffeetown Press, 2013.

Farabee, Charles R. "Butch," Jr., *National Park Ranger: An American Icon.* Lanham, MD: Roberts Rinehart, 2003.

Ford, John, Sr., *Suddenly, the Cider Didn't Taste So Good: Adventures of a Game Warden in Maine.* Yarmouth, ME: Islandsport Press, 2013.

Lankford, Andrea, *Ranger Confidential: Living, Working, and Dying in the National Parks.* Guilford, CT: FalconGuides, 2010.

Lee, Bob H., *Backcountry Lawman: True Stories from a Florida Game Warden.* Gainesville, FL: University Press of Florida, 2013.

Information Security

Bayles, Aaron, et al., *InfoSec Career Hacking: Sell Your Skillz, Not Your Soul.* Rockland, MA: Syngress, 2005.

Butler, Chris, et al., *IT Security Interviews Exposed: Secrets to Landing Your Next Information Security Job.* Hoboken, NJ: Wiley, 2007.

Cowan, David, *Computer Forensics: InfoSec Pro Guide.* New York: McGraw-Hill Osborne Media, 2013.

INDEX

WITHDRAWAL